Textual Intervention

Reading is a form of re-writing. Every interpretation is an act of intervention. These are the premises which inform this challenging yet accessible textbook. In effect this is both a critical guide and a creative manual, for it provides students with a wide range of strategies for exploring texts through re-writing as well as analysis. Such 'textual interventions' include:

- Production of parallel, alternative and counter-texts
- 'Re-centring', 're-genreing' and cross-media adaptation
- Exercises in imitation, parody and collage

A series of 'preludes' on poetry and advertising establishes the basic method and the key concepts: difference and preference; choice and combination; challenge and change; creativity and constraint. The main body of the book then engages with texts ranging from Shakespeare and the nineteenth-century novel to Modernist and Afro-Caribbean poetry, as well as pop and film. The central sections are:

- From narrative to narration and beyond
- Dialogue, discourse and dramatic intervention
- Selves and others, subjects and agents

Textual Intervention draws on a combination of discourse analysis, performance techniques, critical theory and creative writing. While engaging with current debates about cultural production and reproduction, it also encourages students to go beyond them and become analysts, critics and writers in their own right. This is a book about reconstruction as well as deconstruction. Its 'user-friendly' organisation and remarkable range make it a stimulating textbook for a wide variety of courses in language, literature and cultural studies.

Rob Pope is Principal Lecturer in English Studies at Oxford Brookes University.

The INTERFACE Series

> A linguist deaf to the poetic function of language and a literary scholar indifferent to linguistic problems and unconversant with linguistic methods, are equally flagrant anachronisms. – Roman Jackobson

This statement, made over twenty-five years ago, is no less relevant today, and 'flagrant anachronisms' still abound. The aim of the INTERFACE series is to examine topics at the 'interface' of language studies and literary criticism and in so doing to build bridges between these traditionally divided disciplines.

Already published in the series:

The Series Editor

Ronald Carter is Professor of Modern English Language at the University of Nottingham and was National Coordinator of the 'Language in the National Curriculum' Project (LINC) from 1989 to 1992.

Textual Intervention

Critical and Creative Strategies for Literary Studies

Rob Pope

London and New York

First published 1995
by Routledge
2 Park Square, Milton Park, Abingdon, Oxon, OX14 4RN

Simultaneously published in the USA and Canada
by Routledge
270 Madison Ave, New York NY 10016

Transferred to Digital Printing 2006

Typeset in Monotype Baskerville by Florencetype Ltd, Stoodleigh, Devon

British Library Cataloguing in Publication Data
A catalogue record for this book is available from the British Library

Library of Congress Cataloging in Publication Data
A catalog record for this book has been applied for

ISBN 0–415–05436–2 (hbk)
ISBN 0–415–05437–0 (pbk)

Посвяшаю Татьяне
И
всей нашей большой семье

Contents

Series editor's introduction to the Interface series

There have been many books published this century which have been devoted to the interface of language and literary studies. This is the first series of books devoted to this area commissioned by a major international publisher; it is the first time a group of writers have addressed themselves to issues at the interface of language and literature; and it is the first time an international professional association has worked closely with a publisher to establish such a venture. It is the purpose of this general introduction to the series to outline some of the main guiding principles underlying the books in the series.

The first principle adopted is one of not foreclosing on the many possibilities for the integration of language and literature studies. There are many ways in which the study of language and literature can be combined and many different theoretical, practical and curricular objects to be realized. Obviously, a close relationship with the aims and methods of descriptive linguistics will play a prominent part, so readers will encounter some detailed analysis of language in places. In keeping with a goal of much work in this field, writers will try to make their analysis sufficiently replicable for other analysts to see how they have arrived at the interpretative decisions they have reached and to allow others to reproduce their methods on the same or on other texts. But linguistic science does not have a monopoly in methodology and description any more than linguists can have sole possession of insights into language and its workings. Some contributors to the series adopt quite rigorous linguistic procedures; others proceed less rigorously but no less revealingly. All are, however, united by a belief that detailed scrutiny of the role of language in literary texts can be mutually enriching to language and literary studies.

Series of books are usually written to an overall formula or design. In the case of the Interface series this was considered to be not entirely appropriate. This is for the reasons given above, but also because, as the first series of its kind, it would be wrong to suggest that there are formulaic modes by which integration can be achieved. The fact that all the books address themselves to the integration of language and literature in any case imparts a natural and organic unity to the series. Thus, some of the books in this series will provide descriptive overviews, others will offer detailed case studies of a particular topic, others will involve single author studies, and some will be more pedagogically oriented.

This range of design and procedure means that a wide variety of audiences is envisaged for the series as a whole, though, of course, individual books are necessarily quite specifically targeted. The general level of exposition presumes quite advanced students of language and literature. Approximately, this level covers students of English language and literature (though not exclusively English) at senior high-school/upper sixth-form level to university students in their first or second year of study. Many of the books in the series are designed to be used by students. Some may serve as course books – these will normally contain exercises and suggestions for further work as well as glossaries and graded bibliographies which point the student towards further reading. Some books are also designed to be used by teachers for their own reading and updating, and to supplement courses; in some cases, specific questions of pedagogic theory, teaching procedure and methodology at the interface of language and literature are addressed.

From a pedagogic point of view it is the case in many parts of the world that students focus on literary texts, especially in the mother tongue, before undertaking any formal study of the language. With this fact in mind, contributors to the series have attempted to gloss all new technical terms and to assume on the part of their readers little or no previous knowledge of linguistics or formal language studies. They see no merit in not being detailed and explicit about what they describe in the linguistic properties of texts; but they recognize that formal language study can seem forbidding if it is not properly introduced.

A further characteristic of the series is that the authors engage in a direct relationship with their readers. The overall style of writing is informal and there is above all an attempt to lighten the usual style of academic discourse. In some cases this extends to the way in which notes and guidance for further work are presented. In all cases, the style adopted by authors is judged to be that most appropriate to the mediation of their chosen subject matter.

We now come to two major points of principle which underlie the conceptual scheme for the series. One is that the term 'literature' cannot be defined in isolation from an expression of ideology. In fact, no academic study, and certainly no description of the language of texts, can be neutral and objective, for the sociocultural positioning of the analyst will mean that the description is unavoidably political. Contributors to the series recognize and, in so far as this accords with the aims of each book, attempt to explore the role of ideology at the interface of language and literature. Second, most writers also prefer the term 'literatures' to a singular notion of literature. Some replace 'literature' altogether with the neutral term 'text'. It is for this reason that readers will not find exclusive discussions of the literary language of canonical literary texts; instead the linguistic heterogeneity of literature and the permeation of many discourses with what is conventionally thought of as poetic or literary language will be a focus. This means that in places as much space can be devoted to examples of word play in jokes, newspaper editorials, advertisements, historical writing, or a popular thriller as to a sonnet by Shakespeare or a passage from Jane Austen. It is also important to stress how the term 'literature' itself is historically variable and how different social and cultural assumptions can condition what is regarded as literature. In this respect the role of linguistic and literary theory is vital. It is an aim of the series to be constantly alert to new developments in the description and theory of texts.

Finally, as series editor, I have to underline the partnership and cooperation of the whole enterprise of the Interface series and acknowledge the advice and assistance received at many stages from the PALA Committee and from Routledge. In turn, we are all fortunate to have the benefit of three associate editors with considerable collective depth of experience in this field in different parts of the world: Professor Roger Fowler, Professor Mary Louise Pratt, Professor Michael Halliday. In spite of their own individual orientations, I am sure that all concerned with the series would want to endorse the statement by Roman Jakobson made over twenty-five years ago but which is no less relevant today:

A linguist deaf to the poetic function of language and a literary scholar indifferent to linguistic problems and unconversant with linguistic methods, are equally flagrant anachronisms.

Textual Intervention by Rob Pope continues a line in this series of books which directly addresses practical concerns of teaching and learning at the interface of language and literary studies. It is a new kind of textbook requiring, as its title suggests, that teachers and students should intervene in the construction and re-construction of texts in order better to understand them. The central pedagogic strategy is engagement with the processes of the text by an act of re-writing, an act which serves to put readers on the inside of the text and which enables them to write their way into more effective reading. Rob Pope offers a rich range of different types of textual intervention for a rich range of canonical and non-canonical texts, illuminating in the process key issues such as point of view, the nature of literary language, the relationship between text and ideology and the different positions from which texts can be read and interpreted. In a world in which resources for teaching and learning are becoming ever more restricted, a textbook such as this intervenes itself in the trend towards ever more transmissive teaching to ever larger groups by offering the potential for process-based work in which students explore and engage in the kind of textual transformations which enable them to become, rather than passive and compliant, more active and resistant readers.

Acknowledgements

This book has been a long time in the making and many people have had a hand in it. The further reading sections and the bibliography signal my most obvious debts and influences in terms of published work. But perhaps even more important are the numerous instances of unpublished student work, traces of which can be picked up throughout. My most fundamental acknowledgement is therefore to the many hundreds – probably thousands – of students in England, Wales and Russia who have contributed with such energy, enthusiasm and skill (as well as healthy scepticism) to the methods and materials upon which 'textual intervention' draws. In particular, I should like to thank all those at Oxford Brookes University (formerly Oxford Polytechnic) who have made and re-made texts with me and one another on the following courses: Language, Literature, Discourse I: Texts, Problems and Approaches; Language in Advertising and Newsreporting; Chaucer and Women; Shakespeare, Power and Politics; and Modern Drama. I am also grateful to all those with whom I have had such 'serious fun' at conferences and workshops organised by the National Association for the Teaching of English, the 'Connect' scheme in London (especially Islington Sixth Form Centre) and, most recently, the Poetics and Linguistics Association. From amongst the many undergraduate and postgraduate students who have so readily lent support, ideas and materials, I should especially like to thank Belinda Beasley, Helen Coxall, Kathy Doncaster, Dorothy Macarthy, Pat Silver and Jenny Soutter.

All my colleagues in English Studies at Oxford Brookes (as well as many others both inside and outside the School of Humanities) have contributed generously with references, insights and criticism. I have been particularly fortunate in working closely for some years with Stewart Young on modern drama and with Archie Burnett on language and early literature. Moreover, we have all been fortunate in the unfailing support and guidance of a succession of exceptional external examiners in the persons of Douglas Gray, John Lucas, Lisa Jardine and Susan Bassnett. Meanwhile, in my own capacity as external examiner, I have learnt much from working with George Wotton and his colleagues at the University of Hertfordshire (formerly Hatfield Polytechnic).

Terry Hawkes gave the idea of the book an invaluable push at a crucial early stage. And, like so many others, I have benefited hugely from the encouragement and experience of the series editor, Ron Carter. Without his ever-ready patience, understanding and conviction, as first one deadline passed then another, the manuscript would have remained a wild and baggy monster with a lot of past but no future. Continuing to tame and shape the text with Marguerite Nesling was a joy – when it could so easily have been a pain; while Julia Hall, Emma Cotter and all involved in the editorial and production processes at Routledge have overseen the project with great tact, friendliness and expertise. I should like to be able to pass off some of the book's remaining faults on the above people. But in all honesty I can't. The errors at least are 'all my own work'.

My final acknowledgement is to my partner, Tania, from whom I continue to learn far more than I could ever hope to teach.

What the book is about and how to use it

This book is intended for learners and teachers in a wide variety of literary, linguistic and cultural studies courses. It can also function as a textual studies course in its own right. Either way the emphasis is on *using* the book rather than simply reading it from cover to cover.

Basically this is a critical-creative handbook. It offers a range of interactive and interventive strategies in which readers are encouraged to engage in structured yet playful re-writing of any text they meet. Such 'textual interventions' include: 're-centring'; 're-genreing', the generation of various kinds of 'parallel', 'alternative' and 'counter-text' (writing with, across and against the grain of the initial text), as well as exercises in paraphrase, imitation, parody, adaptation, hybridisation and collage. All these strategies are devoted to the exploration of textual differences and preferences, and they are summarised in 'Types of textual intervention' at the close of the book (5.3). This final section is comprehensively cross-referenced and may therefore be used as an alternative 'map' for finding your way around. For the rest, the overall Contents pages identify the main kinds of material treated and methods and models used in the various sections.

The book both features and encourages a synthesis of analytical, critical and creative work. This may be done by people working in groups as well as on their own. Consequently, there is considerable freedom and flexibility as to precisely who does what, when and how. The following study patterns are therefore simply recommendations. Bend them to your own individual and collective designs.

'Preludes' (Chapter 1) are just that – a series of 'foreplays' – and they may be regarded as essential preliminary reading. They introduce the basic method and its underlying principles. The materials used are deliberately very various and differently demanding. The first prelude (1.1) intervenes in a magazine advert, but is framed in such a way as to establish a working model applicable to any text. The second prelude (1.2) reinforces and re-focuses the method by progressively de- and re-centring a literary classic (in this case Robert Browning's poem 'My Last Duchess'). The final prelude comprises a couple of 'work-outs with words'. These help establish a basic critical and linguistic vocabulary, while also exploring very different kinds of text creatively through systematic critique. The materials featured are instances of philosophical discourse and of government health warnings. Both sets of texts are challenged and changed, as well as analysed. And the overall aim is a sharpened sense of the distinctive differences and preferences of these 'base texts' in their various historical moments, as well as an increased awareness of our own capacities and responsibilities when we set about generating counter- or alternative texts in our own moments.

All the terms and techniques practised in these preludes – and in the rest of the book – are summarised and cross-referenced in a **Stylistic checklist** (5.2) and in 5.3. Their theoretical underpinning is explored in a bibliographical essay in 5.1. Meanwhile, each section concludes with suggestions for 'Further re-writing and reading'.

The main body of the book is concentrated in three areas. Each overlaps with the others (so follow up the copious cross references whenever seems appropriate), and each includes an **extensive work-out** on a related cluster of texts. The three central sections are organised as follows.

'Subjects and agents; selves and others' (Chapter 2) explores the construction of subjectivity and agency in and around texts. It also introduces the notion that every text is constituted – and ceaselessly reconstituted – by the interplay of a range of **subject/agent positions: personal, interpersonal** and **depersonalised**. These positions are not only found 'within' the text, but also established by particular readers through active interrogation and negotiation. Whereas 'ideal readers' acquiesce in the text's dominant meanings (as subjects), 'actual readers' always to some extent resist, refuse or re-orient those meanings (as agents). All this is done through individual and group work, exploring both interpersonal and intertextual dynamics. Materials treated range from accounts of the bombing of Nagasaki (2.3); through personal adverts (2.4); to lyric poems (2.5). We conclude with an extended work-out, experimenting with reconstructions of the textual 'I' in poetry, pop, psychiatry and advertising (2.6). The aim here is to recognise and re-think the 'I-that-speaks' as in some measure a contextual and intertextual construct – and one which might be generated and 'genred' differently. Through experiment, we also see that this 'I' is just one position amongst many others that have been marginalised or repressed – or might have been expressed differently. Overall, then, there is an insistence on seeing a shifting configuration of 'selves' always defined by and braced against a shifting configuration of 'others'. The combination of individual and group work ensures that – in practice and not just in theory – we also experience and experiment with our 'selves' and/as 'others'.

'From narrative to narration and beyond' (Chapter 3) starts from the articulation of narrative at the 'micro-' level (e.g. the clause and sentence) and gradually proceeds to explore it at the 'macro-' level of larger stories and histories (ultimately whole mythologies and ideologies). On this basis we proceed in 3.2 to a sustained exploration of a short nonsense-verse narrative – which in the event is revealed to be potentially neither short nor nonsense, but an intriguing blend of poetic and narrative possibilities! This section also features some experiments with narrative in film. We conclude with an extended work-out which involves some very different constructions of Robinson Crusoe's island (3.3). These include versions by Tournier, Coetzee and Wyss – as well as our own. And there is a supplementary review of relevant 'pre-texts' and 'post-texts' ranging from Aphra Behn to the present.

The overall aim of this chapter, then, as its title suggests, is to recognise that narratives (as products) are always subject to successive moments of narration and re-narration (as processes). Consequently, just as every statement begs an infinite number of questions, so every story begs an infinity of untold stories. Unless and until someone decides to tell them, that is. Us, for instance.

'Dialogue, discourse and dramatic intervention' (Chapter 4): this too starts at the 'micro-' level of single exchanges and gradually works up to the 'macro-' level of large-scale inter-actions in conversation and drama, as well as novels and poems. There is a dual emphasis: through **dramatic intervention** we experiment with alternative 'moves' that *might* have been made or 'turns' that *might* have been taken; and through **dialogic techniques** we explore the various 'voices' and 'discourses' in play within and around a work. The approach to drama is therefore 'Brechtian', in that it is concerned with the re-presentation and 'making strange' of interactions. Meanwhile, relatedly, the overall approach to dialogue is 'Bakhtinian', in that it is concerned with the ways in which a text allows us to speak to and through a variety of personal 'voices' and social 'discourses' in a number of historical moments. Once these underlying models have been explained (4.1), we proceed to the joint articulation of a kind of 'assertiveness' or dialectical 'non/cooperative' principle for conversation and drama (4.2). This is both observed and put into practice in the analy-sis and rescripting of a domestic daughter–father dialogue (4.3.1). On that basis we proceed to engage in structured re-writing of the endings of plays by Ibsen and Beckett (4.3.2).

'Cross-cultural dialogues with and within "Eng. Lit."' are explored in 4.4. The main emphasis is on colonial and post-colonial texts (featuring novels by Trollope, Austen, Charlotte Brontë and Rhys, alongside poems by Mnthali, Amryl Johnson and Merle Collins); and the method draws heavily on both Bakhtin's notions of 'dialogics' and 'heteroglossia' as well as Vygotsky on the interplay of 'inner' and 'outer' voices. Again, there is attention to the distinctive potential of a combination of individual and group work – analytically and in performance. The extended work-out in this section is devoted to different moments in the re-production of *Hamlet* over the past four hundred years: as scripts, editions, performances, films, criticisms, allusions, parodies, etc. We start with textual variants of the 'To be or not to be' speech, and finish up with a pack of cigars!

'Review of theories and practices' (Chapter 5): this is a general summary and reference sec-tion. You might in fact *start* here if that seems the best way into your particular course and context. We open with an overview of the main theories and practices which inform the present method (5.1). This is also a critical and bibliographical essay, and offers a blend of models and methods from literary and cultural studies, linguistic and discourse analysis, creative writing and performance arts. Their common concern is ultimately pedagogic: a commitment to learning and teaching as dialogue, and an exploration of 'subjects' which may be conceived as variously intertextual, interpersonal and interdisciplinary. A stylistic checklist is supplied in 5.2. And, finally, all the main modes of textual intervention and alter-native writing strategy used in the book are summarised and cross-referenced in 5.3. For the rest, use the index to follow up individual terms and techniques, authors and genres.

As suggested at the outset, this is a book to *use* – not just to read. It is a *hand*book of criti-cal and creative practices. So, if it looks well thumbed after a little while, it is probably working as it was intended. Or rather, to put the onus firmly back on you as an active user, you are probably making it work for you.

Three last words. Seriously, have fun!

1 Preludes

1.1 THE APPROACH – TEXTUAL INTERVENTION

The highest Criticism, then, is more creative . . . and the primary aim of the critic is to see the object as in itself it really is not.

(Oscar Wilde, *The Critic as Artist* (1891))

Criticism begins with the recognition of textual power and ends in the attempt to exercise it. This attempt may take the form of an essay, but it may just as easily be textualised as parody or counter-text in the same mode as its critical object. As teachers we should encourage the full range of critical practices in our students.

(Robert Scholes, *Textual Power* (1985))

What aspect of the world do you want to disclose? What change do you want to bring into the world by this disclosure?

(J.-P. Sartre, *What is Literature?* (1948))

The approach proposed in this book is basically simple and practical. As the above quotations suggest, it involves criticism, creativity, the exercise of power and the activity of change. I shall describe it from two points of view, *textual* and *educational*. In fact, these are better seen as two intimately related processes: we always do things with particular texts in particular contexts – in our case educational contexts. I shall therefore insist on the necessary link between certain forms of textual theory and certain kinds of pedagogic practice by interleaving this introductory section both with worked examples and with examples for you to work on yourself.

1.1.1 Challenging and changing the text

The best way to understand how a text works, I argue, is to change it: to play around with it, to intervene in it in some way (large or small), and then to try to account for the exact effect of what you have done. In practice – not just in theory – we have the option of making changes at all levels, from the merest nuance of punctuation or intonation to total recasting in terms of genre, time, place, participants and medium. And our analytical tools for discussing all these changes will range from the 'micro-linguistic' (to do with localised choices and combinations of sounds, meanings and grammatical structures) through to the 'macro-linguistic' (to do with the larger-scale organisations of choice and combination we know as narrative, argument and exposition). The emphasis throughout is on exploring possible permutations and realisations of texts in and out of their original contexts.

The initial change may be apparently slight. Perhaps the substitution of a single word or syllable or sound: a 'Hi!' instead of a 'Hello!', 'pretty' instead of 'beautiful', 'freedom' instead of 'democracy' or – more radically – 'she' instead of 'he', 'black' instead of 'white' (or an unmarked space), 'god' instead of 'God', or 'matter' instead of both. It may be as minute – and yet potentially momentous – as the difference between one *style* or SIZE of type-face and another; the presence or absence of inverted commas 'highlighting', 'scare quotes' or 'genuine quotes' (you decide which is which). Or it may be the deceptive finality of the full stop. Which only temporarily invites you to do the same. Like that. As distinct from a string of suspension or continuation dots . . . which . . . again temporarily . . . invite you to do something rather different . . . like this . . . .

But the change may also be something more structural and slightly larger scale. Perhaps choosing a present active construction instead of a past passive one: 'Police shoot ten in Soweto' rather than 'Ten shot in Soweto'. Or deciding to report a text indirectly and with a marked slant rather than quoting it verbatim and relatively impersonally: 'You know, the bit where Marx and that other Commie go on about all the poor downtrodden working classes getting off their backsides and doing something for a change . . .' rather than 'Working men of all countries, unite!' (Marx and Engels, *The Communist Manifesto*, first English edition, 1850). Or substituting a nominalised structure (i.e. one which is noun-based and therefore suggests a more static and object-like phenomenon) for a structure which is more verbal (i.e. verb-based and therefore suggests a more dynamic and process-centred event). For instance, consider the difference between saying 'Inflation up again' and 'Prices and wages continue to chase one another', where the latter lays more stress on the (verbal) action and the former on the (nominal) state.

Still other, wider reaching and more fundamental transformations of text are available to us. These may be as general and pervasive as a complete shift in genre or medium: part of a play recast in the form of a novel, series of letters, legal testimony or psychiatric interview. Or they may involve the adaptation of a printed poem for oral delivery by three voices; or its re-working as part of a song, painting, poster, magazine advert or TV documentary. What's more, you can also – and in fact will constantly be encouraged to – develop the existing characters, scenes, events and arguments of the initial text. In so doing you will automatically need to decide how far you are prepared to write 'with', 'against' or 'across the grain' of what seem to be that text's dominant preoccupations and major strategies, thereby producing, respectively, **parallel, opposed**, and **alternative texts**. In some instances the process of re-writing and intervention will inevitably prompt you to develop characters, scenes and arguments of your own. Consequently and only apparently paradoxically, you will not in fact be led away from your 'original text' (or as I shall henceforth prefer to call it, the 'base text'). Rather, you will constantly and with every tool at your disposal – critical, analytical, theoretical and historical – be forced back into it. Every turning you take, every choice and combination you make will be gauged against one already taken and made in your base text. The latter is therefore, in every sense, the 'base' from which you must depart and to which you must return. But where you go in the meantime – and how and why – is largely up to you. In fact, helping you work out the 'where', 'how' and 'why' of your own critical and textual trajectories is one of the main aims of this book.

The sheer scale and prodigious variety of possible changes to a text should now be clear. As

I have already insisted, the point is that in theory *and in practice* virtually all these options are at your disposal, both as an imaginative reader and an active re-writer. You can opt to change a single word – or the way the 'same' word is delivered (orally or visually); or you can change the whole orientation and mediation of the text. Essentially, it is a practical, material matter – and you don't have to be a genius to do it. Nor do you need to be a genius to explore the consequences of what you have done. You simply need to be systematic, thoughtful and informed (in fact all the qualities needed to write good essays and commentaries). There is therefore no 'mystique' or 'secret' to the approach: it is one which may properly be called **artisanal**. That is, the approach is neither self-consciously 'artistic' or 'creative' (in the commonly elitist, merely subjective and ultimately mystifying senses of these terms); nor one which is self-effacingly 'scientific' (in the commonly clinical, specialist and supposedly impersonal and object-centred sense of that term). Approaching texts as an 'artisan', as a 'crafts/wo/man', means that you treat them with the respect – but also the no-nonsense directness and systematicness – that a skilled engineer or dressmaker approaches their materials and the immediate task in hand. Materials and tools are to be chosen and decisions about how, when and where to use them are to be made. Therefore, this book is indeed a 'hand-book' (a 'manual') in that it puts some tools into your hands – and maybe some handy ideas into your head. But it is finally you who must use them. Put more formally, the precise texts you work on may in part be prescribed and (in that dully resonant phrase) 'set'. But the decisions as to how exactly you might go about challenging and changing them (i.e. *really* criticising them) should largely be yours. So should the choice of critical rationale – to which we shall turn shortly. Other terms for the current project are 're-composition' and 'radical rhetoric'. Before looking at some examples of the approach in action, a couple of central terms need defining. Otherwise, they're likely to cause confusion.

By '**language**' I mean what most people understand by the term most of the time: **spoken, written, printed or otherwise recorded *words***. If I want to refer to some other sign- or communication system (visual, aural, tactile, photographic, cinematic, musical, gestural, architectural, etc.), I shall refer to it as such, by name. By **text** I mean **any more or less cohesive communicative act which involves a substantial verbal component and is in some way recorded (on paper, plastic, electronically, etc.).** A live and *un*recorded – but of course recordable – use of language (i.e. live speech) I shall call an **utterance**. We shall analyse and play around with plenty of 'utterances' – but only once they have been put into recorded, repeatable and therefore more easily studiable form (i.e. as 'texts'). In fact, exploring and exploiting the differences between written texts and spoken utterances turns out to be one one of our simplest yet most powerful critical and creative tools. The acts of speaking the printed and printing the spoken result in revealingly different performances.

1.1.2 Making the first move: from 'What if?' to 'Why?'

In a post-traditional social universe, an indefinite range of potential courses of action (with their attendant risks) is at any moment open to individuals and collectivities. Choosing among such alternatives is always an 'as if' matter, a question of selecting between 'possible worlds'.

(Giddens, 1991: 29)

all imaginative writing springs from one question and one executive recommenda-
tion. The question is 'What if?'. . .

(Nash, 1992: 83)

This section offers a preliminary example of 'textual intervention' at work. The particular material to be worked on is a magazine advert; but the method has been framed in
such a way as to be applicable to any text. Later preludes intervene in and analyse a wide
range of other kinds of text and utterance: poetry, conversation, philosophical propositions
and government health warnings. But the same basic method, as outlined here, is applied
to all of them. Here, then, is the first 'move' and the first text. Only one other thing
need perhaps be added at this stage, and it relates the nature of texts to the function of
education. Both, it is insisted, are basically 'problem-centred'. That is, texts are considered
in the first instance as 'problem-posing' and 'problem-solving' (or 'problem-displacing')
devices. And so is education – though in so far as it 'displaces' problems it, of course, fails.
The crucial thing, therefore, is to decide exactly how to expose the particular problem
posed and resolved (or displaced) in a particular text – and how to relate this to the process
of education. In either event, the strategy is simple and involves an initial act of critical
intervention (*What if?*) followed through by a reasoned explanation (*Why?*). The educational problem is posed in so far as this must be an individual and a collective act. Here,
then, is the first 'move' and the first text.

(1)

What if the text were different? **Intervene in the text in some way so as to 're-
centre' it, thereby deflecting and re-directing its dominant 'ways of saying' and
its preferred 'ways of seeing'. Aim to make two interventions: one subtle; the
other outrageous. If possible do this through discussion in small groups**.

The text in question, which I must here ask you to visualise, is derived from a double-page
car advert in a Sunday newspaper colour supplement. In this case it was a full-colour
advert for a Peugeot 205 as reproduced from the *Observer* magazine (2 April 1986). Similar
ads are still plentiful. In the foreground is a red Peugeot with a young woman standing
nearby wearing an elegant and identically red dress. Both are shot against a summer landscape of cut grass and rolling hills leading to a horizon of neatly pruned and silhouetted
trees. The overall effect might be described as one of high sophistication combined
with pastoral tranquillity: machine, nature and wo/man in perfect harmony. The main
caption along the bottom reads

PEUGEOT 205: LOVE IT!

and to the left of that in smaller letters the corporate slogan appears:

PEUGEOT: the lion goes from strength to strength

Before seeing what other people, literally, 'made of' this ad working to the above brief, try
it for yourself. Take a few minutes, preferably talking over the possibilities with others,
weighing what two critical interventions ('one subtle; the other outrageous') *you* might
make. Do this before reading on.

Here, then, by way of illustration, are some of the interventions in the above Peugeot ad
previously made by other people working in sub-groups. Compare them with your own.

(I leave you to decide which was meant to be 'subtle' and which 'outrageous' – for even tiny changes can have radical effects and pervasive changes need not be unsubtle.)

(a) One group wondered what difference it would make if the woman were in a clashing turquoise dress, rather than one indentically matching the colour of the car.

(b) Another suggested bulldozers and diggers (not trees) in the background, and instead of rolling hills a bypass was being built (like one then being built near our institute, which had been inconveniencing people coming in that way for months).

(c) A third proposed that in view of the comparatively minute space actually devoted to the car and woman (about 10 per cent of total page area, they reckoned) and in view of the correspondingly huge area devoted to the atmospheric landscape, it should really be a 'country holiday advert' – or an ad from *Farmers' Weekly*. All it needed was a change of caption. Having toyed with the rather tame 'THE SOUTH OF ENGLAND: YOU'LL LOVE IT!', they finally went for 'STUBBLE: BURN IT!' (This proved a huge success and caused much merriment.)

(d) A fourth group also intervened in the caption, this time more slyly. They came up with 'PEUGEOT: THE LION*ESS* GOES FROM STRENGTH TO STRENGTH'.

(e) And a fifth group went for a more pervasive change. They simply suggested that the ad be placed in *Green News* (an ecological magazine) or one of the Oxfam publications. The latter change of context – and magazine co-text – from light Sunday leisure reading, chiefly for the middle and upper classes, was reckoned to be immediately arresting and potentially quite politically pointed. Cars and/or high fashion don't easily 'go' with concerns over environmental abuse, starvation and underdevelopment.

And there were others, some more subtle and some more outrageous – but all in one way or another *funny* and all in one way or another *significant*. (As with good graffiti, the point to note is that they are only funny *if* they are significant.) The next step, therefore, is to try to establish why and to what degree each intervention is humorously significant (i.e. 'ludicrous', in the radical sense of 'playfully serious'). The attention now shifts, therefore, to the second question and the second stage, in which analysis and valuation play a more central role.

(2)

Why did you make that particular intervention? What preferences does it imply or assert? Go on to weigh the relative merits of some of the options you considered but rejected. Also identify some other potential differences/ preferences that your particular interventions still leave untouched? Again, do this for your own interventions before hearing how other people understood and interrogated theirs.

Here are the conclusions the above people came to, now reconstituted as a whole group. Each sub-group presented its rationale to the others, who then asked questions, made suggestions, and pointed out assumptions and orientations, etc.

(a) The deliberate mismatching of the colours of the car and the woman's dress revealed that the initial text presented the woman and the machine as a kind of matching set. It implied a close identity between them. Consequently, as soon as the colours were made to clash this more or less unconscious indentification was fractured. The car could no longer be viewed as the matching accessory of a fashion-conscious woman. (As far as the manufacturers and advertisers were concerned, this was obviously the **preferred** or **dominant** reading , the one we were meant to pick up and re-produce). By extension, and perhaps more revealingly, it was no longer possible to view the woman and the machine as though they existed on the same plane of existence, as a matching set, a pair of objects united by colour in the gaze of the spectator. At this point, to make the point, it was suggested that the woman be dressed in a dirty old duffle-coat or, more subtly, that she simply be dressed in routine jumper and skirt. Either way, it was generally agreed that these latter readings – and re-writings – were far from the the ones that we were meant to produce. They were not the 'preferred' readings of the address*ers*. But they were, at least in some measure, the 'preferred re-writings' of the address*ees* – though now having stirred and activated themselves as address*ers* in turn. In fact, this particular, and particularly animated, intertextual and interpersonal dialogue was neatly summed up in the sudden materialisation of an alternative caption:

Would you buy a woman from this car?!

This was felt to be peculiarly appropriate as it also picked up, inverted and recast a familiar gendered collocation associated with sharp practice amongst car salesmen ('Would you buy a car from this man?!'). In this way, as usual, quite routine linguistic resources were picked up and twisted so as both to subvert one way of saying/seeing and to promote another. As long as we stay in language we always fight words with words – fire with fire.

(b) Why had one group opted for bulldozers and bypasses in the background, rather than rolling hills and neatly trimmed trees? This too, it was decided, was not a merely gratuitous choice. In fact, as discussion quickly confirmed, most contemporary car ads present their product in idyllic or at least unusual contexts: on open country roads, up lone mountain tracks or under bare, hi-tech studio lighting – in fact anywhere but snarled up in a 2-mile tailback or groping round town searching for a car-parking space. (The only way in which these latter, potentially unfavourable glimpses of cars in routine situations are accommodated, it was noted, is by the car in question taking on a distinctly fantastic role: flying over, roaring past and squeezing between slow or stationary traffic – and thereby evading the everyday realities of one machine amongst many, many more which are more or less like it.) It was therefore concluded that all these more or less 'unconscious intuitions' (what might more technically be termed these 'traces of internalised cultural competence') had in fact informed the decision to go for a half-built by-pass back-drop. It was just that these 'intuitions/competences' were not fully recognised till they were expressed in specific 'performances', and then made critically and analytically explicit through reflection and discussion. The role of the second stage (presentation to others, question and suggestion) was therefore crucial. This also pointed the way to further inferences and investigations. As far as ads in particular are concerned, the larger inference was inescapable: to sell products you present them in their most attractive light – even if that means substantially marginalising or totally ignoring their routine use. At its most extreme, this means actually inventing a context. The job of radical reading and re-writing is therefore also obvious: to bring the old text into contact with precisely those studiously marginalised or ignored contexts and functions. Invariably the effect is 'funny'. But, as we shall see, this can be a variously teasing or shocking blend of 'funny ha ha' and 'funny peculiar': the comic and the de- or re-familiarised. Genuinely ludicrous in fact.

(c) Further inspection and reflection confirmed that the 'STUBBLE: BURN IT!' sub-stitution for 'PEUGEOT 203: LOVE IT!' had similarly suggestive, essentially critical premises under-pinning the joke. There was so much atmospheric landscape and so little product that you could be forgiven for thinking it was an ad for something else. The enigmatic 'guess-the-product' ad is now, of course, a well-established strategy. You can watch a whole minute's mini-epic on TV till you finally find out what's being sold in the last voice-over, caption or allusion – and even then you may not always be sure! In this case it is the very problem- (even the riddle-) posing and solving strategy of the text which is its greatest strength. Parodically, therefore, this is also potentially its point of greatest weakness. On reflection, the members of this sub-group realised that they had sensed this tendency; and all they had done was push it further, to its il/logical extreme. In this way, exaggeration of a single prominent feature, creative caricature and parodic critique work in harness. The analytical trick is simply to make the processes informing such products explicit: to turn half-sensed 'know how' (skills) into fully formed 'know that' and 'know why' (knowledges and rationales).

But even that is not the end. For, on the basis of the 'STUBBLE: BURN IT' example, it was possible – with only a little prompting – to make two larger and absolutely fun-damental inferences to do with the organisation of language and of texts. First, it was confirmed that strategies of de- and re-familiarisation often involve what can be called 'collocation cracking'. Here this takes the form of linguistic variations on a theme: the same underlying grammatical structure (noun + directive verb + 'it') is used to generate two different 'surface realisations' which are incongruous in that they draw on different discourses ('cars' and 'farming'). The act of superimposing the one on the other there-fore effectively 'cracks' the base text open. The latter is revealed to be an empty – or at least refillable – shell: a form capable of containing no – or another – content. At the very least, this means that the 'PEUGEOT: LOVE IT' formula is readily recognised as a specific '*way* of saying/seeing' (i.e. a configuration of discourses) and can no longer be treated as simply a given state of affairs, how things actually are (i.e. unconstructed reality). Of course, the present example is relatively ephemeral and trivial. It is also, like all deliberately crafted slogans and catch-phrases, a kind of 'pseudo-proverb' – a form of words bidding for the status of recognised **collocation** (a status which 'Coke is it. It's the real thing' and 'Go to work on an egg' achieved for a while).

The other fundamental critical inference that flowed from discussion of the above inter-vention was this: that adverts, like all texts and all other cultural objects, are organised in **genres**; that is, they are recognised as belonging to specific **categories** or **kinds**. What this particular sub-group had done, they subsequently realised, was expose the arbitrary and purely conventional limits within which one of the most familiar genres of car advert was operating. It was all so rural and pastoral (without a road in sight) it might as well be a farming ad! Put more formally, they concentrated on one particu-lar aspect of the image, 'anchored' that aspect by a particular caption – and thereby prompted a reading in terms of a different sub-genre of text (here a different kind of ad). They engineered slippage in the visual sign by means of a new verbal sign. The result: a sense of play in inter- (rather than merely intra-) textual space. Though, of course, such senses of 'genre' and 'sub-genre' are so deeply ingrained in the 'cultural competences' of particular social-historical groups that much of the time they are all but invisible. It is only by deliberately playing with the familiar that that very familiarity is itself recognisable as a construct. Genres appear to be 'given'; but they are in fact 'made'. Which is why they can be – and are constantly – unmade and re-made.

Overall, then, as with the other re-writes, the result of such an intervention is what can be called **the transformation of differences into preferences**. This supplies the moral, political and aesthetic rationale of this whole approach. It also acts as the motor of textual change as well as the motivation behind the various kinds of linguistic, narrative and logical analysis in which we shall engage later. For without such elementary and absolutely fundamental acts of challenge and counter-choice, nothing – literally – changes. With them – potentially everything.

(d) 'PEUGEOT: THE LION*ESS* GOES FROM STRENGTH TO STRENGTH'. Here, with just one tweak of its symbolic whiskers, a whole network of cultural convention was thrown into relief. And again, saying precisely 'why' threw up far more questions and suggestions than the sub-group responsible had anticipated. For instance, through discussion it gradually became obvious that the implied identification of 'Peugeot' with 'lions' (a metaphoric identity which had already been established over several campaigns) did not depend simply on the stereotypical association of 'lions' with 'strength', 'courage', 'wildness', 'regality' and 'exoticism' etc. The 'car/lion' conflation also depended on a specific and equally conventional image of masculinity. For as any even half-attentive viewer of TV nature documentaries can tell you, the 'strength', 'wildness' and 'courage', etc., of the lion may be a potent myth – but it's a long way from the leonine facts of life. It's the *lionesses*, in groups, who do most of the caring for the young *and* the hunting. The lion mainly lazes around all day waiting for sex and food to come to him, cuffs the cubs occasionally, and only stirs himself much when challenged by another male. Of course, again, the larger inferences seem obvious when you point them out: amongst many other things, the Peugeot ad draws on and perpetuates some pretty deep-seated gender stereotypes relating to both cars and lions. The great thing about textual intervention, however, is that it allows you to get to that point fast. What's more, its use in sub-groups who subsequently pool their 'findings' and 'makings' ensures that everyone gets to see that there are always more 'points' (if you like, 'messages') in a text than one. Different 'points of entry' necessarily produce different – though often relatable – interpretations. Hence the singular – yet interconnected – rationale of the next intervention.

(e) Placing the Peugeot ad so that it comes into collision with an inherently unlikely and potentially inhospitable range of co-texts (to do with ecology and developing countries) was recognised as a way of making a number of crucial points simply. Morally and politically, of course, it throws into relief the fact that commodity values, the 'high life' and a high degree of exploitation of human and natural resources (both in the production of cars and the production of advertising images) cannot easily – or at all – exist in the same 'wo(r)lds' as either an ecological vision of humanity, machines and nature genuinely in harmony, or an egalitarian vision of a really fair, free and fed world. Meanwhile, textually, this minimal act of **collage** (placing one item in a new and dynamic relation to others surrounding it) is a sharp reminder that texts are continuous with their contexts; and that therefore the precise meaning and value of a text can be as much a product of *where* it is as *what* it is. With texts as with people, we know them by the company they keep. Consequently, when we see them in new or strange company we may see a whole new side of them that was previously hidden and perhaps unsuspected. The critical point is that we must learn to look at texts not only in their 'original' (i.e. usual, conventional) contexts and co-texts. We must also be prepared to pull them out and look at them again, in others, differently. In fact *re-co/n/textualising* turns out to be one of our most powerful critical, creative and historical tools (cf. 1.2.2–4; 2.6; 3.3.1; 4.5.3).

All in all, then, the kind of composite profile of the Peugeot ad that has been generated above is far more various, searching and valuable than anything a single individual – or even a single sub-group – would produce in ten times the time. It also prevents the facile belief that there is just one 'politically correct' 'decoding' of a text – as if every text carried around with it a 'single sub-text' which it is the mission of the radical analyst to identify, expose and 'name' (often in a particularly exclusive kind of academic discourse). In fact, the results of such triumphant acts of exposure 'decoding' and 'naming' are frequently a mixture of the textually obvious and the professionally obscure. An academic meal is made of it.

Much more valuable, I believe, is the recognition that the play of meanings and values round a text is inherently plural – and that there are therefore many ways into and out of ostensibly 'the same text'. At the same time it is important to insist that a text does not mean anything for anyone; it means and does specific things for and to specific individuals and groups of people at specific historical moments. Its meanings and effects are formed dialogically, through interpersonal and intertextual negotiation, and at any one moment for any one individual or group those meanings will in practice be finite and closed – however infinite and open in theory. For all these reasons, it is crucial that at some point people be obliged to express preferences: to insist that choices are made from amongst the options available; to force an act of 'closure'. This is what we do next.

(3)

Consensus and/or conflict? **The group as a whole must put together an outline of just *one* counter- or alternative text within a strictly limited time** (5, 10, 15 minutes, etc.). In effect, you have two options: (a) to put together a composite text based on elements of all those versions that you consider preferable and compatible; or (b) to choose just one of the alternative texts produced and work that up, incorporating new material and ideas as you see fit. (Clearly, this exercise can only really be done through groups. But if you are working on your own, you can still weigh which option(s) you would prefer. And you can still set about producing a final alternative or counter-text based on one of your own and/or one or more of those offered above. Either way, attempt to join in – not just spectate – this part of the activity).

Now, whether you managed to produce a single 'preferred' version or not, go through the following questions:

If you *did* produce a version, which was it: (a) or (b)? Why and how did you arrive at the choice of this version, and was everybody finally in agreement? Did any individual or group dominate the process of decision-making and, conversely, did anybody feel marginalised or underrepresented? (If so, what could have been done to remedy this?) Finally, would you describe the overall process as 'democratic', 'authoritarian' or something else?

If you *did not* produce a version, why not? At what point did negotiations break down – or never get going!? Was this because you were being 'under-' or 'over-' 'democratic', 'authoritarian', etc.? And if you attempted to do something like this again, what ground rules might be helpful to produce a tangible result?

The reason for stage (3) should be obvious, because of – rather than despite – the pressured conditions in which it was executed. For the awkward fact is that texts are produced (and especially published) in the most actual of all actual worlds. That world includes 'ideals' and 'desires' and 'personal preferences', of course. But it also includes pressures of time, place, publishing space, technology, economics, politics, etc. There were only a few of these pressures to consider in this exercise. Consider how much more complex – yet also in a strange way, perhaps easier – the decision-making process might have been had it been necessary to take all these aspects into account. This is a simple but fundamental point. It may be expressed more abstractly as follows:

In the actual world of textual production and re-production differences must always be resolved into preferences; that is, if the textual process is finally to lead to a textual product.

Anybody who pretends otherwise is simply not living in that world.

Incidentally, the result of the whole group working together for 15 minutes so as to produce just one alternative version of the Peugeot 205 advert was as follows: they didn't. However, after splitting up with a mixture of good humour and acrimony into three groups (sigificantly different from the initially randomly constituted sub-groups), they did come up with *three* very interesting alternatives the respective merits of which they hotly contested. Significantly, then, the demand for a single, all-purpose and all-embracing fiction produced faction, and not one fiction but many. In other words, in flouting the rules of the game they were given, the group(s) made up another one (three?!). What's more, as their revised game(s) was (were) even more productive of insight into the essentially fraught nature of textual production, from an educational point of view it was (they were) *better*. The difficulty I have just had – and am still having – in describing it (them) is a measure of its (their) success!

There is yet another fundamental and often overlooked *pedagogic* point in all this too, another lesson in learning. It relates to the often woeful gap between sublime theoretical possibilities and actual teaching practice. Put bluntly – and somewhat parodically – it is not enough simply to *tell* people that 'texts are plural', 'heteroglossic', 'multivalent', 'the product of an open series of processes of intertextual and interpersonal dialogue', and so on. (These are all potentially very valuable terms, to be sure, *as long as* they are not merely parroted to echo a new critical orthodoxy). Nor should it then be necessary – because people may have got hold of the wrong end of the stick and believe that 'a text can mean anything' or 'what I say it does' – simply to *tell* them that texts are also to some extent explainable and even predictable as socio-historical constructs; that 'texts are always already implicated in a range of potentially convergent but also problematically divergent discourses'; that they 'both reveal and attempt to conceal the site of their own inner contradictions'; that 'they offer "points of closure" which may be "opened up" so as to expose the play of the text's differences', and so on. Again, these are all insights which if properly internalised – and proper internalisation necessarily involves sceptical interrogation and transformation too – can be very useful indeed. But again, as merely ritual gestures, the dutifully delivered antiphonal responses to the revised liturgy of a new critical priesthood, they are worse than useless. They are dangerous – as are all unchallenged dogmas. In fact, none of this needs be the case, especially as the really radical ideas are really and radically liberating. With properly structured group work, designed to empower all and not act as the forum for the few; and above all given the opportunity and framework in which to challenge and change, intervene in and analyse texts for yourself (but not on your own), all that is needed is some encouragement, some occasional prompting and some guidance on 'where to find out more'. Not because you're told to, or generally feel it's expected of you; but because you genuinely want and need to; because your own part in the activity of asking 'What if?' has given you strong personal and social reasons to ask 'Why?'

1.1.3 Summary of the method

I'll now summarise the method. It is essentially very simple and comes in three stages (with an optional fourth stage, depending on the nature and resources of the course in which it is used). As has already been suggested and will shortly be demonstrated with another example, it can be used with any text at any level from that of the smallest, micro-linguistic feature ('lion*ess*' is pretty small) through to the largest, macro- (and non-) linguistic matters of genre transformation, re-contextualisation and medium transfer (there were instances of these in the suggested recastings between specific advertising genres, as well as in the unusual 'placing' of the ad). The same basic principles therefore apply to interventions in other sign- and communication systems. In fact, the imaginative act of asking 'What if?' and the critical act of then asking 'Why?' can be usefully – devastatingly, liberatingly – applied to just about every aspect of life as we (might) live it.

(1)

Intervene in and in some way transform the text. Deliberately put it 'off balance' and alter its emphasis. Try to make it address a different aspect of the same problem, or even a different problem entirely; and do not be afraid to try it out in – and against – different styles, discourses and co(n)texts.

(2)

Consider what light these changes throw on the structures, meanings, values and functions of the base text. Discuss and compare the changes you generated with those generated by other people. Be prepared to recognise other 'points of entry' and other points of view, and to modify your version accordingly. And above all be prepared to see the text as a series of sites of potential struggle and/or celebration.

(3)

Try to arrive at a final act of explicit preference – however provisional. This may, of course, include a preference for choices and combinations made in the base text. Either way, whether you admit it or not, there will always be at least some implicit act of preference involved in your response, however apparently active or passive that response may be. Intellectually, morally and politically it is better to come clean with yourself and others. And when working through groups it is always better to acknowledge and seek to resolve genuine conflicts of interest rather than pretend to some bogus consensus. From a more specifically educational point of view, it is the sheer activity of expressing a preference and the open exploration of the process of valuation that is important – not the act itself. For this reason some **commentary** on the process of decision-making is always necessary, explaining the decision-making process and registering routes *not* taken as well as those that were.

(4)

Follow up with further reading so as to improve your grasp of the critical, historical and theoretical issues thrown up by the exercise as a whole. This material may be fed back in to produce a more sophisticated set of interventions in the text and a more considered rationale. Alternatively, as we shall see shortly, it may suggest you should switch attention completely and concentrate on another kind of text and activity. In this case the initial text is not only de-centred internally, it is de-centred externally – and re-centred on another text altogether (see 1.2.3).

1.1.4 'Catch 23'

Now that the basic method is laid out and everything, perhaps, seems straightforward, I should like to mention a 'catch'. I call it 'catch 23' in homage to Joseph Heller and the kind of insight that his novel of that name (minus 1) gives into authority as it makes up the rules by which its authority is imposed and maintained. Foucault (1986) observes something similar in institutional discourses of all kinds.

In the present case 'catch 23' is that the text of the Peugeot ad that you and the previous students intervened in was *not* 'the original'. It had already been intervened in – by me, in fact. In the class exercise I deliberately removed and blurred out (or in your case deliberately 'omitted to mention') a small yet highly significant part of the accompanying image. To the right of the woman and car in the landscape there was a camera and tripod, and the camera was pointing at them both. No camera operator was in sight. In other words, the initial image had already incorporated its own self-reflexive gesture. There was an acknowledgement that it was part of a process of image-making. It was a text with a built-in 'metatext'. It had 'intervened' in itself.

When the deliberate removal of this part of the image was revealed to the students concerned their reaction was perhaps as yours may be: a mixture of curiosity and anger, fascination and frustration. 'Why haven't we been given the real, original image earlier?' 'What are you playing at?!' To which my answers were – and are – as follows:

(1) What was the 'real', 'original' image anyway? Aren't all images constructs of

reality, and themselves constantly subject to processes of production and reproduction – always more or less differently? So which point of the 'original' would they (or you) like to identify as its 'origin': the car, the landscape, the woman, the photographic apparatus; their/your first, second, last or next encounter with this text/these texts . . .?)

(2) Much contemporary image-making has already made its own kind of self-consciously metatextual gesture towards its own constructedness. Many 'post-modern' texts – and not a few earlier ones – therefore partly anticipate and manipulate a critical, 'knowing' and sceptical response. They 'intervene' in themselves, but they make that intervention in their own terms and manipulate it towards their own ends.

(3) Consequently, characteristically, the Peugeot ad still only gestures to *part* of its own constructedness. We still do not see the camera which and the photographer who takes the photo of the photographic apparatus. The artificially contrived and *openly* acknowledged act of looking *within* the image is still subject to an artificially contrived and *concealed* act of looking from *outside* the image.

There are also, I suggest, some more general lessons to be learnt from the above sleight of hand:

(4) Never believe that the text you are presented with is merely mediated or transferred; it will always have been re-presented and transformed in the process, whether incidentally or, as here, deliberately. If in no other way, to isolate and foreground a text in a particular context is in effect to reorient that text and change its meanings and functions. Educational con/texts are no exception.

(5) *Caveat lector!* – which in this case might be mangled to mean 'Be aware of the lecturer!' as well as, more accurately, 'Reader beware!' For teachers, like everyone else, have their own axes to grind and their specific, albeit broadly 'educational', reasons for re-presenting texts. Usually, of course, these reasons are not acknowledged or are passed off as totally 'impartial', 'neutral', etc. And yet this latter position, I suggest, is even more of a sleight of hand – and far more dangerous and insidious. For then the act of pre-selection and framing has not been signalled as such. The subject, it is thereby maintained, just 'is'. 'Catch 23' is at least the one you are shown. All the other 'catches' you are not shown, because they are claimed not to exist. You must therefore make your own interventions to 'catch' them for yourselves.

(6) All in all, then, we are hardly ever the first, nor the second, nor the third . . . to be engaged in intervening in a particular text. But at any particular moment we are the latest and the last. And that gives us all, at that moment, a peculiarly immediate and potentially wor(l)d-shaking power.

The first and last question for all of us, therefore, is 'What are *we* playing at?'. And how seriously, with whom and to what ends do we wish to 'play the game'? Which – and whose – game?! Carry on playing and you will be able to see – and say – for yourself.

Further re-writing and reading

Identify a magazine or newspaper advert which you find in some way arresting. Go through the same operations on it as those outlined in the above Summary (1.1.3). This can be done on your own. But if possible do it with at least one other person, and preferably in groups of three and four.

The general methods and models informing the practice of textual intervention are outlined in 5.1. Particularly relevant to the above example and referred to there are: 'commutation (substitution) techniques'; strategies of 'opposed and alternative decodings'; 'uses and gratifications' theory; and Eco's notion of 'semiotic guerrilla warfare'. Other relevant work on kinds of 'intervention' across a wide range of verbal–visual materials includes: Burgin (1986); Hutcheon (1985, 1989); Caws (1989); Hillis Miller (1992) and Graddol and Boyd-Barrett (1994: 224–38). On advertising in particular, see Barthes (1977: 32–51), Williamson (1978), Davis and Walton (1938: 166–204), Goldman (1992) and Cook (1992). More specifically 'literary' instances of intervention are referred to at the close of 1.2.6.

1.2 DE-CENTRING AND RE-CENTRING A LITERARY CLASSIC

so many utterances of so many imaginary persons, not mine
> (Robert Browning's advertisement to his *Dramatic Lyrics* (1842))

Henceforth, it was necessary to begin thinking that there was no center . . . that it was not a fixed locus but a function . . . in which an infinite number of sign-substitutions came into play.
> (Jacques Derrida, *Structure, Sign and Play in the Discourse of the Human Sciences* (1966))

We now turn our attention to a very different kind of text: a poem from the mid-nineteenth century. Our basic method and rationale remain the same as with the preceding advert, however. What we shall do initially, therefore, is simply reinforce these by applying them to different materials. Then, as the section proceeds, we gradually extend and refine them into a more fully articulated working model of intertextual and inter-personal processes. As usual, this is a model which you too must 'work' if it is to make anything worthwhile. The present text also involves a visual image (here a verbal repre-sentation of a painting); so once more we are obliged to work across the verbal–visual interface – albeit in a different dimension and direction.

Over the course of the previous activity one thing became particularly clear: the apparent 'centre' of attention and valuation in a text is not the only one possible. Browning and Derrida in the above quotations agree in that respect, albeit in different terms. In *our* terms we may say that the address*er*'s 'preferred reading' (or viewing) need not agree with the address*ee*'s 'preferred reading' (or viewing) – in part or at all. Moreover, if the addressee chooses to take a more active role and become an address*er* in turn, then the re-centring s/he prefers may well materialise as a slightly or very different version. In this way the grounds and the extent of the dis/agreement are literally 'realised' – in another text.

However, if the exposure of differences and the expression of preferences is not to be an utterly arbitrary, haphazard or capricious affair we clearly need to go about it systemati-cally and responsibly. What's more, even when we have escaped the comfort or tyranny of a single 'centre' and the illusion of a single problematic, how exactly do we go about re-centring and re-problematising the text? More particularly, how do we 'fix' both our-selves and it in a specific historical relation which is not just 'different' but actually and historically, as far as we can see, *preferable*? In short, how *should* we *de*- and *re*-centre texts? And how are we to do this so as to respect the imperatives of our several moments in time: the moment of the text 'there and then' – and our own moment 'here and now'? Neither exists independently and in isolation. Both, as we read, exist interdependently and in dia-logue. The critical-historical challenge is to bridge the gap.

In this prelude we engage in three movements and 'moments' of intervention: **textual**; **contextual**, and **cross-textual**. These may be glossed as follows:

Textual: *intervention from 'within' the text* – re-constructing around other textually available centres.

Contextual: *intervention from 'outside' the text* – bringing the text into contact and collision with other centres of interest in the contemporary context.

Cross-textual: *supervention of the text* – shifting the centre of attention to another text (and perhaps author and discourse) entirely – albeit ones that are still obliquely related (NB '*cross*-textual', as distinct from '*inter*textual', in that the former points to a deliberately motivated switch, whereas the latter implies a merely 'given' frame of textual reference).

1.2.1 Textual de- and re-centring

Here, then, is Robert Browning's poem 'My Last Duchess' (1842; in Browning 1991: 25–6). In it a sixteenth-century Italian Duke is represented addressing a servant on the subject of a painting hanging on the wall before them. The painting is of the Duke's previous wife, the 'last Duchess' of the title. The servant is in the service of a Count and appears to be involved in negotiations for another marriage, as yet only proposed, between the Duke and the Count's daughter. The poem, like the situation, is quite complex. It usually requires several readings before anything like the full implications of what is being said and – equally importantly – what is not being said are grasped. With this in mind, do two things.

As you read, ask yourself:

1 how far you personally are prepared to adopt the Duke's position (e.g. his 'voice' and self-image);

2 what other position(s) you feel yourself drawn to adopt (even though they may have no 'voices' or self-images directly available).

As always, experiments in reading aloud followed each time by discussions of the experiences of reading and listening are a good way of establishing the kinds of emotional distance and perceptual difference in play.

> *My Last Duchess*
> *Ferrara*
> That's my last Duchess painted on the wall,
> Looking as if she were alive. I call
> That piece a wonder, now: Fra Pandolf's hands
> Worked busily a day, and there she stands.
> Will't please you sit and look at her? I said   5
> 'Fra Pandolf' by design, for never read
> Strangers like you that pictured countenance,
> The depth and passion of its earnest glance,
> But to myself they turned (since none puts by
> The curtain I have drawn for you, but I)   10
> And seemed as they would ask me, if they durst,
> How such a glance came there; so, not the first
> Are you to turn and ask thus. Sir, 'twas not
> Her husband's presence only, called that spot
> Of joy into the Duchess' cheek: perhaps   15
> Fra Pandolf chanced to say 'Her mantle laps

Over my lady's wrist too much,' or 'Paint
Must never hope to reproduce the faint
Half-flush that dies along her throat:' such stuff
Was courtesy, she thought, and cause enough   20
For calling up that spot of joy. She had
A heart – how shall I say? – too soon made glad,
Too easily impressed; she liked whate'er
She looked on, and her looks went everywhere.
Sir, 'twas all one! My favour at her breast,   25
The dropping of the daylight in the West,
The bough of cherries some officious fool
Broke in the orchard for her, the white mule
She rode with round the terrace – all and each
Would draw from her alike the approving speech,   30
Or blush at least. She thanked men, good! but thanked
Somehow – I know not how – as if she ranked
My gift of a nine-hundred-years-old name
With anybody's gift. Who'd stoop to blame
This sort of trifling? Even had you skill   35
In speech – (which I have not) – to make your will
Quite clear to such an one, and say, 'Just this
Or that in you disgusts me; here you miss,
Or there exceed the mark' – and if she let
Herself be lessoned so, nor plainly set   40
Her wits to yours, forsooth, and made excuse,
– E'en then would be some stooping; and I chose
Never to stoop. Oh sir, she smiled, no doubt,
Whene'er I passed her: but who passed without
Much the same smile? This grew: I gave commands: 45
Then all smiles stopped together. There she stands
As if alive. Will't please you rise? We'll meet
The company below, then. I repeat,
The Count your master's known munificence
Is ample warrant that no just pretence   50
Of mine for dowry will be disallowed:
Though his fair daughter's self, as I avowed
At starting, is my object. Nay, we'll go
Together down, sir. Notice Neptune, though,
Taming a sea-horse, thought a rarity,   55
Which Claus of Innsbruck cast in bronze for me!

Now firm up some ideas about how you might intervene in this text. Re-read the preceding brief and use the summary of moves in 1.1.3 to help get some initial bearings. Then turn to the 'Types of textual intervention' (5.3) to decide on an effective strategy for the purposes you have in mind (e.g. 'alternative summaries', 'supplementary conversations', 'diaries', 'letters', 'trial', 'altered titles', etc.). Don't draft anything in detail at this stage. But at least sketch the kind of parallel, counter- or alternative text you have in mind, and give some indication whether it is to take the form of (another) monologue or a dialogue. Do this before reading on.

You have now established your own initial bearings with respect to this text. The activities which follow are designed to help you fix those bearings more precisely or, as appropriate, shift them.

(1)

'Translate' the whole thing into a conversational idiom with which you are more familiar, presenting the results on the page or in live reading as you see fit. This is a crucial move to make if you are to gauge the stylistic, perceptual and historical distances between your own characteristic language use and that offered by the text. Even experimenting with 'translation' of just a few lines (the first five, for instance) helps to register the various 'voices' and 'discourses' in play – the text's and your own. After all, it is one thing to be *told* or *see*, analytically, that this poem is written in decasyllabic rhyming couplets; employs language which is conversational but also formal and sometimes archaic; that word-order is often inverted and that sentences are arranged so as to stop and start part way through the line or 'run over' from one line to the next. However, it is quite another thing to experience all these features by actually *saying* them – and then to experiment with their transformation by *saying them differently*. Reading aloud and 'translation' are often the quickest ways of grasping what a text is – and is not – to you. Such simple strategies are used throughout the present method (see 4.4.1 for more detail).

(2)

Draw up a list of all the people actually presented or referred to in the text (the Duke, the Count's envoy, the 'last Duchess' etc.). These may be called the **included participants**, and each of them is a potential 'centre' or 'growth point' in her or his own right. For each *could* be envisaged as the centre of her or his own worlds, and therefore re-written and represented through her or his own words (thoughts, actions, etc.).

(3)

Go on to distinguish these 'included participants' in so far as they are represented in the text as 'speaking', 'spoken to' or 'spoken about'. In other words, in terms of personal pronouns, how far are they aligned with first, second or third person positions (respectively, 'I'/'we', 'you' and 's/he', 'they/it'). To give visible structure to these differences, try plotting each included participant in so far as she or he can be placed at one of the points of the triangle in Figure 1.1 on p. 18.

Doing this gives a basic sense of the kinds of communicative circuits and perceptual relations involved. If you add the status of these participants in terms of rank, gender, occupation and age, it also confirms the kinds of power relation in play (see 2.2 for developments of this model).

(4)

Now look again at the text and draw up a list of references to all those *artefacts* and *practices* which must at some point have required human labour – even though the labourers themselves are absent and their existence is merely assumed or ignored. The latter may be called the **excluded participants**. They are the

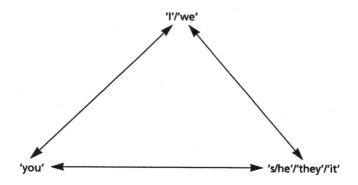

Figure 1.1 **Simple interpersonal triangle**

'other' people of the text – the ones who exist merely as material traces in someone else's story. They can therefore only be recovered by processes of deliberate **inference**. And yet, crucially, they too are also potential 'centres' of interest and textual 'growth points' in their own right. They too have their own potential wor(l)ds.

NB By 'excluded participants' I do not mean, say, 'Fra Pandolf' or 'Claus of Innsbruck' or the Count's daughter; for these are all referred to directly and in that sense are 'included'. What is at issue is the assumed or ignored existence of all the people who built 'the wall' (l. 1) and 'the terrace' (l. 29); who made 'Her mantle' (l. 16); who tended 'the orchard' and 'the white mule' (l. 28); and who gathered, refined and made the materials for the 'paint' without which 'My last Duchess' could not be painted. Every text is teeming with thousands of 'excluded participants'. By definition they cannot be found in explicit references. The challenge is to reconstruct them through systematic inference.

(5)

Go on to add the actual writer (here Robert Browning) and some actual readers (e.g. you and me) to the picture. These are what may be generally called the **extra-textual participants** and they/we clearly have a considerable – though not necessarily identical – say in what the text means. In fact, in so far as we (as readers) choose to *agree* with what we perceive to be the 'preferred position' of the writer (Robert Browning), we may be termed **ideally cooperative readers**. However, in so far as we tend to *disagree* with – or at least *diverge* from – that position, we may be termed *uncooperative readers*. (cf. 4.2). We are therefore talking about dialogically *negotiated positions* for both writer and reader. These positions were – or are – only realised through the very activity of writing and reading. And in our case the latter includes re-writing.

With all this in mind, try to model your relation to the various participants in the text alongside what you perceive to be Browning's relation to them. Use the diagram (Figure 1.2) as a rough matrix. Notice that you are asked to rank what you perceive to be first Browning's and then your own 'preferred centres' on scales of 1 to 10(+). Whether and how far the two of you agree is for you to speculate and decide.

A similar matrix of intra-textual and extra-textual participants can be drawn up for any text. It is a handy way of registering that: (a) there are many actual and potential 'centres'

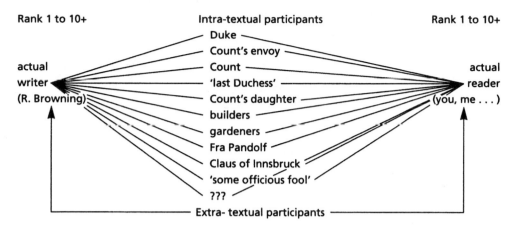

Rank 1 to 10+   Intra-textual participants   Rank 1 to 10+

actual writer (R. Browning)

Duke
Count's envoy
Count
'last Duchess'
Count's daughter
builders
gardeners
Fra Pandolf
Claus of Innsbruck
'some officious fool'
???

actual reader (you, me . . .)

Extra- textual participants

Figure 1.2 Actual writers and readers, intra- and extra-textual participants

available within a text; (b) there are far more participants recoverable through inference than are actually referred to; and (c) the apparently 'preferred centre' offered by the initial writer may – but need not – be the 'preferred centre' of the subsequent reader.

(6)

Now re-consider what participant(s) you personally would prefer at the 'centre' of a parallel, counter- or alternative text. Go on to refine or revise the version you first thought of, this time working towards a more fully artic-ulated text. Notice that whichever 'centre' you opt for, this will automatically entail the construction of a new 'interpersonal triangle'. For instance, if you were to privilege the Duke's 'last Duchess' as a speaking, writing or observing 'I' you would then need to re-configure other people around her in a range of 'spoken/written-to' and 'spoken/written-about' positions. They would become 'you's and 'he's, 'she's and 'they's expressed through different 'voices', implicated in different 'discourses' and located in different perspectives. Perhaps return to the 'interpersonal triangle' (Figure 1.1) above to remind yourself of this simple yet fundamental fact. You would then, of course (as before) need to decide which is the best textual mode for your proposed effects: diary, letters, conversation, trial, alter-native summary, 'altered ending', 'prelude', 'interlude' or 'postlude', etc. (see 5.3). You might even wish to interview, interrogate, chat or correspond with the initial writer (Robert Browning) more directly. For clearly there are some points on which you might seek enlightenment, some on which you might agree – or agree to differ – and yet others on which you might disagree entirely. All this can be done through a critical mix of research, reflection and recreation (see 1.2.4).

(7)

Sketch and draft your refined or revised version now. Put a provisional title to it. Go on to add a commentary comparing your version with the base text, explaining your critical rationale and chronicling the decision-making process. Do this before reading on.

Here, for comparison and by way of further illustration, are the titles of some of the versions of 'My Last Duchess' produced previously by students. They are accompanied by brief descriptions indicating the overall emphasis and strategy adopted in each case. It must be insisted, however, that these are no more than the suggestive tips of some substantial pieces of critical-creative work. Their function is simply indicative.

(a) *The work journals of Fra Pandolf and the private diaries of Lucrezia de Medici (the Duchess)* Entries from both treating events on the same day's sitting from very different points of view: in very different styles and with very different functions in mind. The Duke is represented in the background as a variously threatening or laughable presence. Presented on facing pages.

(b) *He gave commands* (cf. ll. 45ff.) Letters from a nunnery in which the incarcerated 'last Duchess' (not dead in this version) tries to contact the prospective 'next Duchess' to warn her of the Duke's paranoia, and incidentally reveal some of her former husband's rather unsavoury personal habits.

(c) *Gardeners' Question Time?!* The title is an allusion to a former long-running radio programme. But the actual text presented episodes from the Duke's marriage to his 'last Duchess' through the eyes, ears and words of the gardeners in the orchard: the breaking of the cherry bough; the ride on the white mule on the terrace; a final hurried abduction one stormy night – through the orchard itself. These conversations were expressly modelled on a combination of the gardeners' scene from Shakespeare's *Richard II* (III. iv, where the gardeners compare an unruly kingdom to an uncultivated garden) and the gravediggers' scene from *Hamlet* (IV. v, where the gravediggers give a shrewd and searching labourers'- (and clowns'-) eye view of goings-on at court.

(d) *'The Count, my master' (The envoy's response)* (cf. ll. 49ff.) Comprising, on the one hand, a formal letter to the Count advising his master to proceed with the marriage of his daughter (which the envoy knew was financially and politically expedient and so virtually inevitable anyway) and, on the other hand, the envoy's conversation with his fellow courtiers (in which he expresses personal anxiety about the girl's chances of either happiness or long life).

(e) *'My own fair self?'* (cf. ll. 48ff.) A 'postlude' in which the Count's daughter, now installed as the 'next Duchess', meditates upon the portrait of the 'last Duchess'. She concludes that she too has never been any more than a counter in dynastic property deals – but at this stage in history is not sure what she can do about it. The final narrative 'framing' is of a twentieth-century female art student looking at a painting of a Duchess looking at a painting of another duchess. It included allusions to the 1992 film of Virgina Woolf's *Orlando*, which features a trans-historical, transsexual hero/ine.

(f) *'Patriarty': objets d'art and male objects of desire* A collage of heavily cropped images featuring fragments of women from portraiture of the sixteenth, nineteenth and twentieth centuries. This was over-laid with blown-up fragments of Browning's text in which the disembodied parts of the Duchess are referred to (esp., ll. 14–22: 'spot of joy', 'cheek', 'wrist', 'throat', 'heart', etc.).

The above interventions and your own illustrate just some of the possibilities of textual intervention *from within* a text. Once we have got all these various participants ('intra-textual' and 'extra-textual', 'included' and 'excluded') back in play, virtually anything might happen. Though at any one moment, as we see above, for any one reader/re-writer (Browning or you or me) it is always something – not anything – that is made to happen. Potentially infinite differences, maybe – but always resolved as finite preferences.

Before turning to the next section (intervention 'from outside' the text) it is perhaps worth recording the general effect that such interventions as those above had on their composers' views of Browning's text. Significantly, virtually without exception, the result was increased admiration for it. Or at least fascination – albeit sometimes tempered by frustration. For not only does the activity of intervention, systematically and attentively engaged in, force us to wrestle with the text; it also, in every sense, obliges us to come to grips with that text's peculiar strengths as well as weaknesses (and its linguistic detail too, as the above versions generally attest). Indeed, in their commentaries, all the above re-writers saw themselves as in some way *complementing* or *supplementing* Browning's text – generating **parallel** or **alternative** versions. No one actually claimed to be engineering an outright opposition to it: an utter **counter-text**. This is important. For it may be casually assumed that intervention is automatically a negative activity; that it only draws attention to perceived short-comings or failures. In practice, this turns out to be far from the case. The outcome of the critique can just as well be an enhanced as a depressed valuation of the base text. Certainly it results in a genuinely critical-creative engagement with the text which is very different from the acts of merely embracing or attacking its values.

Incidentally, the main reason Browning's 'My Last Duchess' was chosen as a a preliminary example is to do with its hybrid status as a 'dramatic monologue'. That is, on the one hand it is 'dramatic' (and therefore implicitly dialogic) in that it presents one figure speaking to another in a particular situation and context. On the other hand, it is 'monologic' in that the immediate addressee (here the Count's envoy) either says nothing and simply listens or does not have his responses registered – except in the reactions of the speaking Duke. The overall result is therefore a tension or unresolved contradiction; in short, a **dramatic monologue**, with the emphasis falling equally on both terms. As a result, in reading we tend to put ourselves in the position of the silent addressee: full of questions and observations perhaps – but denied a voice within the text as such. Indeed, artfully constructed 'dramatic monologues' such as Browning's tend to produce peculiarly active and engaged responses from their readers – most palpably in the form of a desire to 'answer back'. Placed in the position of the speechless (and often the powerless), we feel impelled to speak out.

The trick, therefore, is to treat every text as a 'dramatic monologue'! For every text – whether 'literary' or otherwise, and however artful or artless – has its muted voices and marginalised discourses. Every text must therefore be 'answered back' with questions it did not propose – as well as those it did. That is what we proceed to do next, in another textual dimension. (For the activity of 'answering back' in ways which are both 'response-able' and 'responsible', see Bakhtin (1990); and for some awkwardly dialectical discourse questions, see 4.1.)

1.2.2 Contextual de- and re-centring

There are basically three ways of intervening in a text 'from the outside' so as to de- and re-centre it. All of them involve the actively critical invocation of various kinds of histori-cal context. For instance, we can:

(a) bring the socio-historical 'background' of the initial moment of production into contact – and perhaps collision – with the textual 'foreground';

(b) trace the variable fortunes of the text's subsequent moments of reception – seeing precisely how it has been viewed and reviewed;

(c) shift attention almost entirely from the base text so as to focus on other texts entirely – perhaps by other authors.

Taking these three moves in turn, there is therefore a kind of progression from the absence closest to the base text to the absence which involves its virtual displacement. In terms of the base text, of course, this is not so much a *progression* as a *regression*. But however we perceive this process, as increasingly eccentric motions with respect to the assumed 'centre' which is the base text or as the establishing of new and virtually independent 'centres' of textual and contextual interest, it clearly has to be engaged in if we are to locate and model a text dialectically and dialogically. That is, in order to grasp what a particular text said and says, we also have to grasp what it did not say then, and does not say now. 'Noisy' on some things and in some ways – it will have been utterly silent on and in others. And as when listening to music, we must be attentive to both the sound and the silence. In this section we make the first of the above overtly extra-textual moves.

(8)

Bring the socio-historical 'background' into the textual 'foreground'. This can be done by putting two crude – even rude – questions to the text in hand:

(a) What *else* was happening at the time and why has it *not* been mentioned? What was everyone else doing at the time and why have they *not* been mentioned? (Putting the 'content' of the base text off-centre)

(b) Who was the author *not* addressing – and what *other* specific genres and channels would s/he have needed to use in order to communicate with them? (Putting the initial communicative circuit in question)

Such questions need to be crude if they are to dislocate the base text from its privileged position of assumed centrality – and thereby re-locate it in an awkwardly alien yet illuminating critical-historical environment.

For instance, if the above questions are put to Browning's 'My Last Duchess' we come up with something like the following.

For convenience, this material is organised around the year 1842, the year of the text's first publication in *Dramatic Lyrics*. It is broken down into **references** (basically, 'data', 'facts') and **inferences** (interpretations of those 'data/facts' so as to produce usable information). All the references were gathered in the library from standard reference books, biographical and historical dictionaries and critical introductions before the group session (e.g. Pascoe, 1974; Litzinger and Smalley, 1970; Ousby, 1993). All the main inferences were teased out over some 20 minutes in that session.

References

1842 was the year Dramatic Lyrics *was first published in London* with a print-run of 500, partly subsidised by the author himself (then aged 30). It received mixed notices and 200 copies were left unsold five years later. Browning was at this time and for most of his subsequent life known chiefly as 'the poetess's husband', the 'poetess' being Elizabeth Barrett Browning (of whom more later).

1842 in Britain was also a year of: Chartist demonstrations and riots in Britain in support of the vote for all adult males; the passing of a British parliamentary act forbidding the working of women and children underground in coal mines; 2 years before the Factory Act which cut the working hours of women and children to 10 hours per day; 3 years before Engels' *Condition of the Working Class in England*; 6 years before the first Public Health acts demanding covered sewers and the 'relief' of over-crowded housing – and much more . . .

1842 in the rest of the world was also the year of: the declaration of South Australia as a Crown colony; a Maori revolt against infringements of the Treaty of Waitangi by New Zealand settlers; a massacre of British and Indians in the Khyber Pass; the Ashburton Treaty settling a boundary dispute over the US–Canada border; one year before the 'Rebecca Riots' in Wales, and the Anglo-Irish Government's prohibition of meetings in support of O'Connell's agitation for repeal of the Irish Act of Union – and much more . . .

1842 in the arts and sciences was also the year of: the first publication of the *London Illustrated News* and of Gogol's *Dead Souls*; the first showing of Turner's *Steamer in Snowstorm*; the composition of some of Schumann's best known chamber pieces; when Doppler showed that wavelength changed depending on the relative motion of source and observer (the 'Doppler effect'); the first use of general anaesthetic for an operation; Henson's first aerial steam carriage – and much more . . .

The crude answer to a crude question, therefore, is that Robert Browning wrote about *none* of these things and *none* of these people in 'My Last Duchess' – or for that matter anywhere else in *Dramatic Lyrics*. In fact, merely to present such a list is to remind ourselves of a number of fundamental, palpable absences from his text. It thereby helps us more clearly see the nature and range of its 'presences'. In other words, faced with such a barrage of relatively raw 'references', we may feel moved to make some broad inferences. These you should challenge or change as you see fit.

Inferences

Browning's text is *not* about urban and industrial conditions in contemporary Britain and therefore *not* about the lives of the great majority of the labouring population. But it *is* about personal relations and court politics as imagined amongst the Italian aristocracy nearly 300 years earlier. It *is*, we may further infer, about personality and the past – *not* about the massively depersonalising forces of the then-present, nor the various popular resistances to those forces.

We may also infer that 'My Last Duchess' is *not* set in those countries which were foreign and 'other' to Britain in quite different ways from Italy: the new and old colonies in Australia, New Zealand and North America, Wales, Ireland and Scotland. However, it *is* about one of the traditional centres of Western European power and the neo-classical culture associated with it: about a taste for court intrigue, aristocratic portraiture and expensive, exclusive monumental sculpture on classical themes. Furthermore, this text is most certainly *not* about current changes in the knowledges and practices of physics, medicine and steam travel (though in principle – and increasingly in practice – all of these were perfectly legitimate subjects for paintings, engravings, novels and poems).

Now to some critical-historical inferences about the communicative circles in which Robert Browning's text did – and did not – move. Manifestly, Browning was *not* writing for any of the prolific, 'mass' publications of the day such as newspapers and popular magazines (e.g. *London Illustrated News*). But he *was* publishing in a privately subsidised and tiny circulation book form to be read by a few literary reviewers, friends and family. He was *not* writing in prose, the then-dominant literary medium of the novel, the essay and the feature; *nor* was he publishing in popular ballad form for singing in public or circulating in song-sheets. But he *was* writing in a decasyllabic couplet form of great conversational and psychological sub-tlety, chiefly designed for silent and carefully considered reading by individual intellectuals. ('Mr Browning has never been a popular poet, and never can be. Perhaps he does not desire to be', remarked a contemporary reviewer; see Litzinger and Smalley, 1970: 372.)

Overall, then, what can we learn from these numerous – but by no means exhaustive – references, and the many inferences they occasioned? For one thing, it might be argued that the same references could be marshalled so as to generate very different inferences. However, *I* would argue that it would be very difficult to make utterly opposed inferences by citing this information. We may therefore be reasonably sure that if anyone wanted to oppose such a view of Browning they would simply *omit* reference to such events altogether. In other words, simply to bring such information into the foreground in this way would – and doubtless will – be considered by some people a 'barbarous', 'irrelevant', 'gratuitous' or 'unnecessary' act. Meanwhile others would persist in finding such references/inferences both illuminating and highly significant. (Clearly, by heavy implication, I subscribe to the latter view. You must decide for yourself.)

Notice, however, that none of the above references and inferences actually tells us whether we should *like* or *dislike* Browning's text. They do, however, help us to see that text histor-ically for what it was and was not; what it could and could not do, and whom it was and was not for. Moreover, these are constitutive historical differences which we are much less likely to be aware of simply by scrutinising 'the words on the page'. In fact, it is only when we bring the wor(l)ds of a particular page into contact and collision with other contem-porary wor(l)ds that we really become aware of what Browning was and was not saying, there and then in that medium. To be sure, Browning may have meditated long and hard on all the above-mentioned issues. It is just that from reading this particular text you would not know it.

1.2.3 Cross-textual de- and re-centring

The first part of this section is in effect an extended reminder about 'catch 23' (see 1.1.4). It points to the fact that the printed text we meet has always already been 'intervened in'. It is also a reminder that we can be aware of this, and set about some counter- and alternative interventions of our own.

Most texts studied on literature courses come complete with some kind of critical-scholarly apparatus of introduction and notes, and some suggestions on 'further reading'. (The present textbook is no exception.) The function of this apparatus is twofold: (a) to provide what the editor considers basic information on the text, its author(s) and period, etc. (i.e. 'terms of reference'); and (b) to point out, or at least suggest, how you should interpret and evaluate this information (i.e. 'terms of preference'). We may therefore call these the dually *referential* and *preferential* aspects of the scholar-critic's role: the supporting and guiding (or dominating) tasks of the textual apparatus. Inevitably, these aspects get thoroughly mixed up and in practice are often virtually indistinguishable. Hence the hybrid coinage 'terms of p/reference'.

Put another way, we may say that texts come *pre*-centred and *pre*-disposed towards the cultivation of certain readers and certain readings in a more or less institutionalised way. They also come pre-packed. For texts are not only cultural objects and elements in communicative – e.g. educational – processes. They are also commodities, products for purchasing.

By way of illustration, here are extracts from the critical introductions to the sections on Robert Browning in two of the most highly influential modern anthologies of English Literature. The first is from the *Oxford Anthology of English Literature*, Volume 2 (Kermode and Hollander, 1973). The second is from *The Norton Anthology of English Literature* Volume 2 (Abrams, 1993). The latter, as you can see, was revised some twenty years after the former. As you read over these passages, reflect what changes in editorial taste, historical emphasis, public demand and marketing strategy seem to have intervened in the meantime:

(A) Browning, in this editor's judgement, is the most considerable poet in English since the major Romantics, surpassing his great contemporary rival Tennyson, and the principal twentieth-century poets, including even Yeats, Hardy and Wallace Stevens, let alone the various fashionable modernists whose reputations now are rightly in decline. But Browning is a very difficult poet, notoriously badly served by criticism.

(Kermode and Hollander, 1973: 1279)

(B) During the years of his marriage Robert Browning was sometimes referred to as 'Mrs. Browning's husband.' Elizabeth Barrett, who has been regarded in the twentieth century as a lesser figure, was at that time a famous poet, while her husband was a relatively unknown experimenter whose poems were greeted with misunderstanding or indifference.

(Abrams, 1993: 1182)

These are instances of the active formation of the 'literary canon' at its most overt. They are also characteristic of two major kinds of critical history. The *Oxford Anthology* entry offers an essentially fixed and monolithic hierarchy. Robert Browning is installed firmly at the top, with all the other figures who preceded or succeeded him spread out in graded positions below. The *Norton Anthology* entry is quite different. It offers a view of a variable and potentially dialectical historical process. Robert Browning is firmly braced against Elizabeth Barrett, his wife, and the reputations of both are presented as fluctuating inversely over time. We may therefore say that while the introduction in the *Oxford Anthology* forecloses the play of differences by the open assertion of preference, the introduction in the *Norton Anthology* keeps the play of difference open (at least between the two poles represented by Robert and Elizabeth).

Now, I should point out straightaway that my own preference, with some qualifications, is very much for the latter kind of critical history – dialectical, historical and differential. However, that is not the main reason for featuring these two extracts here. Rather, it is the very mechanics of canon-formation that I wish to draw attention to: the precise ways in which critics and editors intervene in a certain body of knowledge with a certain form of evaluation. We have just seen the two main strategies by which this is achieved: fixed monolithic hierarchy versus fluid dialectical process. We shall now concentrate on the tactical differences at a smaller linguistic level. Basically, as in the previous section, this comes down to examining the relation between specific *references* and different forms of *inference*. We shall then be in a position to intervene: to recover the references – but invert or divert the inferences. Same 'data' – different interpretations.

Here is what I suggest you do. (Use the checklist in 5.2 and the index to follow up technical terms.)

(9)

(a) Go through each text (A) and (B) in turn identifying all the words which carry highly specific references to individuated persons, times or places. Basically, this means noting all the **proper nouns**: 'Browning', 'English', etc. These provide the basic framework of named historical entities: the primary 'frames of reference'.

(b) Now go through each text identifying all the individual words which carry overt valuation. Many of these will be adjectives, including comparatives and superlatives, or adverbs (e.g. 'great', 'most', 'lesser'; 'relatively'). Some valuations will be implicit in the choice of a particular verb or noun (e.g. 'surpassing', 'indifference'). Taken together, all these are the most obvious carriers of inference, the interpretive counters which weight the surrounding references. They supply 'frames of preference'.

(c) Extend this analysis so as to take in combinations or patterns of words and the larger structurings of perception these entail. For instance, consider the use of different tenses (present and past) in the two extracts; and the deployment of **active** or **passive** constructions. Cumulatively, these are all ways of establishing particular 'distances' between the editors and their subjects of study. They therefore affect how we in turn relate to the various *participants* involved (the intra-textual participants, e.g. 'Browning'; and the extra-textual participants – the respective editors).

The next step is to **intervene** in these critical introductions: to introduce the same historical *references* – but supported by different critical *inferences*. In effect, this means shadowing each of the above analytical operations with a corresponding critical-creative operation. This is what I suggest you do.

(d) Re-write each of the above texts so that the references are maintained but the inferences are inverted or in some way diverted. That is, make the texts refer to the same persons but in ways which suggest an opposed or alternative valuation. Do this by systematically challenging and changing those features observed in (9b)–(9c); i.e. value-laden adjectives, adverbs, verbs and nouns; tenses and active/passive structures. However, do this so as as to leave the proper nouns ('names') identified in (9a) intact – but in a very different informational co-text.

The *Oxford Anthology* version (A) might therefore begin thus:

Browning has been reckoned by many people as the least considerable poet . . . (counter-text: now generalised, passivised, past tense and inverted valuation)

or

The most unusual poet in English since the Romantics may have been Browning . . . (alternative text: now with differently 'fronted' structure; 'Browning' is delayed; and subtly different – not utterly opposed – valuations in the choices of adjective and modal verb).

Carry on along similar lines for yourself, re-writing each text so as to introduce the same figures in slightly or very different configurations of information. How far you have developed a counter- or alternative text can be gauged retrospectively.

The purpose of the above activity is to encourage you to experiment with and thereby experience the linguistic construction of critical-historical 'preferences' ('tastes', 'values'). It is then up to you to gauge how far it is you or the editors of the Oxford and Norton anthologies who are engaged in the most *perceptive* or *deceptive* moves. For clearly all changes in critical *reception* can involve both. Or rather, to put that more actively, people change the history of reception through a deceptively natural combination of reference and inference.

The overall lesson, then, is that critical histories and anthologies may be made for us. But it is also we ourselves who make critical history – as we do any other history. Moreover, the choice is never between histories that have and those which have not been 'intervened in'. They all have. Every reference is automatically implicated in an inference – and therefore a preference. Rather, it is a choice between those histories which for moral, political and aesthetic reasons we actively prefer – and those we do not. Consequently, where a suitable critical history or anthology does not already exist, we must make it our business to put one together. The history we do not find, we must look for and make.

1.2.3 Cross-textual de- and re-centring

We now make a couple of decidedly *cross*-textual moves. The first one involves us in considering the very different critical introductions to the work of *Elizabeth Barrett* Browning in the same two anthologies. Once you have read over the extracts which follow, carry out exactly the same analytical and critical-creative operations as those applied to the extracts devoted to her husband ((A) and (B)).

(C) Educated at home, Miss Barrett became an invalid (for still mysterious reasons) from 1838 to 1846 when, Andromeda to Browning's Perseus, she eloped with the best poet of the age. Her long poem *Aurora Leigh* (1856) was much admired, even by Ruskin, but is very bad. Quite bad too are the famous *Sonnets from the Portuguese*, . . .

(Kermode and Hollander 1973, vol. 2: 1475; from part of a tiny section called 'Other Victorian Poets')

(D) During her lifetime, Elizabeth Barrett Browning was England's most famous
woman poet. Passionately admired by contemporaries as diverse as Ruskin, Swin-
burne and Emily Dickinson for her moral and emotional ardor and her energetic
engagement with the issues of the day, she was more famous than her husband,
Robert Browning, at her death.

> (Abrams *et al.* 1993, vol. 2: 1029; here with a separate
> section and some 'room of her own')

The next cross-textual move follows the same 'ex-centric' – some would say eccentric –
trajectory. For we now completely de-centre our base text, Robert Browning's 'My Last
Duchess'. At the same time, inevitably, we also *re*-centre on other things and other people. The critical aim, however, is to select points and trajectories which also help us plot
the location of that base text from a different vantage point. We must therefore try to
choose texts and historical moments which have at least enough in common to 'talk with
one another' (what conversation analysts call some 'shared knowledge'). At the same time,
these texts and moments must be different – perhaps even divergent – enough to make
the resulting dialogue both animated and significant. Below are just two suggestions in this
line. Each text is prefaced by a catch-line. This is meant to signal the grounds of my own
'preferred reading' and the proposed relation to 'My Last Duchess'. For the rest, I shall
leave you to revolve the potential connections as you read. Some suggestions on further
activities follow.

Perhaps re-read 'My Last Duchess' before reading these extracts. This will help put the
'voices' and 'discourses' of all three texts in play more or less simultaneously.

A feminist response to marriage?

(Aurora Leigh is explaining why she refuses to marry the philanthropist Romney)

> 'Farewell, Aurora? you reject me thus?'
> He said.
> 'Sir, you were married long ago.
> You have a wife already whom you love,
> Your social theory. Bless you both, I say.
> For my part, I am scarcely meek enough
> To be the handmaid of a lawful spouse. [. . .]
> You misconceive the question like a man,
> Who sees a woman as the complement
> Of his sex merely. You forget too much
> That every creature, female as the male,
> Stands single in responsible act and thought
> As also in birth and death.

> (Elizabeth Barrett Browning, *Aurora Leigh* 1856: ll. 1044–65)

A socialist response to the Duchess's mantle?

> With fingers weary and worn,
>   With eyelids heavy and red,
> A woman sat in unwomanly rags,
>   Plying her needle and thread
>   Stitch! stitch! stitch!
> In poverty, hunger, and dirt,
>   And still with a voice of dolorous pitch
> She sang the 'Song of the Shirt'. [. . .]
>
>   'Work – work – work
> Till the brain begins to swim:
>   Work – work – work
> Till the eyes are heavy and dim!
> Seam, and gusset, and band,
>   Band, and gusset, and seam,
> Till over the buttons I fall asleep,
>   And sew them on in a dream!
>
> (Thomas Hood, 'The Song of the Shirt' (1844), in Bold, 1970: 66–8)

Engels in his *Conditions of the Working Class in England in 1844* wrote that this 'beautiful poem, "The Song of the Shirt" . . . drew sympathetic but unavailing tears from the eyes of the daughters of the bourgeoisie' (see note in Bold, 1970: 519).

1.2.4 Large-scale re-textualisation

There are many ways of bringing the texts of Robert Browning and, say, Elizabeth Barrett Browning, Thomas Hood and Friedrich Engels into a dynamic and overtly dialogic relation (see 5.3 for further detail). **Textually**, the possibilities include various kinds of 'collage' and 'montage': simultaneous, alternating, sequential or overlapping. Various kinds of 'hybrid' – with or without contextual information spliced in – are also possible. **Performance** versions can readily be devised for four, five or more voices (e.g. Browning's Duke; Barrett's Aurora and Romney, Hood's sempstress and Engels). These too could be simultaneous, sequential or overlapping (cf. 2.3). They could also be set in a scene comprising, say, the Duchess's portrait, a half-finished 'mantle', 'shirt' or 'shroud'; with various other paraphernalia of marriage and death strewn around. The theatrical and filmic possibilities for variously convergent and divergent words, images and sounds are, of course, considerable (cf. 3.2).

Textually and in performance this is also an opportunity to draw some of the other items in the socio-historical background into the foreground of the interpretation. Review the lists under the year 1842 above (1.2.2). Schumann's chamber music; Turner's painting; specific details on the laws relating to the labouring poor – even the 'Doppler effect': these could all be invoked in the form of distinctive voices, or cited as instances of competing discourses under 'the year in question'. For what *is* the question you wish to put to 'My Last Duchess' in and around the year of its first publication?

In all these ways – and many more hardly gestured to here – we can grasp the base text, 'My Last Duchess', not just as an isolated aesthetic object, but also as an instance of one set of cultural practices and processes amongst many. And we can thereby perceive what it is (or appears to have been) in dynamic relation to what it is not (or appears not to have been). After all, historically, it can hardly serve as its own 'frame of reference' or, in terms of value, its own 'frame of preference'. Some comparative or contrastive activity is always required if we are to see and make sense of both; and if we are to genuinely bridge – not merely fill in or ignore – the gaps between various 'theres' and 'thens' and equally various 'heres' and 'nows'.

Like the questions, our answers must be both multiple and subtle: *Whose* 'last Duchess'? The Duke's? Fra Pandolf's? Her own? The gardeners' and sempstresses'? The editors' and critics'? Mine? Yours?

The overall question, then, is not 'to intervene or not to intervene?' But how and why?

1.2.5 Summary

1 *Text* Re-centre the text 'from within', developing a subject/agent position which is marginalised or merely assumed in the initial text.

2 *Context* Place the text in relation to all those areas of life at the time and all those communicative modes it does *not* explore and exploit. See how this act of negation helps identify what the base text *is* saying, how and for whom.

3 *Cross-text* Shift or switch focus to a relatable yet distinct body of texts and practices (e.g. another author or body of writing). Different anthologies, guides and reference books can themselves be the focuses of study at this point. The main thing is to look for a centre of attention which is different and even perhaps, for you, preferable.

4 *Re-textualise* the products and processes of these various moments of de- and re-centring in forms and materials which seem most appropriate and effective for your purposes

5 Add an analytical commentary examining what you have done, how and why.

Further re-writing and reading

Apply the method just summarised in 1.2.5 to any literary text which fascinates or perhaps frustrates you. Comparative exercises similar to that on Robert Browning and Elizabeth Barrett can be carried out with respect to, for instance, Percy and Mary Shelley (also husband and wife) and William and Dorothy Wordsworth (brother and sister). In these cases, too, valuations and reputations have varied markedly, to some extent in inverse proportions.

For further fictional/factual materials and models treating Elizabeth Barrett and Robert Browning, see Henry James's short story, *A Private Life* (1892); Terence Rattigan's classic domestic drawing-room drama, *The Browning Version* (1948), and Michelene Wandor's feminist stage adaptation of *Aurora Leigh* (1982).

Group intervention at the micro-linguistic level of literary texts is finely exemplified by Burton (in Carter, 1982: 195–216), featuring systematic student re-writes of Sylvia Plath's *The Bell Jar*. On a larger scale, Dollimore and Sinfield use what they call 'creative vandalism' to explore the possibilities of subversive re-writing with Shakespeare's *Julius Caesar* (see Sinfield, 1992: 16–24). For further references on general theory and method, see 5.1; and for extended work-outs on and around Defoe's *Robinson Crusoe*, and Shakespeare's *Hamlet*, see 3.3 and 4.5.

1.3 WORK-OUTS WITH WORDS

A system network is a theory of language as choice. It represents a language, or any part of a language, as a resource for making meaning by choosing.

> (M.A.K. Halliday, *An Introduction to Functional Grammar* (1985))

As a writer I know that I must select studiously the nouns, pronouns, verbs, adverbs, etcetera, and by a careful syntactical arrangement make readers laugh, reflect or riot.

> (from *Conversations with Maya Angelou* (1985))

If we are to analyse and play around with words freely yet systematically we need some kind of flexible yet consistent terminology. The practical purpose of this section is to begin assembling just such a terminology – one which we can add to and refine as we go along. The more theoretical aim is to build up a sense of language as the interplay of *choices and combinations* at all levels. The concepts of **play** and **interplay** are also central. We play with language, like the rest of life according to various **rules** and in various **roles**: rules of sound system, word choice, grammar, etc.; and roles of perceived appropriateness to occasion and function. At the same time, we are in some measure free to make decisions about how precisely we shall play: the exact choices and combinations of move we shall make – using precisely which words, where, when, how and to whom, and with what potential effects. Significantly, this freedom (or creativity) sometimes even extends to changing the rules (or roles) of the game. Moreover, there is always some *inter*play or **dialogue** or **exchange** in all this. For we invariably 'play' language (like the rest of life) with other people – or with different parts of ourselves conceived as other people. And all these dialogues, as we have already seen repeatedly, involve not just exchanging words but also changing them in the process.

All these theoretical aspects of language will be handled practically in the brief activities which follow. Our immediate aim, then, is to turn existing linguistic *know how* (what you already know how to do with words) into a more precisely analytical *know what* (some terminology for explicating and refining that knowledge). Put more formally and fully, this is a matter of using existing linguistic and cultural **competences** to generate particular **performances** – and then going on to analyse the one in relation to the other. In the process, we shall experience ourselves being both used by and *subjected to* other people's words (and worlds) – even as we, as active agents, move to make them our own.

One last preliminary remark on the model of language used here: it is a combined **generative-functional** model. That is, the approach is **generative** (or **transformational**) in so far as it explores our capacities to generate infinite rule-related variations from substantially finite materials. At the same time, the approach is **functional** (or **pragmatic**) in so far as it explores not just the abstractable meanings and formal structures of words; but also what people actually do with words in real historical contexts – and what words do to people. (For references and reading, see 1.3.4.)

1.3.1 Critiqueing Descartes

If opponents of all important truths do not exist, it is indispensable to imagine them and supply them with the strongest possible arguments.

> (J.S. Mill, *On Liberty* (1859))

I should have liked to write a philosophical work consisting entirely of jokes.

(attributed to Ludwig Wittgenstein, on his death bed (1951))

'Critique' is the traditional term for critical re-writing of a text. It is not just a critical commentary on another text; it is a direct challenging and changing of the words of that text. In that sense most of the practice in this book involves 'critique'. In this section we shall critique one of the most famous philosophical one-liners, and perhaps the only line of Descartes many people know, even if they do not know it is by Descartes: 'I think, therefore I am.' Another, slightly later French philosopher, Rousseau, will accompany us in the early stages of this critique; for he too, in a modest yet significant way, directly challenged and changed Descartes' formula to make his own point in his own historical moment.

Again, the immediate aim of this prelude is a further work-out with the basic terms and techniques of critical-linguistic analysis. And again the method is both creative and dialogic in that we explore other people's words by generating our own related yet alternative versions. A further aim of this section is to push language up to – and beyond – its strictly logical limits. This is by way of preparation for the many experiments with 'non/sense' in the main body of the book (see esp. 3.2. and 4.3.2).

René Descartes (1596–1650) said: 'I think, therefore I am.'

Jean-Jacques Rousseau (1712–78) said: 'I feel, therefore I am.'

(1)

What kind of existential statement would *you* care to make:

'I ? therefore I am.'

Put in a word or phrase – almost any verb will do – and be prepared to defend it, however implausibly. Go on to consider what your intervention shows up about the specific interests of Descartes and Rousseau in *their* acts of self-definition.

(2)

Now tinker with the second verb ('am'). What other verbs are possible in this slot? Try some. What in this case are Descartes and Rousseau agreed on as an aim of their self-definition; but you – by your substitution – are not?

(3)

Play around with the personal pronouns (other than 'I') which were not chosen by Descartes and Rousseau. Do this by

(a) using a different pronoun to 'I' in both slots;

(b) using a different pronoun in each slot.

Again, what does this show about their common preoccupations? Specifically, what light is thrown on their view of identity and the dis/continuity of the subject position filled by the first-person singular speaking subject.

(4)

Change the tenses, aspects and modality of the verbs, and perhaps add circumstance items (e.g. adverbial or prepositional phrases). For instance, if we do all these things to the simple sentence 'I love you' we might come out with something like this: 'I should be loving you in ten years time' (i.e. 'should be' – future tense + modality of obligation; 'in ten years time' – prepositional phrase of time; see 5.3 and the index for further guidance on technicalities). Now carry out similar operations on Descartes' or Rousseau's texts.

(5)

On the basis of the above interventions, how would you now characterise Descartes' and Rousseau's intellectual positions? What differences are there between them. And what aspects of life (and language) do they both centre, marginalise or exclude? (Ignore for the moment the fact that these words were first written in Latin and French. This is a matter to which we return shortly; see D below.)

The last activity in this preliminary work-out gives you a much freer hand. However, it is important that you at least sketch some provisional responses in order to get the best out of the examples which follow.

(6)

Finally, generate *two more* variations on Descartes' 'I think, therefore I am' - and in any way that you choose. Be as subtle or outrageous as you wish. But perhaps read over the following remarks first, so as to remind yourself of the full range of options. For instance, you already know that you can experiment with localised changes at the level of choice of individual items: substituting different words or phrases for 'I' or 'think' or 'therefore' or 'am', as in the preceding activity. But remember that you can also engage in more pervasive and full-scale recasting, through re-combining larger structures within the sentence (e.g. reversing the sequence of elements, modifying the grammatical structures, deleting or adding clauses, etc.). Also notice that you have a number of speech and performance dynamics at your disposal, depending who you project these words as being delivered by and in what circumstances. In short, be adventurous! The only practical limitation is that you are asked to do all this more or less within the bounds of a single sentence – however long or short, complex or simple, 'standard' or 'deviant'. Do this before reading on.

Here, for comparison and by way of illustration, are some versions produced by other people working to the same brief. They were working in groups of two or three, and short summaries of their rationales and the subsequent analyses and discussions are attached to each. (As usual, these were much longer, more detailed and often much livelier than there is space to chronicle here.) Compare their versions with your own, and use their analyses to help shape analyses of your own versions. Each version or group of versions is identified by the main linguistic feature and textual strategy it exploits. I leave you to decide which of these travesties are 'subtle' and/or 'outrageous'!

A. Discourse acts

'I think – therefore I *am*!!', she said, with a glint in her eye, iron in her soul and a plastic lemon squeezer in her hand.

Descartes has thus been recast as an *exclamatory query*, with a specifically *gendered* speaker ('she'), and with a gesture towards manner of delivery and immediate situation. The contrast with Descartes is marked. And what it points up is precisely the fact that Descartes' dictum is usually treated as a *present tense declarative* and the most routinely privileged of speech acts – but that it needn't be! Refracted through a converse, Descartes' words suddenly look relative and maybe vulnerable. Maybe they too should really have inverted commas round them, an ascription and some clue as to mode of delivery?

B. Permutating the verbs

I (think) /feel/love/laugh/eat/consume/fart/write/act/keep on typing . . ., therefore I *do*.

Each of the substituted verbs entails distinctive premises which underpin a distinctive worldview. Think about them, then review the wor(l)ds you yourself proposed. Of course, there is virtually no end to the existential statements we can make in this way. Notwithstanding, whether you consider such alternatives serious, ludicrous or merely scurrilous, they certainly throw light on the purely intellectual and cerebral nature of Descartes' choice: 'think'. Notice, too, how the substitution of 'do' for 'am' (i.e. 'I think, therefore I *do*') signals a radically *pragmatic* rather than an *existential* approach to life – not as a question of 'being' but of 'doing'.

C. Extending the verbal process ('going transitive')

	think deep thoughts		an intellectual
	feel hungry		going to eat
I	laugh a lot	therefore I am	easily amused
	consume chocolate		fat and spotty
	write words		a writer

All these versions use verbs transitively; that is, with some 'carry over' or 'extension' from one participant to another (e.g. 'I' + 'think' > 'deep thoughts'; 'I' + 'am' > 'an intellectual'). They therefore highlight the fact that both the verbal processes in the base text are essentially *in*transitive: they lack extension or carry-over to another participant. Descartes' 'think' has no object (what is thought) and his 'am' has no complement (some counterpart or attribute of the subject 'I'). Clearly, then, the verbal processes in the base text are presented as self-sufficient.

D. Tinkering with tense, messing with modality and conjuring up circumstances

I shall think tomorrow in London, therefore presumably the day after I should have been being yesterday in Oxford.

Clearly, this version has made all sorts of radical interventions in Descartes' framing of time, space and perception. You may also find some of it grammatically 'anomalous' or 'deviant'. As a result, rather than simply castigate the person responsible for 'bad grammar', you might like to ponder the problems it poses about any assumed direct connection between 'correct grammar' and 'being logical'. For instance, is it (a) necessary or (b) helpful to insist on a direct connection between 'language' and 'logic'? You might also like to reflect that neither Descartes' French version (*Je pense, donc je suis*) nor his Latin version (*Cogito, ergo sum*) admits such a distinction in purely verbal terms; for neither language distinguishes between progressive and non-progressive forms of the present tense (though each does have other means of signalling duration). Consequently, is it here the case that users of English (which has non-progressive *and* progressive forms of the present tense) are left with a problem – and a possibility – not routinely available to the users of French and Latin? And there is still the question of whether the above version is, for you, 'unacceptably anomalous' or 'suggestively deviant'? Does the pure logic of reason meet its match in impure linguistic non/sense?!

E. *Personal pronouns, subject positions and some secret agents*

(a) i think, therefore I am. (i/I);

(b) It thinks, therefore we are. (It);

(c) She thought for the first time in her life, therefore she/. . . ;

(d) René thought he was Descartes – but his mother called him Cyril. (Cyril's mother)

These are just some of the versions generated over the years which explore and in large measure explode Descartes' model of the unitary human subject. Basically, this model assumes or asserts the continuous and constant identity of the two 'I's in the initial proposition: '*I* think, therefore *I* am.' In effect Descartes offers them as single, self-evident realisations of the same phenomenon. In fact, all groups agreed that what most irritated them about the base text was that it seemed to offer a wholly *self*-centred and *self*-validating argument. If you accepted the two 'I's on their own terms and accepted that they could stand in for anybody and everybody, anytime anywhere, then the proposition was closed and virtually impregnable.

Some more specific and peculiarly illuminating observations were made on each of the above variants. The gist of each is therefore worth repeating.

(a) '*i think therefore I am.*' *(i/I)* Due homage was made to the poet ee cummings and his example of a consistently unassuming, lower-case 'i'. In these cases, however, the 'I' was represented as *first* 'lower' *then* 'higher'. The argument was that this particular 'i/I' could be visibly seen growing in confidence and therefore size over the course of the proposition.

(b) '*It thinks, therefore we are.*' *(It)* So what might this 'It' be? What mighty and markedly *im*personal force has the power to determine not just what but *that* 'we' are – and then 'sign' the proposition?! God? Freud's 'Id' – the capitalised Latin version of 'it', signifying the sum of subconscious drives which pervade every action and reaction of the psyche? (If so, what has happened to Freud's 'Ego/I' and 'Super-ego/I'?) Or perhaps we should take a more political less psychoanalytic tack: perhaps the 'It' here is really

Althusser's 'Ideological State Apparatuses' or that even grander, though equally deterministic and reified abstraction, Hegel's 'History'. 'No', say a few separatist feminists, 'It' is really 'Patriarchy' – to which yet others rejoin with *'We think – despite them (men) – therefore we (women) are.'* And so on. Crazy? Maybe. But no more so than Descartes.

(c) *'She thought for the first time in her life, therefore she . . .'* Here's an enigma, a puzzle, a gap waiting to be filled, an absence begging a presence: . . . What might have happened here, between the first main clause and the unresolved and 'empty' dependent clause? First fill it, write it, as you see fit.

(d) *'René thought he was Descartes – but his mother called him Cyril.' (Cyril's mother)* This too plays happy havoc with the supposed stability of Descartes' speaking subject(s), 'I . . . I', and in a wide variety of ways. More particularly, we can note: (i) a telescoping of the base text's clausal structures so as to omit the 'therefore' and turn the verb 'thought' into a transitive; (ii) a thoroughgoing transformation of the verbs from the simple, 'universalising' present tense into the simple, non-progressive and thereby 'closed' past ('thought', 'was', 'called'); (iii) a shift from first-person self-reference to third-person narration, 'I' to 'he', thus separating out the speaking subject from the spoken subject (Descartes is now the object not the source of the text); (iv) a switch from personal pronouns to proper and common nouns ('René, Descartes, Cyril, Cyril's mother'), with a corresponding increase in referential specificity which humorously highlights the context-dependent generality of the initial proposition; (v) a deliberate play on the differing statuses of fore-names and surnames.

F. Chrono-logic chopping and games of con/sequence

(a) 'I think . . . – ,;:. I am;

(b) I think and/or/but I am;

(c) I, who am, think;

(d) Because I think, I am . . . ;

(e) If I think, then I am . . .

This is an attempt to compress a number of diverse yet relatable possibilities within a single section. What they have in common is that they all sport with different ways of combining the two mini-statements of which this proposition is composed: 'I think' and 'I am'. These examples therefore provide a basic work-out in ways of building compound, multiclausal sentences. They explore the relation between **chronology (sequence in time)** and **logic (consequences)**, the relations between causes and effects). At the same time they pick up and play around with the differences between grammatical **coordination** and **subordination** (cf. 3.1.6). Below is a check-list of the principal connectors (coordinators and subordinators) in modern English. Try some more out yourself, experimenting with inverted sequences of clauses as well as the sequence in the base text.

coordinators: and, (either. . . .) or, but, and yet.

subordinators:

   time: when, then, now, whenever, after, before, since, till, while, etc.

place: where, here, there, wherever, everywhere, anywhere, etc.

conditional, concessional or *hypothetical*: if, unless, in case, as long as, however, even though, although, despite the fact that, etc.

reasoning: therefore, because, so, for, thus, etc.

comparison: like, as if, as though, as . . . so, etc.

(For fuller listings and discussion, see Crystal, 1988: 189–9).

G. Non-propositional logics – alternative universes of discourse

What if I am a butterfly thinking that I am a human being a butterfly?!

This resulted when three people 'crossed' Descartes' words with one person's somewhat mangled memory of a famous Chinese conundrum: 'What if I am a butterfly *dreaming* I am a man?' The hypothetical 'What if . . . ?!' clearly has the effect of turning the whole discourse act into an exclamatory question rather than, as in Descartes, a declarative. It thereby implicitly poses the question: are 'truths' better expressed through questions rather than through statements? Proponents of formal, propositional logic and of certain empirical versions of 'common sense' would tend to the latter view. Everything really worth saying, they maintain (or more usually simply assume), can be stated. 'Truths' (or 'facts' or 'universal laws', etc.) are thus supposed to be expressible wholly and solely through statements: propositions. However, proponents of a wide range of alternative epistemologies and teleologies (extending from Zen Buddhism to dialectical materialism) would pose the whole problem quite differently. In fact, they pose *all* problems as questions and contradictions, challenges and conundrums – *not* as statements and propositions.

H. Cartoon capers and do-it-yourself dialogics

Thinks (thought bubble): 'I AM!'

This is yet another, overtly dialogic way of translating and transforming the relation between the base text's two primary processes: 'thinking' and 'being'. It also plays in the spaces between supposedly 'high serious' culture and 'popular pleasure' culture. Here, however, the discourse through which we re-write and read Descartes' *Discourse* is that of the comic or cartoon, and more particularly the device of the 'thought bubble'. You may also recall that 'thought bubbles' are conventionally differentiated from 'speech bubbles' in that the former have an interrupted 'bubble' link to the 'thinkers', whereas the latter are linked by a continous point or flash to the 'speakers'. These two graphic resources therefore represent the two main parameters of all verbalised thought: 'inner speech' (conscious thought) and 'outer speech' (speech proper). Vygotsky, Bakhtin, *Marvel Comics* and the *Beano* agree on this much at least (see 5.1). And so apparently does Lacan. Here is his critique of Descartes, from the lecture 'The insistence of the letter in the unconscious' (in Lodge, 1988: 96):

'I think therefore I am' where I think, there I am.

Or perhaps you prefer the cartoon version.

I. Sound on sense – sound non/sense

Oi-oi-oi-oi-OI! (the Yiddish connection)

This is both the simplest and the most complex version so far. For, though initially enigmatic, this string of letters and the speech pattern it represents actually takes the line of
least resistance where language is concerned: from sense to sound and back again.

So why *this* sound? Or perhaps – by way of a clue – I should say 'Whoi oi?' The process
of composition is worth describing in detail. It all started with someone trying out
Descartes in a stereotypically southern English 'yokel's' accent: something like 'Oy thenk
theferr oy yam – Oo Aa!!' This was funny in its own right. The suddenly superimposed
image of 'sophisticated French philosopher' dressed in the linguistic garb of 'simple
English yokel' was reckoned to be witty and, in its way, potentially significant (an instance
of 'carnivalisation', in fact; see Bakhtin (1968) and 5.1). But it didn't stop there. The
suggestive confusion of 'Oy' and 'I' prompted yet another member of the group, who was
Jewish, to chip in with 'Oi-oi-oi-oi-OI!' In Yiddish, she explained, this is an exclamation
meaning roughly 'Well I never!' or 'Fancy that!' (It is used similarly in Slavonic languages.)
And with each alternating syllable there should be a corresponding shaking of the head
and raising of the hands.

On reflection, and after several spirited demonstrations, 'Oi-oi-oi-oi-OI!' was generally
adjudged to be a wholly appropriate summary response to Descartes. In fact 'Well I
never!' or 'Fancy that!' – in a distinctly Yiddish formulation and with the accompanying
body language of 'folk' surprise mingled with disbelief – seemed to express the general
feeling quite neatly.

**Now return to the two alternative versions you produced in (6) (p. 33). Analyse
the linguistic resources you have drawn on in each case, and the rationales
and effects they seem to entail.**

Ideally we would now go on to explore Descartes' words in verbal co-text and social-
historical context. For reasons of space, it has been impossible to do this here. Those
who wish to, however, are urged to do so for themselves (see Descartes, *Discourse on Method*
(1637: IV)). There you will see that this famous philosophical one-liner and apparently
free-standing statement is perhaps no more than a passing aside. Certainly no more than
one amongst many subclauses in a long and complexly structured sentence – which itself
is embedded in a passage which can be described variously as 'meditation' and 'diary' as
well as 'philosophical treatise'. In fact, all famous quotations invariably turn out to be both
far less and far more than they appear in isolation. For they too – like our critiques – are
embedded in specific dialogues with both surrounding co-texts and enabling contexts.
Again, it's a complex matter of wor(l)ds.

However, I shall at least make a couple of parting gestures in these directions. (You, of
course, might make others.) With Descartes' proposition in mind, respond to the reso-
nances of the following counter- and alternative propositions:

> The philosophers have only *interpreted* the world in various ways; the point, however,
> is to *change* it.

> (Karl Marx, *Theses on Feuerbach* (1845: XI))

And these, from the Martiniquan pyschologist and revolutionary, Frantz Fanon – attacking the 'European mind' in general and French colonial rule in particular (1967: 252):

> All European thought has unfolded in places which were increasingly deserted and more encircled by precipices . . . A permanent dialogue with oneself and an increasingly obscene narcissism never ceased to prepare the way for a half-delirious state, where the intellectual work became suffering and the reality was not at all that of a living man, working and creating himself, but rather words, different combinations of words, and the tensions from the meanings contained in words.

Of course, these passages too can be subjected to systematic critique, just as they can be debated *for*, *against* and *alternative*. They may even be knit, along with Descartes' and Rousseau's propositions, into a single composite – whether in the form of an essay or some other critical mode (cf. 1.2.4; also 2.3).

1.3.2 Changing government health warnings

All language in use changes over time. More actively, we may say that 'people change language'. In this final work-out we look at government health warnings on cigarettes as instances of changes to language firmly in the public domain. We also engage in some publicly challenging activities of our own. This section therefore marks a shift from the more overtly philosophical preoccupations of the previous section to those which are more overtly political. However, as we saw from the above comments by Marx and Fanon, even the most apparently metaphysical argument has its political implications. Conversely, as we shall now see, even the most apparently mundane text can become the subject of the most profound reflections. Again our immediate aim is a work-out with a mixture of analytical, critical and creative apparatuses. What your own ultimate aims might be is your responsibility – as you are reminded at the close of play in this prelude.

Here is a common British 'government health warning' which until 1992 appeared on cigarette advertising and the packs themselves:

H.M. Government Health Warning:

SMOKING CIGARETTES CAN SERIOUSLY DAMAGE YOUR HEALTH

(1)

Consult with someone else and come up with *two* alternative versions: one stronger and more intense; the other weaker and less intense. Be as subtle or outrageous as you like. Once you have experimented with some possibilities, write down your two preferred alternatives here:

Stronger (A1):

Weaker (A2):

---

(2)

(a) **Now describe as precisely as possible the differences between each of your versions and the base text.** Draw on the terms and techniques explored already in 1.3.1 and use the checklist in 5.2.

(b) **Go on to consider what medical, legal, commercial, consumer group, governmental and generally social pressures might be brought to bear on each of your versions.** Whose immediate interests would or would not be served by such a warning. What institutions would come into play – and who, in your view, might 'win' – and why?

Do all this before reading on.

(3)

Go on to compare your hypothetical versions with the following actual versions. These appeared in Britain from January 1992 as a direct result of the implementation of European Community guidelines on the advertising and sale of tobacco products.

> (a)   5 mg TAR 0.5 mg NICOTINE
> SMOKING CAUSES CANCER
> Health Department's Chief Medical Officers

> (b)   8mg TAR 0.75 mg NICOTINE
> PROTECT CHILDREN:
> DON'T MAKE THEM BREATHE YOUR SMOKE
> Health Department's Chief Medical Officers

(4)

What are the chief differences between these actual, later versions and the earlier British Government Health Warning? Would you say they are stronger or weaker? And what other differences of emphasis or orientation do you notice?

(5)

Now compare your versions with the following pairs of re-writes produced by small groups of students working to the same initial brief (1).

(B1) *Stronger*: H.M.Government Health Warning:

SMOKING CIGARETTES WILL VERY SERIOUSLY DAMAGE YOUR HEALTH

(B2) *Weaker*: H.M.Government Health Warning:

SMOKING CIGARETTES MAY SOMETIMES DAMAGE YOUR HEALTH

(C1) *Stronger*: GOVERNMENT LAW AND ORDER: SMOKE! DIE!! DON'T!!!

(C2) *Weaker*: Westminster bureaucrats are told to say: There is some evidence to suggest that in certain cases the inhalation of tobacco fumes could have detrimental effects.

(D1) *Stronger:* DE BLACK QUEEN SAY: COUGH YO' LUNGS OUT, BABY!

(D2) *Weaker:* The Queen's annual message: To smoke or not to smoke, that is the question?

---

(6)

Go through each of the above pairs noting their differences and the difference between each of them and the base text. What specific choices and combinations do they involve and how, formally, would you account for their various effects? Also consider in what ways the communicative relations and discourses implied in the base text have been subverted, inverted or diverted? Towards whom and what – from whom and what?

Finally, we turn to some versions which were the product of research and reflection (drawing on Chapman (1986), for instance). These particular versions were generated by the same groups responsible for versions (B)–(D) above. The brief this time was both more challenging and more open.

(7)

Research any aspect of smoking which interests you (tobacco growing and manufacture; taxation; health policies; consumer or manufacturer pressure groups, advertising, etc.). Then come up with your own 'PREFERRED HEALTH STATEMENT'. This is what the above group came up with. A summary of their rationales and the ensuing discussion is appended to each.

(B2) TOBACCO IS A CASH CROP YOU CANNOT EAT AND IT MAKES THOSE WHO GROW IT ECONOMICALLY DEPENDENT. ARE YOU DEPENDENT ON TOBACCO TOO?

Generated by reading about the economic dependency of numerous countries on tobacco and other cash crops (e.g. coffee, tea, sugar, poppies/heroin). Pun on 'dependent'; general statement followed by direct address to reader/smoker. The group added, 'Our version is too wordy and too specialist for general distibution – but alright as part of a larger consciousness-raising campaign.' 'You can see how the base text concentrates on *use* rather than *production*. Ours points to "damaging" effects at the other end of the process.'

(C3) WHY ISN'T THIS GOVERNMENT HEALTH WARNING IN HUGE BLACK LETTERS ON EVERY SIDE OF AN EMPTY PACK?

Generated by reading about the protracted negotiations between government and tobacco firms on the precise size, design and location of the warning. The result in 1991: it should occupy one side of the pack and not more than 15 per cent of the total area, in black on white, at the base of a billboard or magazine advert. The above alternative was a deliberately metatextual and auto-referential intervention in this state of affairs. The 'empty pack' sought to draw attention to the 'liberality'/'inconsistency'/ 'contradiction'/'hypocrisy' – all these words were invoked – of a policy which officially warned against but didn't prohibit cigarettes. The group acknowledged that their warning had a distinctly 'counter-cultural' feel to it: 'handy as an irritant, but its shock-value would soon wear off', as one person observed. It could, however, they suggested, easily appear on an 'alternative postcard' or a 'trick packet'. Again, the sheer blandness, 'the total lack of shock' in the base text was recognised as 'the secret of its success'. There was some pained awareness of the general utility and essential 'colourlessness' of official broadcast discourses of all kinds: for everyone in general – and therefore no one in particular.

(D3) IT IS YOUR GOD-GIVEN, DEMOCRATIC AND COMMERCIAL RIGHT IN A FREE SOCIETY WITH A FREE MARKET AND FREEDOM OF EXPRESSION TO SMOKE ANYWHERE, ANYTIME.

Generated by reading some of the huge quantity of material, often sponsored by the tobacco industry, which is dedicated to the equation 'freedom of expression' = 'freedom to smoke'. The group admitted to writing this to some extent 'tongue in cheek' and with deliberate exaggeration (hence 'free/dom' × 3, 'anywhere/time' and the potentially incongruous mixture of religious, political and commercial references). They also said they had resisted the temptation to add graffitti (e.g. 'and choke other people' immediately after 'smoke'). The rest of the group did not share their reserve and volunteered many, many more (e.g. tagged on to the end: ' – So how come cigarettes aren't "free" too?!'). It was also observed that if the address*ees* of this message actually believed in the peculiar configuration of religious, political and commercial values it offers, then it would command assent (if taken seriously) or occasion offence (if taken parodically). Again, the intimate and variable connection between text and context and between meaning and social function was highlighted. And again the bland 'offend-nobody-please-nobody' nature of the base text was thrown into relief.

That last point, returning to the base text, brings us back to the beginning of this series of exercises. It may also usefully prompt a restatement of the rationale for these preludes in particular, and for textual intervention in general. It should be clear by now that textual intervention is far from being a wholly negative and destructive activity. Dialectical and dialogic, certainly – but ultimately both *decon*structive and *recon*structive in aim. For the method combines the analytical-critical *un*doing of differences with the creative-critical *re*making of preferences. Moreover, as the students' own commentaries on their initial and final re-writes repeatedly attest, the result may just as easily be increased, qualified or begrudging respect for the base text as opposition to or dismissal of it. In this case, for instance, many who did the most outrageous and inventive or subtle and specialist re-writes eventually came round to the conclusion that the actual 'H.M. government health warning' was *in its own terms* highly effective. It represented a highly skilful resolution of – or compromise among – competing legal, medical, commercial and educational demands. Meanwhile, though all of the alternatives proved hugely interesting to produce and analyse, and each had something distinctive to recommend it, many were palpably preaching to or by the converted; they were messages caught in the circuit of specific pressure and interest groups.

On the other hand, some felt that the collective process of re-writing and analysing, researching and further re-writing pointed to some genuinely alternative possibilities. They felt that they had not just explored existing arenas of discourse but had actually extended them in viable directions (the move to include the effects of 'secondary smoking' in the actual, post-1991 revisions was another instance of this; see examples in the initial

'Prelude' to this section). In other words, new agendas were not just hypothetically possible; they were being realised – after considerable pressure – all the time. Today's potentially Utopian version might still become tomorrow's reality. At the same time, reviews of the various medical, legal, commercial, etc., interests involved had given everyone some foretaste of what was really involved in transforming official public pronouncements. To be sure, all participating felt in some real sense *empowered* through working in small groups in an educational context. But they none the less had a realistic sense of where the actual political and economic *levers of power* were and are to be found: in the commercial, governmental, legal, medical and educational institutions through which various vested, socio-historical interests are confirmed and, in some cases, contested. The overall result was as it should be. People had an exhilarating yet also chastening grasp of a number of vital issues: a sharpened sense of their own responsibilities both to know how words work and simply to 'know' more when it was necessary; as well as an acute sense of their pressing yet also playfully serious need to contribute to the making and remaking of the 'worlds' within and beyond the words.

At this point, therefore, you might like to carry out the final brief, (7), for yourself (see p. 41). Explore the differences constituted by the words and worlds associated with smoking, and express your own preferences on the subject. As always, the most immediate subject of discourse in this course is yourself.

1.3.3 Summary

Language, like other communication and sign-systems, entails the interplay of *choices and combinations* at all levels. Consequently, even the smallest part of a word always refracts a whole world of social and historical relations. Its very existence both presupposes and helps constitute the language as a notionally whole system. And yet this is always a 'whole' which is full of 'holes' – an apparently stable totality which in reality is constantly subject to change.

For all these reasons we are primarily concerned in the present practice with *language as discourse* (i.e. language as a part of a social-historical *dialogue* involving both exchange and change) as well as language as a *creative* resource. At the same time, we are engaged with the *play* between infra-textual *participants, processes* and *circumstances* (e.g. nouns, verbs, adjectives and adverbs) and the extra-textual participants, processes and circumstances to which they refer or in which they are implicated (e.g. addressers, addressees and the subject matter of the address). This brief introduction to language has therefore been *interactive*. For we find ourselves working not just **upon** but also **within** a variety of dialogic and discursive processes. We recognise ourselves being used by language (as historical subjects) even as we realise our own power actively to use language (as historical agents). In grasping the *constraints* which regulate and guide us, we also grasp the resources of our own *creativity*. In theory, history may always have had the last word. But in practice, in the present, we always have the first . . .

FURTHER RE-WRITING AND READING

A. Critiqueing famous philosophical one-liners (cf. 1.3.1)

Here are some more or less well-known philosophical axioms. You can doubtless think of or look up others, perhaps drawing on dictionaries of quotations and histories of philosophy. Use some of these short texts as focuses for the kinds of re-writing activities used to critique Descartes' 'I think therefore I am'. Do this adventurously yet systematically, exploring alternative word-choices and combinations, sound patterning and visual presentation, discourse acts and contexts. A stylistic checklist is supplied in 5.2.

(1) The good is the beautiful.

(Plato (429–347 BC), *Lysis*)

(2) Man is by nature a political animal.

(Aristotle (384–322 BC), *Politics*, Bk I)

(3) Question: In clapping both hands a sound is heard: what is the sound of the one hand?
Response: . . . (Any suggestions?)
(Koan of the Zen Master, Hakuin (1685–1768); for traditional responses and commentary,
see Hoffmann, 1977: 38, 208–10)

(4) God is dead: but considering the state the species Man is in, there will perhaps be caves,
for ages yet, in which his shadow will be shown.
(Friedrich Nietzsche (1844–1900), *The Gay Science*)

(5) Philosophy is not a theory but an activity.
(Ludwig Wittgenstein (1889–1951), *Tractatus Logico-Philosophicus*, section 4)

(6) Matter – a convenient formula for describing what happens where it isn't.
(Bertrand Russell (1872–1970), *An Outline of Philosophy*)

(7) He is the Subject, he is the Absolute – she is the Other.
(Simone de Beauvoir (1908–86), *The Second Sex*, Introduction)

B. Changing public pronouncements (cf. 1.3.2)

Here are some more short texts for exploring using the same method as was used with the government health warnings. That is, generate 'stronger' and 'weaker' versions, then, on the basis of further research and reflection, proceed to your own 'preferred pronouncement'. You can no doubt identify comparable texts more directly relevant to your own situation. Many occur in the discourses of politics, public relations and advertising. Again, draw on the stylistic checklist in 5.2 to help explore alternatives.

(1) BUY BRITISH!

(Slogan periodically appearing on goods in campaigns sponsored by government and trade since the mid-nineteenth century. Counterparts can be found in most modern nation states.)

(2) DON'T DRINK AND DRIVE

(British government public health slogan since 1970s; cf. next.)

(3) Practise safe sex. Use a condom.

(British AIDS-related public health slogan, from 1990)

(4) WORKERS OF THE WORLD UNITE! – YOU HAVE NOTHING TO LOSE BUT YOUR CHAINS!

(Slogan current since its first appearance in Marx and Engels' *Communist Manifesto* (1845); e.g. on front of *Pravda* till 1992.)

(5) We hold these truths to be sacred and undeniable; that all men are created equal and independent.

(Thomas Jefferson (US President 1801–9), first surviving draft of the Declaration of Independence)

Relevant *introductions to language* are Farb (1975) and Fromkin and Rodman (1993). Good overviews of *language and power* are Montgomery (1986), Kramarae, Shulz and O'Barr (1984) and Andersen (1988); also see Orwell's essay 'Politics and the English Language' (1946). *Language and logic* are treated, often with an emphasis on 'serious play', in Wittgenstein (1953), Thouless (1953), Posner (1982), Hintikka and Kulas (1983), Fisher (1988) and Harris (1989). For the movement now known as *critical linguistics*, to which the present book is in part a contribution see Fowler *et al.* (1979), Kress and Hodge (1993), Kress (1989), Fairclough (1989, 1992) and Fowler (1991). *Literary stylistics*, to which it also contributes, can be very usefully approached through Haynes (1989, introductory), Traugott and Pratt (1980, advanced), Fowler (1986), Birch (1989) and Carter and Nash (1990).

Relevant *grammars* are Crystal (1988, introductory), Halliday (1985, advanced functional) and Quirk and Greenbaum (1976, advanced traditional).

Handy *reference books* on language, stylistics and discourse are Carter (1993, introductory) and Walcs (1989, advanced). More specific or advanced work on *dialogue, discourse analysis* and *pragmatics* is referred to in 4.6; and there is a discussion of key works by Vygotsky (1934), Voloshinov (1973) and Bakhtin (1981) in 5.1.

2 Subjects and agents; selves and others

The text exposes for representation the extreme moment characteristic of all process as practice. In so doing it 'speaks' to every subject moving through this practice in various domains.

(Julia Kristeva, *Revolution in Poetic Language* (1984))

The aims of this chapter are fourfold:

1 to use the **personal pronoun system** of English (I/me/mine/my; we; you; she; he; they; it) to illustrate the ways in which language offers us specific, structurally inter-related choices;

2 to explore the ways in which this personal pronoun system helps us to focus the kinds of **subject position** we can take up with respect to a particular text or other event;

3 to promote a sense of readers as **active agents** rather than just passive subjects, negotiating their own 'orientation' rather than simply accepting the 'positions' offered by the text;

4 to do all this, as usual, through experiment and exploration as well as exposition, drawing on the example and inspiration of previous work by students and aiming ultimately to enhance all these capacities in the current reader as re-writer. Most immediately and importantly that means *you*.

2.1 SUBJECTS AND SUBJECTION; AGENTS AND AGENCY

Some provisional definitions of those crucial terms 'subject' and 'agent' will help get our bearings and prevent confusion. Basically, three meanings of 'subject' are current:

(a) subject meaning **grammatical subject**: what controls the verb and is traditionally distinguished from grammatical 'object' and 'complement' (e.g. '*She* started the car'; '*The car* was started easily');

(b) subject meaning **subject matter**: 'topic', 'what something is about'. This can have a generalised sense, as in 'The subject of this book/film is . . .'; or a specialised educational sense, meaning 'subject of study' or 'academic discipline';

(c) subject, as in psychological, ideological and modern philosophical usage, meaning **subject position: a perceptual location within or orientation towards an event, usually unconsciously and habitually assumed.** Partially equivalent traditional terms are 'point of view' and 'perspective'. But these are limiting in their reliance on a narrowly visual analogy. They also tend to presuppose a fixed 'object' or unified 'event' around which the various 'points of view' are organised and on which a particular 'perspective' converges. They posit a more or less stable and given 'centre'. The advantage of talking in terms of alternative 'subject positions' within or around an event is that each one is in effect *its own centre*. It is therefore axiomatic that each subject position offers not just a slightly different version of 'the same event' but substantially 'different events'.

It is primarily this last meaning of subject position (perceptual, social-historical and ideological) we shall use in the present chapter. I shall therefore explain it at greater length (for references, see 2.8 and 5.1).

For instance, consider all the potential subject positions involved in a supermarket transaction. Notice that these include not only those people *obviously present and immediately implicated* (customer and cashier with perhaps manager, shelf-fillers and security guard in the background) but also those people *remotely absent yet ultimately implicated* (the growers of fruit and vegetables and the rearers of animals; the miners of metal and oil and the paper- and plastic-makers – and the processors and distributors of all of them). Moreover, on the holistic principle that 'everyone and everything is eventually connected to everyone and everything else', this latter category of *remotely absent yet ultimately implicated subject positions* extends in principle to everyone, everywhere and at all times. That is, not only does it embrace all those people directly involved in the various agricultural, industrial and commercial processes worldwide (for supermarket commodities, like most others, are global in provenance); it also embraces members of the governments, armies, police forces, and all the various political, religious, legal and educational systems, etc., which underpin those commercial processes, and are in turn underpinned by them. Ultimately, therefore, each and every supermarket transaction – and most other transactions – involves *you* and *me*. What's more, that 'you' and 'me' needs to be read historically as well as in some present time frame. For clearly, all these processes of growing and rearing and preparing and packing (and governing, and policing and legislating and educating, etc.) do not happen all at once. They – and the people involved – are themselves the result and latest representatives of historical processes stretching from the infinitely remote past to the infinitely remote future. In sum, everyone everywhere – past, present and future – may be 'remotely absent' from a particular event; but they/we are most definitely 'ultimately implicated'.

Such a 'totalising' and 'world-historical' view of something as apparently limited and localised as a supermarket transaction may be initially difficult to grasp. Indeed, in practice – if not perhaps in theory – it is mind-bogglingly impossible to grasp. Genuinely holistic comprehension always is. And yet, it is clearly crucial at least to make the effort to 'think the whole' if we are to avoid the peripheral blindness of concentrating only on the 'part' we see and misconceiving *that* as the whole.

For all these reasons it is analytically convenient as well as theroretically (and morally) imperative that we recognise the various dimensions in which subjects operate: in an immediate situation and context *and* as figures in a range of world-historical processes. Initially, then, it is helpful to think of the 'subjects' involved in, say, a supermarket transaction as they can be plotted on a number of axes in a number of temporo-spatial and socio-historical dimensions. These may be realised diagrammatically as in Figure 2.1.

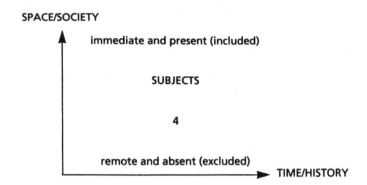

Figure 2.1 A model of social-historical subjects

Put more discursively, we may say that the subjects involved in an event may be distinguished as immediate and present or remote and absent, relative to whatever centre we choose; but that ultimately everyone everywhere – past, present and future – is implicated in that event in so far as all spaces and societies are interconnected, and interact and change historically.

However, being a 'subject' of any kind is only the half of it. In order to fully grasp the process whereby subjects are not only **transform*ed by* society and history** but also actively engage in **transform*ing* society, history and themselves** we need another term and another set of concepts.

Agents and agency

Agent and its abstract noun *agency* derive from the Latin verb *agere*: 'to act' or 'to do'; 'to cause', 'to make happen' – hence '*agen*da', meaning 'things to be done', and 'to *agi*tate', 'to get things moving'. **Agents**, then, are **people who make things happen**; and **agency** is the generalised **power or capacity to make things happen**. Agents are 'causers'; agency is 'causation'. 'Subjects', on the other hand, are those persons 'thrown under' someone or something else (from the past participle, *subjectum*, of the Latin verb *subiacere* – 'to throw beneath'). Hence the close similarity of meaning between being, say, a 'royal subject' and 'royal servant'; and the sense of being a 'British subject' as one 'subject' to the laws and obligations, as well as privileges, of that particular nation state (see 4.1). For this reason we need to recognise agents as the 'flip-side' of subjects in the two main positions for the latter distinguished earlier. That is,

> *immediately present agents/agencies* are those people/forces we see making things and making things happen and whom we can *directly refer to* in a particular situation;

> *remotely absent agents/agencies* are those people/forces that we cannot actually see but whom we must *indirectly infer* as having made related things happen elsewhere at some other time.

With all this in mind, I shall therefore invite you to practise this theory.

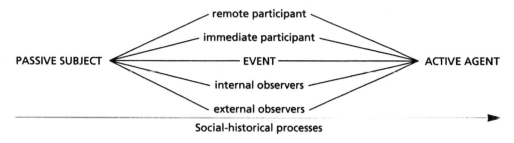

Figure 2.2 Event-centred model of perception

Simply add '/AGENTS' to 'SUBJECTS' in Figure 2.1 or recast the diagram more radically – completely replacing it if you see cause to. In any event, exercise your own judgement and agency in this matter.

Two further overarching positions need to be distinguished, both of which have a subject/agent (passive/active) dimension. In the above generalised account of the supermarket encounter, it was assumed that the event was just sort of 'happening', 'over there' – independent of any observer, commentator or analyst. However, this is clearly an artificial and practically impossible state of affairs. Every observation, commentary or analysis presupposes an observer, commentator, or analyst – someone *doing* these things. And here the emphasis, notice, is on *observing, commenting* and *analysing* as *active transitive processes*: someone observes, comments upon or analyses someone or something. These are *acts*, not simply events.

Figure 2.2 above, for instance, is a substantially recast model which attempts to incorporate all these dimensions. It may be 'read' in the following ways. Everyone is potentially both a participant and an observer; and everyone, at the same time, is potentially both an active agent and a passive subject. In any particular event, however, there are always some participants who seem to be more immediately or remotely implicated than others. Similarly, observers can appear to be more or less 'internal' or 'external' to the event – with an 'insider' or an 'outsider' view. The crucial point, therefore, is which of these roles we see ourselves as playing with respect to a particular event. In what ways do we reckon ourselves to be participating and/or observing? Above all, how far do we reckon ourselves to be the passive subjects or active agents of the event – whether in our role as participant(s) and/or observer(s).

Before proceeding to apply and test this model, we shall supplement it with another one. However, even before that, you yourself are invited, again, to refine, recast or replace it. For once more the only really worthwhile model will be one that works for you: one for which you feel some responsibility: one in which you have had a hand yourself. Experiment with some alternative shapes and words before reading on.

2.2 PERSONAL, INTERPERSONAL AND DEPERSONALISED

At this point we extend and refine a model of subjects/agents introduced in 1.2.1. There we saw that it is convenient to think of a text (and more generally any instance of representation) as a construct resulting from the interplay of three major types of subject/agent position:

personal; **interpersonal** and **depersonalised**. Using the personal pronoun system of modern English as a framework, we may characterise each position in so far as it is overtly oriented from or towards one of the three major pronoun positions:

personal, centred on the first-person 'speaking subject': 'I/me/mine/my; we/us/ours/our';

interpersonal, centred on the second-person 'spoken-to subject': 'you/yours/your';

depersonalised, centred on the third-person 'spoken-about subject': 'she/her/hers/her; he/him/his; they/them/theirs/their; it/its'.

Another way of formulating these distinctions is in terms of, respectively, **addresser-centred**, **addressee-centred** and **message-centred** (referential and textual) emphases. The basic principles are not hard to grasp. We thus finish up with an array of positions which can be provisionally plotted as in Figure 2.3:

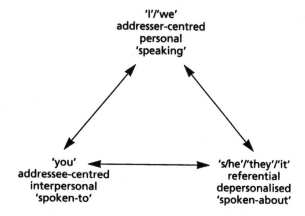

Figure 2.3 'Triangular' model of subject/agent relations

Note: The two-way arrows are a way of signalling that all these positions are in fact simultaneously interrelated, reciprocally defining and ceaselessly changing.

For instance, each of the following groups of texts may be said to open by being centred upon or focused through just one of these three major positions:

(1) (a) I got up this morning, and my woman she was gone . . .

(blues)

(b) I wandered lonely as a cloud/That floats on high o'er vales and hills,/When all at once I saw a crowd/A host of dancing daffodils;.

(poem)

(c) Here we go, here we go, here we goooo!

(football chant)

(2) (a) In the event of fire, make your way out of the building by the quickest route. Do not use the lifts. Do not stop to collect personal belongings . . .

(public notice)

(b) You are the sunshine of my life . . .

(pop song)

(3) (a) Litmus Test. When litmus paper is immersed in an acidic solution it turns pink; in an alkaline solution it turns blue . . .

(text book)

(b) He was an old man who fished alone in the Gulf Stream and he had gone eighty-four days now without taking a fish . . .

(novel)

All the examples in (1) are delivered by an overt 'I' or 'we', are centred on the addresser/speaking subject and therefore primarily *personal*. All those in (2) are overtly directed towards 'you', are centred on the addressee/spoken-to subject and therefore primarily *interpersonal*. All those in (3) refer wholly to something or someone else ('litmus paper/it'; 'He/an old man') without any overt acknowledgement of either addresser or addressee (a speaking 'I/we' or a spoken-to 'you'). These are therefore primarily, by contrast with the examples in (1) and (2), *depersonalised*.

These distinctions among relatively personal, interpersonal and depersonalised modes of address are neat and they make a rough kind of analytical and perceptual sense. As the above examples show, they also have the advantage of being applicable to a wide range of texts, irrespective of the other formal characteristics or functions of those texts.

HOWEVER (a big one), it is essential to recognise and re-emphasise those repeated words 'overt' and 'primarily' in the above commentary. That is, by heavy implication, there are always other 'secondary' and more or less 'covert' subject positions to take into account and knit into the picture. More particularly, on closer inspection we shall always find that there are potential traces of precisely those *other* subject positions (personal, interpersonal and depersonalised) which at first seemed not to figure in the foreground. That is, to every foreground there is a defining background; to every centre there is a surrounding margin.

Here, by way of example, is a fairly detailed interrogation of (1a). The grounds for labelling this a *primarily* and *overtly* 'personal' text are obvious enough. There is clearly a speaker/singer all rolled together and identified with that first word, 'I'. This primary subject/agent position is confirmed in the follow-up first person pronoun 'my'. Attention is thus drawn firmly to the 'I who speaks/sings/suffers'. But, no less clearly, there are also accompanying references to a third person ('woman . . . she') as well as to such circumstances as 'this morning' and such processes as 'got up' and 'was gone'. In other words, there is also a markedly referential dimension to 'an other' in this song, even though we may say that it is primarily concerned with expressing the singer's own sense of 'self'. Put yet another way, the text is 'I'-centred, with the addresser as 'speaking subject' in the immediate foreground; but we can also readily discern and, if we so choose, draw attention to a third person who is available as an alternative 'spoken-about subject'.

What's more, remembering the potential for personal, depersonalised *and interpersonal* dimensions to every communicative act, we may then go on to ask who is the person (or persons) being addressed in this song: the 'spoken-to subject(s)'. Who is the implied 'you' the song is for? Is it being sung to someone else present (a friend maybe)? To the absent woman (hoping perhaps she may return)? To the singer her- or himself? Just one of these – or all three in various measure? Indeed, to take a still broader view of the communicative process, perhaps the 'you' being addressed and sung to is not immediately present at all. Perhaps s/he is or they are the sorrows and souls of all the previous blues singers with whom this particular singer, by adopting this form of words and mode of performance and genre, is aligning himself and thereby communing with? Or perhaps the 'you' being sung to and for is an audience seated at home listening to a recording? And so on. In any event, each of these 'you's may be the clinching link in the communicative chain which fixes the then-meaning-there for whichever and however many of the many potential addressees are actually being addressed.

We are therefore left with some fascinating and potentially infinite complications to what at first looked like a neat and finite formulation. The blues line 'I got up this morning and my woman she was gone . . .' may indeed be primarily and overtly personal: centred on the speaking/singing subject. None the less, for the purposes of anything like a fuller understanding, we can and must use that subject position as a point of departure rather than arrival. And what we shall pick up on our journey, very quickly and in great profusion, will be a complex sense of all sorts of other, actual and potential subject/agent positions (spoken-to and spoken-about), crowding in and around – and even threatening to displace – that initial centre from which a first perception flowed. What may have looked like a straightforwardly 'personal' message turns out to be much much more. In place of one, routinely privileged subject position we begin to perceive a complex and at any one time highly variable interplay of personal, interpersonal and depersonalised trajectories.

Moreover, still further consideration may convince us that in fact *none* of these subject positions needs be automatically privileged. The initial or apparent centre (here the 'I-who-sings') can, *if you so choose*, give way to alternative centres – alternative, 'secondary', 'covert' subject positions – which to you are more important. For notice that it is *you, as the latest observer and participant*, who have final control over which textual positions shall be emphasised, and in what order or hierarchy. Similarly, it is *you* who have the immediate and ultimate control over who or what in the message is to be credited with agency, causality and responsibility for whatever is adjudged to be happening or have happened in the event being represented. In the case of this blues line, for instance, do you identify and sympathise with the 'I-who-sings' and cast her or him in the role of a figure of suffering: an innocent 'done to'? Or do you identify with the 'woman', 'she' who has 'gone', and cast her in the role of a sorely tried or a wilful woman? In short, who is to 'blame' for the break-up; and who is to charged with responsibility (whether as active agent or passive subject)? Obviously, in any given instance, we should need to explore the rest of the song in performance and in immediate situation and larger cultural context before we came to a conclusion. But even then it would still be up to us as active observers (analysts, commentators) to hang on to or rupture or re-forge the chains of events we discerned.

On yet another hand (we always need three or more hands when juggling complex concepts) perhaps the subject position you most identify with is that of listener, audience and remote or surrogate confidant: the role of confided-in and sung-to? Yet again, relatedly, perhaps what you are engaged with is the 'aesthetic' pleasure of the message as a more or less arbitrary or merely formal representation: a more or less depersonalised yet none the less affecting pattern of musical notations, words and sounds? Maybe it is the music or song in and for 'itself' (and to that extent depersonalised) that actually ensures *your* engagement with the message?

In sum, then, each and all of the above responses, each and all of those centrings and fore-groundings is not only possible but, if you choose to make it so, actual. The resulting prospect can be both exhilarating and terrifying. What initially appeared to be a single centre and unproblematic foreground (an instance of 'personal' expression) can be ceaselessly – though in practice always determinately – reactivated by the exercise of your own responsibility as an observer/participant: your own capacity as a personal, interpersonal or depersonalised agent: your own power to intervene in the patterns of agency which you find in the text's meanings.

Here, then, are two further steps into and out of a text:

(a) Identify the dominant subject/agent position apparently 'preferred' by the writer (or speaker) using the 'triangular model' on p. 50 (Figure 2.3).

(b) Explore that position by drawing attention to other positions which you, as actual reader, perhaps prefer (these again may be plotted as 'personal', 'interpersonal' or 'depersonalised').

Now apply these questions to the remaining texts in (1)–(3) (pp. 50–1 above). Which 'subject/agent' positions are (not) privileged in each – and which might yet be, and how?

A further result of this practical activity may well be the sense that we need to modify or at least extend the above 'triangular model' of subject/agent relations. We need to incorporate *actual writers and readers*; and we need to indicate that the interplay between them effectively dynamises and dialogises the relations held to obtain 'within' the text.

Figure 2.4, then, is a possible modification of the 'triangular model' (Figure 2.3). As before, once you have got hold of it, try twisting and turning it to suit yourself. Or throw it away and start from scratch.

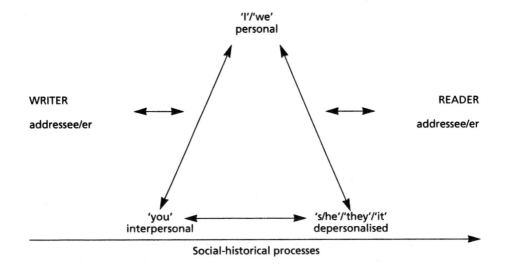

Figure 2.4 'Mobile' and 'flexible' triangle of intra- and extra-textual relations

At the centre is the triangular model of subject/agent relations as in Figure 2.3. This applies to those positions made available 'within' the 'text' as address or message (ie, *intra*-textually). To either side are the 'writer' and 'reader', each of whom is in a specific dialogue with the positions offered by the text in so far as s/he may be identified with a certain range of *extra*-textual subject/agent positions (e.g. as woman or man, black or white, poor or rich, young or old . . . student or teacher, etc.) (cf. Figure 1.2, p. 19).

The *two-way arrows* after and before 'writer' and 'reader' are a pointed reminder that both have a dialectical and negotiated relation with the subject/agent positions realised by the text. Neither can therefore be wholly identified with what appears to be going on there. The recognition that the text's address*ee* (e.g. reader) is also potentially an address*er* of that text (e.g. as interpreter, commentator and re-writer) is crucial. By the same token, the text's address*er* (e.g. writer) may be indirectly interrogated by the reader and thereby in turn become an address*ee*.

At the same time, however, the fundamental directionality of 'social-historical processes' is not being denied. 'Time's arrows' do indeed run from past, through present to future; there is indeed a before, a during and an after. However, this most definitely does *not* mean that the moment of the 'writer' takes absolute *precedence* over the moment of the 'reader' in interpretative and evaluative terms, even though it does in temporal terms. Addresser and addressee are 'placed' but *not* 'privileged' by virtue of speaking from and in their respective historical moments. The writer may seem to have the 'first word'; but the current 'reader/re-writer' always has the 'last word' – or at least 'the latest'.

Overall, then, this is *a dialogic and historical model of the construction and reconstruction of subject/agent positions 'within' and 'around' a text*. It is based on a 'triangle' which 'moves' and 'flexes'. Put more actively, it is a 'triangle' that we, as active readers, must learn to move and flex for ourselves – assertively yet with a sense of historical responsibility. The fact that this is not the only possible such model will have been confirmed by your own efforts. It is also attested by the development elsewhere in this book of relatable yet distinct models (see 3.1.5 and 4.1). After all, it would be an odd interactive model that could not be changed! It would also be a pretty useless one if it did not work. That is what we find out next.

2.3 VERSIONS OF NAGASAKI, 9 AUGUST 1945

Here are two versions of 'the same event': what happened at Nagasaki on 9 August 1945.

Read over these passages several times noticing how each in effect constructs that event as a 'different event'. More particularly, consider how far each account is 'personal', 'interpersonal' or 'depersonalised'? And begin to think how you might intervene in and re-write each account so as to re-model the subject/agent positions involved.

(a) As the first mushroom floated off into the blue, it changed its shape into a flower-like form – its giant petal curving downward, creamy-white outside, rose-colored inside. It still retained that shape when we gazed at it from a distance of about two hundred miles.

(b) My brother and sisters didn't get to the shelter in time, so they were burnt and crying. Half an hour later my mother appeared. She was covered with blood. She had been making lunch at home when the bomb was dropped. My younger sisters died the next day. My mother – she also died the next day. And then my older brother died.

How is it, then, that 'the same event' can be realised so differently? What are the various subject positions and agencies involved? Which version – if any – are we to prefer? And what can all this mean to each of us in our various 'heres and nows'? The following activities will help you work through these questions both critically and creatively.

Textual

(1)

Go through both texts identifying their principal differences in terms of: *vocabulary* (literal or figurative); *sentence structure* (long or short, coordinated or subordinated); *personal pronouns* (choice, range and distribution of 'I', 'me', 'we', 'it' etc. – also noting those which do not occur in each text). (See the checklist in 5.2 for further guidance.)

(2)

Plot each text in terms of personal, interpersonal and depersonalised subject/ agent positions using the basic 'triangular model' in the previous section (2.2). Notice that you have already identified the choice, range and distribution of personal pronouns, so that is an initial basis.

(3)

What kind of writer–reader (addressee–addresser) relation seems to be offered in each text? And are you, as an actual reader, able or prepared to accept the positions offered to you? What other positions would you like to open up and find out more about? (This is an initial opportunity to 'flex' the 'mobile triangle' model in the last section.)

Contextual

(4)

Version (a) is by William Laurence, consultant to the US war department and science correspondent for the New York Times. He was viewing the event through arc-welder's glasses up in an 'observer' plane. His article was filed immediately and published three days later in the New York Times – an 'eye-witness account' quickly picked up and reproduced by many papers worldwide.

Version (b) is by Fujio Tsujimoto, a boy at Yamazato Primary School, Nagasaki, who was in the playground at the time the bomb was dropped. His account was gathered through an interview with a Japanese pacifist organisation ten years later, published six years after that in Japanese, and another nine years after that (i.e. in 1970, twenty-five years after the event) in a pamphlet produced by a British-based anti-nuclear group. And that's where I first came across it (Thompson and Smith, 1970: 32–3).

How far does this contextual information help to explain the textual features you discerned in (1) and (2)? And how far does it help you understand your acquiescence in or resistance to the different implied addressee positions already weighed under (3)?

Intervention

(5)

Re-write version (a) so that the referent is clearly a bomb-blast and the imagery is human and mechanical rather than natural and organic. Try this in two ways: one celebrating the awesome power of human science and technology; the other deploring them. Consider the supplementary use of diagrams, maps, photographs and other audio-visual aids.

(6)

Re-write version (b) so that it is systematically depersonalised, perhaps in the form of a clinical medical or military account. Adopt exclusively third-person reference, avoiding all first-person pronouns. Substitute other nouns, verbs, adjectives and adverbs, and re-model sentence length, structure and complexity as you see fit. Do your utmost to obscure or 'defamiliarise' the family relations. Again consider audio-visual aids.

(7)

Now settle on a subject/agent position which you feel has not yet been explored but needs to be. Write it up, adding a rationale and commentary.

(8)

Hybrids. Consider how you might combine and perhaps supplement these two accounts of the bombing of Nagasaki so as to make a critical point creatively. For instance, previous hybrids have taken the written form of collage (with visuals) and interlinear or marginal glosses; while perfomance versions have used – or scripted the use of – alternating or overlapping voices, spatially differentiated speakers (higher and lower), and back projection. They have also drawn on such materials as can be found in Hackmann and Marshall (1990: 146–53) and Kanda (1989). Decide on your own 'hybrid' before reading on.

Here, for comparison and by way of illustration, is one 'hybrid' with 'supplement' developed for a follow-up session. Sentences from the beginning of the following novel were read out loud alternating with sentences from the two base texts ((a) was read by a man; (b) by a woman). The result was a peculiarly effective and affecting experience: a kind of 'mobile triangle' in performance in which subject/agent positions (and voices) kept on breaking in and out, up and down.

> Listen: *(A line each from versions (a) and (b))*
> When I was a younger man two wives ago, 250,000 cigarettes ago, 3,000 quarts of booze ago . . . I began to collect material for a book to be called 'The Day the World Ended'.
> The book was to be factual. *(Another line each from versions (a) and (b))*
> The book was to be an account of what important Americans had done on the day when the first atomic bomb was dropped on Hiroshima, Japan. *(Another line each from versions (a) and (b))*
> It was to be a Christian book. I was a Christian then.

I am a Bokonist now. *(Another line each from versions (a) and (b))*

(Vonnegut, 1963: 7)

The reading concluded with the following questions put by a chorus of two women and two men: 'Which I? You – me? Which eye? Mine – yours? American –Japanese – British . . .? Christian – Bokonist? Hiroshima – Nagasaki? *What's the difference?*'

2.4 PRESENTATION OF 'SELF' AND 'OTHER' IN PERSONAL ADS

Portraits as we see you – £6
Portraits as you see yourself – £25

(Sign in a photographic studio window, Manchester, 1990)

Funny things happen to people in the media: the personal is made public and the public is made personal. This process is nowhere more apparent than in the 'personal' columns of newspapers. Here we meet individuals who are consciously presenting themselves to others in the hope of finding that 'special other' with whom they can get along, have fun, just sex, or a long-term relationship. In any event, the 'self' is seeking or being sought by 'another', and the individual is constituted as a figure firmly in the public domain. S/he is palpably an interpersonal and social construct. In this section we look at this presentation of 'self' to, for and by 'other' in a selection of adverts. We then write some 'serious' and 'parodic' versions of our own; and go on to analyse them. This section is also by way of prelude to the tuning of our own 'personal/public voices' in the activities with lyric poems which follow.

First, then, some personal ads from a local weekly newspaper (*Oxford Star*, 8 November 1990).

Read them over a few times, asking yourself how far they observe a common pattern. (What is it?)

(a) *Attractive Male*, 38, fair hair, hazel eyes, non-smoker, seeks relationship with warm, affectionate Lady. Photo, please.

(b) *WELL DRESSED*, well travelled, honest, sincere, divorced, young 41 Male seeks slim attractive Female for possible lasting relationship. Prove to me that there is life after divorce.

(c) *ATTRACTIVE BUBBLY* FEMALE, 40, would like to meet caring, humorous Male for friendship and evenings out.

(d) *CHUNKY BUILT*, curly haired professional Man, sought by considerate, clever, fanciable career woman. Fit forty. Let's begin with the safety of an anonymous phone conversation.

(1)

Now write a 'personal ad' for yourself, using the above examples as rough models (maximum 25 words). Present yourself, an imagined ideal partner and what kind of relationship you are seeking. Try to do this as seriously as possible in the first instance. There will be more playful opportunities later. Do this before reading on.

(2)

Compare your ad with those above, using the following analytical questions as prompts. Have you also:

> adopted a clipped, *elliptical style*, omitting indefinite articles ('a', 'an') and overt references to a speaking 'I' and an addressed 'you' (e.g. 'I am a . . .', 'You may be . . .')?

> gone for a predominantly *third-person presentation of 'self'* and of desired *'other'*, thereby to some extent depersonalising both?

> opted for an information sequence of *participant 1* (self), *process* (linking verb), *participant 2* (other), followed by a *circumstance item* (typically an adverbial phrase) specifying the range or scope of the proposed relationship (e.g. (b) 'for possible lasting relationship'; (c) 'for friendship')?

> *or* opted for an *inverted information sequence*, as in (d), leading with the 'other' and following with the 'self'? (any potential confusion here, in this immediate co-text?);

> used a *highly nominal (noun-based) structure* which is *heavily pre- and/or post-modified*? (Notice that listing the adjectives in these ways often has the effect of giving them semi-nominal force, as though they are almost nouns in apposition.)

> added a second sentence supplying further information and perhaps altering the mode of address? (For instance, (a), (b) and (d) opt for more directly interpersonalised ways of signing off.)

If you have done all or most of the above then you have, in effect, written within the genre supplied. Some of this will have been conscious (after all, I did ask you to use these examples as rough models); and some perhaps less so (simply through previous exposure to similar kinds of text). Either way, you may be surprised by the high degree of structural consistency between what you and the composers of these ads produced.

Another thing you will have become acutely – even embarrassingly – aware of in the above activity is that all these 'selves' and 'others' (including your own) are intrinsically social constructs. In fact as soon as we 'go public' in language of any kind, acts of inter/personal definition inevitably get caught within a play of differences which in some measure already exists. More dynamically and with the emphasis on ourselves as agents (i.e. our 'selves' engaged in active self-making), we are constantly aware of a tension between the game which is already in play and the game as we wish to play it. In short, we are aware of actual constraints as well as potential creativity. It is the latter we explore more concertedly now.

(3)

Write an alternative personal ad. Do this in as wild and weird or subtle and insinuating a manner as you wish. In other words, play around with your 'self', your prospective addressee(s), and any other aspect of the language, genre and discourse of personal ads that you feel inclined to challenge and change. Seriously, have some fun! But again do it in a maximum of 25 words and before reading on.

(4)

Compare your *alternative* ad with your initial ad. Note major differences of strategy, using the analytical checklist in (2) as a basis for detailed comparison. For instance, have you gone for *third- or first-person* presentation of self? and used *direct or indirect address* to your addressee? Are your speech acts stating, questioning, exclaiming or directing? More subtly, are they promising, threatening, cajoling, pleading, ingratiating, challenging, feigning insult or im/modesty, etc.? What kind of *information structure* do you use: with participants, processes and circumstance items in what order or hierarchy? Are your noun groups heavily modified or your verb groups heavily modalised? And so on. (For a more detailed checklist, see 5.2.)

(5)

Finally, write an '*anti*-personal ad'. Emphasise all your *bad* points and sketch the kind of person you would *not* want a relationship with. Compare this with your other two versions in terms of overall strategy and specific tactics (see (2) and (4), above).

Other 'selves' and other 'others'

Here are some further examples of published personal ads for comparison and analysis. Some will probably strike you as unconventional or in some way unusual. Others will point to the existence of *counter- or alternative genres of personal ad* – some of which are decidedly 'unpersonal' according to dominant Western models of 'the person as individual'. They will therefore remind you that constructions of 'self' and 'other' are the product of pressures which are both culture-specific and idiosyncratic. That is, each culture (or subculture) has its peculiar constraints and its peculiar forms of creativity ((e)–(g) are from *India Today*, 30 April 1992; (h) and (i) from *Oxford Star*, 8 November 1990; (j)–(n) from *Private Eye*, 27 March 1992 and 8 May 1992).

(e) Correspondence invited from Protestant Christian, well-educated, well-placed teetotaller boy for 31-year-old girl fond of music and reading, postgraduate, presently teaching in the Gulf.

(f) Mother seeking good-looking educated girl for clean-shaven Sikh male, cultured, US citizen, 40, 5ft 11in, divorced. Hotel management, studying accountancy.

(g) Aunt invites suitable match from professional men physicians/engineers/scientists.

(h) BLOKE, 36, quite frankly ain't got a lot going for him, seeks romantic, beautiful, silly Lady of substantial means.

(i) BUSY professional single mother, 39, seeks Man who shares doubts about ads like these.

(j) FLOPPY OLD HOUND on long leash, bored with fantasies, seeks Earth mother, object letters, chats, occasional meets for sniffs and scratches.

(k) BRIGHTON BIKER, 36, hairy, large motor cycle, seeks bored housewife for wild rides while the kids are at school.

(l) LEMON CAKETTE seeks professional man for afternoon tea.

(m) CZECHMATE – 500+ cultured, sophisticated ladies – doctors, teachers, lawyers, radio, TV producers, 'the Arts' from Czechoslovakia, seek sincere gentlemen for marriage. As featured on BBC News, Anglia TV, BBC World Service, Sunday Observer.

2.5 LYRIC VOICES

We now switch focus to some genres of text which appear to be very different from personal adverts: short lyric poems. Our overall aim and method, however, remain the same: to explore representations of 'self' and – or as – 'other'; and to do this by investigating the interplay of subject/agent positions within and around a text, most notably through the personal pronouns and the various positions they privilege, marginalise or exclude.

Specific texts in specific genres make specific demands, however. In this case, as the compositions we are engaging with are in some sense 'poetry', we shall ourselves need to engage in processes of poetic re-composition – and even prosaic de-composition! Or at least we shall if we are to grasp these texts in their unique specificity as well as their general applicability – as instances as well as illustrations.

2.5.1 Who speaks?

Read the following text through a few times, preferably aloud. Experiment with pace, volume and tone till you settle on a manner of delivery which feels satisfying. Meanwhile, think about who might be saying these words and in what circumstances.

Last night
got a peek
at the moon
last night
an didn't think of lovers

got a peek
at the moon
last night
an saw
a man with a load on his back

got a peek
at the moon
last night
an cried

Once you have established your own initial bearings, go on to plot – and re-plot – them through the following operations.

(1)

Who speaks? As is common in song and conversation, the grammatical subject of 'got' and the other verbs here is not specified. It is 'deleted'. In principle, therefore, the grammatical subject slot could be filled by a wide variety of items: any personal pronoun ('I', 'we', 'you', 'she', 'he', 'they', 'it'); a common noun or noun phrase (e.g. 'a boy', 'this girl', etc.) or a proper noun (e.g. someone's name – yours, mine or someone else's). Try out some of these possibilities by adding them to the beginning of all three blocks of text, noticing that each will have a subtly or markedly different effect on the text's potential meaning.

Once you have settled on a choice which in your view best fills the slot and suits the role, say why you prefer it: on the grounds of what implied perceptions and perspectives?

(2)

How far, then, would you characterise the dominant subject position in the text as 'personal', 'interpersonal' or 'depersonalised'? (See Figure 2.3 in 2.2.) Which subject positions therefore seem to be marginalised, excluded or merely implicit?

(3)

How do you envisage the dominant voice behind or within the text in terms of, say, gender, race and class? What prompts your inferences? Compare your inferences with those made by other people.

(4)

Information sequence. What would be the effect of re-shuffling the three blocks of text so that the last came first or second? Is there, therefore, any discernible or arguable rationale to the specific progression of the last lines of each block as currently constituted? What expectations are set up or thwarted by this sequence?

(5)

Multiple context(s): person(s), time(s), place(s) and occasion(s). You will already have considered some of the possible persons involved in and around this text. There is also an explicit – albeit context-sensitive – reference to time in the title and throughout (i.e. 'last night'). What other possible clues are there as to the place and occasion for the poem? (For instance, how would it change the implied situation if the first line of each block were '*Gazed* at the moon' or '*Glanced* at the moon'?) And who – or what – might be the 'man with a load on his back'? (A metaphorical or literal 'man'? A metaphorical or literal 'load'?)

In addition, you might like to consider the fact that there must be at least *three* moments involved in the production, reproduction and perception of this text: (a) the moment referred to 'last night'; (b) the moment of the text's initial composition, presumably the day after; (c) the moment(s) of the text's subsequent reproduction(s) – including this one. Each of these moments therefore might entail a slightly – or very – different configuration of subject/agent positions. Which moment(s) are you concentrating on?

(6)

Re-titling: determining the indeterminate. The present title is very 'open' (i.e. context-sensitive and highly indeterminate). **Draw together all the inferences you made in (4) as to the possible persons, times, places and occasions involved and turn them into a massively extended title.** This might take a form something like 'A speaks to B in place C at time D about subject E in manner F'. The result will, of course, be ludicrously cumbersome and grotesquely explicit compared with the present title. However, simply doing this will serve to demonstrate just how important it can be for certain kinds of 'literary', 'poetic' or generally 'playful' text to offer an extremely wide, open and to some extent highly indeterminate range of subject/agent positions.

At the same time, you might like to consider the ways in which the text none the less does determine some positions more than others. It means *some* things not *any* things. It is 'open' – but not totally. It is creative – yet also constrained.

(7)

Re-write the text as continuous prose. For instance, perhaps compress it so that 'got a peek / at the moon / last night' is used just once (not three times), and then modify the grammar, spelling and punctuation in line with the formal written standard with which you are most familiar. You would therefore finish up with a short, single sentence running between one side of the page and the other.

What is lost or gained by doing this? And what does this activity show about the relation between the formal patterning and presentation of the initial text and its potential meanings and effects?

(8)

Finally, on the basis of all the above activities, debate the following proposition in the preferred way – *for*, *against* and *alternative* (i.e. by substituting a different proposition):

The ultimate 'subject' of a poetic text is not its content (what it is about) but the poetic form itself (how it is done).

(For relevant reading, see Jakobson and Shklovsky in Lodge (1988: 15–61). 'Last Night' is by the Jamaican poet and performer Oku Onuora, as printed in Burnett (1986: 83, also see 389–90). He has performed it in various versions, accompanied and unaccompanied.)

2.6.2 Who speaks back?

Read this short text over a few times silently to yourself. Meanwhile, weigh what kind of text it is and what function(s) it could perform.

> This is just to say
> I have eaten
> the plums
> that were
> in the icebox

and which
you were probably
saving
for breakfast

Forgive me
they were delicious
so sweet
and so cold

Once you have got your initial bearings, retrace them using the following interlinked activities.

(1)

GENRES **How would you categorise this text?** What kind(s) of text is it?

(2)

FUNCTIONS What clues are there that this is not just an *instrumental, informative* use of language – but also a *playful, 'poetic'* use. In other words, how far is it the 'content' or the 'form' of the message that engages you?

(3)

Use the 'triangular model' (Figure 2.3) in 2.2 to plot all the main subject/ agent positions through the personal pronouns. Is one position prominent and another marginalised – or are they fairly evenly balanced? Go on to consider which other words, apart from personal pronouns, carry traces of a specific interpersonal relation. (For instance, 'Forgive' is a directive request, and the plums must have been 'delicious', 'sweet' and 'cold' to somebody.) Feed these analytical insights into the next, more speculative activity.

(4)

What do you infer about the identity of the 'I' and the 'you' in the base text in terms of gender, race, age, social position, country and period? And what kind of relationship do you imagine as obtaining between them? (Could the 'you' be plural, for instance?) Discuss the grounds for your inferences with others.

(5)

What does the previous exercise suggest about the differences and similarities between you as an *actual reader* 'outside the text' and the 'you' as an *implied addressee* 'within the text'? (Cf 3.1.4.) For instance, how much do these two 'you's appear to converge or diverge with respect to gender, race, age, country and social position? Or perhaps you more readily align your 'self' with the address*er* of the text – the apologetic poet and plum pilferer? Or neither? Which – and why?

(6)

The final act of practice is this. Write a note back to the addresser of 'This is just to say' on behalf of its addresee. That is, decide what *you* (the actual extra-textual reader) would like *her* or *him* or *them* (the implied intra-textual addressee(s)), 'just to say' in return. Opt for any genre or discourse, medium or material, which seems to you to register an appropriate response.

(7)

Consequently, the final act of theory is this. Return to the 'mobile' and 'flexible' triangle of intra- and extra-textual subject/agent relations in 2.2 (Figure 2.4). How adequate is this as a model of the operations you actually experienced when writing on behalf of the implied addressee of 'This is just to say'? If this model *does* correspond to your experience, then perhaps use it again? If it *does not* correspond to your experience, then refine or replace it with another experimental model – and test that instead.

All this is just to say that

> each of us together

>> must use practice and theory to help

>>> one another

('This is just to say' is by William Carlos Williams (1934) in Williams (1976: 72). This poem/note/apology is frequently featured in both analytical and theoretical work on the interfaces of language, literature and discourse, e.g. Hawkes (1977: 139–40); Carter and Nash (1990: 11–12); Cook (1992: 144). Follow up some of these references to see both *what* these writers say about 'This is just to say' and *how* they say it – describing and re-inscribing it in what discourses and using it to what ends.)

2.6 EXTENDED WORK-OUT: RE-GENREING THE 'I' IN POETRY, POP, PSYCHIATRY AND ADVERTISING

The following activities provide further practice in exploring a wide variety of intertextual strategies along with a corresponding variety of subject/agent positions. Our especial focus is the first person, 'I/me/my/mine'. We plot the many ways in which this apparently singular 'speaking subject' can be oriented and understood within different *contexts* and *co-texts*. We also see how its *intertextual* alignment with specific **genres** and **discourses** can lead to a highly pluralised and potentially creative – or constrained – sense of the individual and/or collective 'self'.

Presented below are extracts from four texts. One would be conventionally categorised as *poem*; another as *TV advert* (verbal script); another as *pop song* (the words); and another as *psychiatric disorder* (patient's account). They are not necessarily presented in that order.

Read and comment on each *one* of the following in *four* ways: as though it were (a) a *poem*; (b) a *TV advert*; (c) a *pop song*; and (d) an account of a *psychiatric disorder*. The result will therefore be a total of 16 readings and, in a sense, 16 distinct texts. Keep a record of each reading, at least in note form. In each case identify and comment on:

potentially 'poetic' features of form and content;

what the text might be helping to sell (selecting an appropriate product and accompanying images);

what style of 'popular' music and type of singer or band (plus promotional video) it might draw on;

what might be psychologically 'deviant' or 'abnormal' about the speaker/writer.

If you recognise any of these pieces, try to ignore this for the moment. Simply treat each one in turn as a serious candidate for each of the four categories.

(A)   Today I am
a small blue thing
Like a marble
or an eye

With my knees against my mouth
I am perfectly round
I am watching you

I am cold against your skin
You are perfectly reflected
I am lost inside your pocket
I am lost against your fingers

(B)   One's-Self I sing, a simple separate person,
Yet utter the word Democratic, the word En-Masse.

Of physiology from top to toe I sing,
Not physiognomy alone nor brain alone is worthy for the
Muse,
I say the Form complete is worthier far,
The Female equally with the Male I sing.

Of Life immense in passion, pulse and power,
Cheerful, for freest action form'd under the laws divine,
The modern man I sing.

(C)   There is no gentleness, no softness, no warmth in this deep cave.
My hands have felt along the cave's stony sides, and, in
every crevice, there is only black depth.
Sometimes, there is almost no air.
Then I gasp for new air,
though all the time, I am breathing
the very air that is in this cave.
There is no opening, no outlet.
I am imprisoned.
But not alone.

(D)   At night I dream of many things
Some of which I plan and save for

Some of which I achieve

When I was young I wanted to see Africa
To run away
And so I travelled but never left
my dream
changed
and I became us
became a family
And while dazzling things dazzle still
My values hold dear

Only read on when you have at least sketched 16 different readings (4 for each text).

The general theoretical question might be framed as:

What does this activity show about the *speaking subject* as a *con/textual* and *intertextual construct?*

But that sounds too ponderous. So here are some more specific questions and suggestions to help build more discriminating principles on the basis of your own in part peculiar practices.

(1)

Text/texts? What does the above experience tell you about the value of traditional notions of 'the text' (singular) and the value of 'close attention to the words on the page'? Should each text rather be considered plural ('text*s*'), depending on assumed contexts, genres and discourses, etc.? Or are there indeed things *within* each text which mark it out as having one meaning and function rather than another, and as belonging to one genre rather than another? Which features in each text did you find most 'open', 'context-sensitive' and 'indeterminate'; and which did you find most 'closed', 'context-free' and 'determinate'? And were there any features that could be both – depending how you read them?

(2)

Mobile and flexible triangles (cf. 2.2, Figure 2.4)

(a) Re-write *two* of the above texts deploying different ranges of personal pronouns. For instance, substitute 'we/our', 'you/your', 'one', 'she', 'he', 'they' and 'it', etc., where the base text currently uses 'I, me, mine, my'. Do this initially so that the changes are consistent with one another (e.g. in (B) '*Our-Selves we* sing . . .'). But then experiment with more variegated permutations, changing the verbs accordingly (e.g. '*Our-Selves she* sings . . .'). In each case work over the text till you achieve an alternative form of textual cohesion and an alternative coherence of meanings that you find in some way satisfying. Then say why. (For a similar exercise using Descartes' '*I* think, therefore *I* am' as base text, see 1.3.1.)

Go on to consider what your alternative subject/agent configurations show up about that in the base text? How far is the latter thereby more readily conceivable not so much as a single-voiced monologue but as an internal dialogue 'within the self' or an external dialogue between 'self and others' (cf. 4.1).

(b) **Concentrating on *one* of the base texts, identify just one of the 'not-I' positions which has been marginalised or excluded (e.g. 'you', 's/he' 'them' and/or 'it'). Then attempt to reconstitute the text around that 'centre'.** Use the 'mobile triangle model' to help articulate this subject/agent position as the centre of its (your, her, his, their) own universe of discourse. This may be done in the same textual mode as the base text or in another (see 5.3 for some possibilities).

(3)

'I'dentity? **What provisional inferences have you made about the identity of the 'I's in the various texts?** Try categorising each in terms of the following criteria: gender; age; class; nationality; period; religion/moral-political outlook; education; temperament; anything else.

What warrant does there appear to be in the text for these inferences? And how far is there consensus within the group on the interpretation of these criteria and the grounds for inference?

(4)

Marginalia, heckling, graffiti, voice-over, critique. . . ? **Turn the questions and comments you have so far generated on one of the base texts into an actual dialogue with it** (cf. 4.5.3). This may take a variety of textual or performance forms: marginal comments or interlinear glosses, underlinings and footnotes; a dramatised speech imagined as though spoken by the text's implied address*ee*; a voice-over or palimpsest in which the base text is heard, seen or intermittently 'glimpsed' beneath the critical commentary – or even a conventional essay or linguistic analysis! In any event, try to speak back to the 'I' addressing you, the actual reader.

(5)

Hybrids. **Experiment with ways of *framing*, *mixing* and *fusing* all four of the above base texts** (cf. 1.2.4). There are many ways of putting these texts together and bringing them into complementary or contrastive relations. For instance, consider doing it so that:

(a) all the various 'I's are to be identified with one another as different aspects of the same person;

(b) each of the 'I's is distinguished as a different person caught in some kind of multivocal dialogue;

(c) an audience or readers are not sure whether they are being confronted by the various 'inner voices' of a single person or the various 'outer discourses' of a number of social institutions.

All the above re-workings may be framed as narrative and/or dramatically, textually and/or in performance, in one genre, medium and set of discourses or more. In any event, weigh all the main co/n/textual and intertextual variables before settling on a strategy.

(The base texts used in this section are: (A) Suzanne Vega, 'Small blue thing' from her LP, *Suzanne Vega* (1985); (B) Walt Whitman from *Leaves of Grass* (1855); (C) extract from journal of schizophrenic in Laing (1968: 146); (D) female voice-over from TV ad for Nationwide Anglia building society, United Kingdom, November 1990.)

2.7 SUMMARY ACT

Re-read the four aims stated at the very beginning of this chapter (p. 46, (1)–(4)). Then re-write each of them substituting the words 'I can' or 'We can' for the infinitives 'to use', 'to explore', etc. ((1) will therefore now begin 'I/we can . . .'). If the statements personalised and modalised in these ways now strike you as true, then you have in effect both summarised and practised the methods of this chapter at the same time. If you cannot yet say this with confidence, then review some of the preceding exercises and explanations. Either way, the further reading and re-writing which follows should help both reinforce and refine the above models and practices.

FURTHER RE-WRITING AND READING

A. Making history (cf. 2.3)

(1)

Drawing on your responses to the two accounts of the bombing of Nagasaki, write two markedly different accounts of the utter devastation of the place where you live. Go on to analyse each account using the 'mobile flexible triangle' (2.2, Figure 2.4). Finally, debate the following propositions *for*, *against* and *alternative*:

There is no Event – only versions of events. No real History – only more or less imagined histories.

(2)

Who or what 'finished' the Second World War – or any other war you choose? Use reference books, news reports and discussion to help formulate possible answers, then identify at least *two* 'causes' under each of the following headings:

   (a) a *single person* was responsible (name two or more);

   (b) a particular *group of people* (party, class, section, nation, etc.) was responsible (two or more);

   (c) a particular, long-term *historical process* was responsible (two or more);

   (d) a specific *occasion or circumstance* was responsible (two or more);

   (e) any *other kinds of agent/agencies* – including perhaps yourself as historian.

Go on to ask the further question: **Who or what started the Second World War – or the other war you chose?** Again, sketch at least two potential agents or agencies under each of the above categories. Finally, debate the following proposition *for*, *against* and *alternative*:

Everyone is responsible for history.

B. More 'selves' in search of 'others' (cf. 2.4)

Gather and explore some more instances of personal ads. What information structures and verbal patterns do they use (are there discernible super-, sub- and anti-genres, for instance)? And what kinds of personal relationship and world do they presuppose or propose? (For reading, see Bhaya Nair in Toolan (1992: 227–58.)

C. Who speaks . . . back? (cf. 2.5)

Select a short lyric poem (or song) and explore the question of 'Who speaks?' Use some of the techniques already used for the lyrics by Onuora and Williams, including the 'subject positions triangle' (2.2, Figure 2.3). Also consider the possibility of a written or sung response.

D. Re-genreing and reco(n)textualising (cf. 2.6)

Select three or four texts from a variety of sources and devise a series of activities similar to those featured above. Often it is convenient to choose texts built round the same personal-pronoun position (e.g. 'I' or 'we' or 's/he' or 'they'). The challenge then is to subject them to a variety of pressures and operations. Get your readers actively involved in the exploration of variable contexts, co-texts, genres and discourses. (A variation on this activity is to settle on three or four texts *at random*. Then go through similar processes of re-genreing. Alternatively you might shape all these constituent texts into some hybrid 'megatext'.) Either way, conclude by analysing what you have made and by reviewing what you have learnt about the nature of textuality.

Influential studies of the significance of *personal pronouns* include Benveniste (1966: 195–204, 223–30), Brown and Gilman in Giglioli (1972: 252–82) and Mühlhausler and Harré (1990). Analogies with the above model of *personal, interpersonal* and *depersonalised* positions can be found in Jakobson in Lodge (1988: 36–7), Moffett (1968: 18–22) and Halliday and Hasan (1989: 15–18); also see Mead (1934) and Simpson (1993). For a range of 'event-based' *communication models*, see Fiske (1982: 6–41) and McQuail and Windahl (1993: 13–57). The formation of *subjects* is treated as a psycho-linguistic process by Lacan (see Lodge, 1988: 79–106); a psycho-political and poetic-semiotic process by Kristeva (1980, 1984); and a political-ideological process by Althusser (1971: 161–6); generally see Coward and Ellis (1977). More pro-active and interactive – rather than simply reactive or resistant – models of *subjects as agents* can be traced in Burke (1945), Pêcheux (1982), Belsey (1980: 56–84), Hall in During (1993: 90–103), Fiske (1987: 48–83) and Giddens (1991). Vygotsky (1934) remains a powerful and influential reference throughout this chapter.

3 From narrative to narration and beyond

3.1 PRELIMINARY PRACTICES AND THEORIES

The aim of this chapter is fourfold:

(1) to introduce the principal terms and techniques of narrative analysis and to relate them not only to purely verbal texts (such as novels, short stories and poems) but also to mixed-media materials such as drama and film;

(2) to explore narrative choices and combinations at every level: from that of the single word or clause, through decisions on where to begin, develop and end stories, where to use speech, report and description, what 'point(s) of view' to adopt; and so on to larger strategic matters of genre and medium;

(3) to recognise that all these decisions and distinctions, at whatever level, are of ideological as well as formal significance, and that in actual texts in actual contexts they always involve the writer in the opening up or closing down of specific personal and social historical problems and the projection of specific subject/agent positions – which the active reader can then open up and close down and project differently;

(4) in short, as the title of the chapter proposes, to re-realise apparently finished narrative products as continuing processes of narration. In shorter, to get the reader in on the act of story-telling. In shortest, to re-tell it your (her, his, their) way.

3.1.1 Participants, processes and circumstances

We begin with the basic building blocks of narrative. A story must involve the relation of at least two connected – or connectable – events. Grammatically, we may say that the minimum requirements for a story are two clauses, whether these occur in a single complex sentence or two simple sentences. Conversely, we may say that it is virtually impossible to imagine a story made up of just one simple event and a single phrase or word. Or at any rate this is about as impossible as trying to imagine an argument made up of a single proposition, or a dialogue made up of just one person speaking. For instance, consider each of the following strings of words:

(1) Dave got up late.

(2) Come here!

(3) I'm going to tell you something.

(4) Russia!

None of these in itself is a story. Of course, it is perfectly possible to imagine each of these strings of words as the beginning or end or as some part of the development of a story. And each may set off a kind of 'unwritten story in the head': *why* Dave got up late; *who* was saying 'Come here!'; who the 'I' might be and *what* s/he is about to tell; and of course that single word 'Russia!', especially when exclaimed, could be filled by all sorts of connotations and fitted to all sorts of imagined scenarios and myths and histories. But all these would still be the essentially 'unwritten' or 'potential' stories, the ones which the actual words written on the page, as such, do not tell. Clearly, then, in each of the above examples what we are waiting for is some additional piece of information, some extra event – or dimension of the same event – to set a story in motion. Linguistically, we might say that what we are waiting for is at the very least *another action or state* (typically a verb) and / or *another participant* (typically a noun) as well as perhaps, for good measure, some sense of *circumstance* (typically an adverbial or prepositional phrase). Basically, what we are waiting for is another clause. Take (1), 'Dave got up late', for instance. This might be set in motion as a story by adding some such items as the following before, after or during the base text:

(1a) *Because he'd been out drinking the night before,* Dave got up late. (*preceded* by adverbial clause)

The event is thus situated in time, with a before and an after, and motivated: there is a sense of consequence as well as sequence.

(1b) Dave got up late *then washed in the kitchen.* (*succeeded* by a coordinated clause)

The event is thus extended, two actions are differentiated and a circumstance or setting is added.

(1c) Dave – *and Sue* – got up late. (*interrupted* by a coordinated clause including another proper noun, 'Sue')

Another actor is added and the implied relationship between the two people leaves us to generate inferences about why they got up late. Notice that the absence of any 'circumstance' leaves that play of inference wide open: add 'from the same bed' or 'on opposite sides of town' and the whole potential surrounding story changes markedly.

Go through a similar procedure for yourself with examples (2)–(4), adding plausible items *before*, *after* and *during* as you see fit. What events and situation can you weave round these materials, using what linguistic resources? What fuller information have you thereby supplied, and what is still open to the play of inference?

All of these extended versions at least begin to suggest the articulation of a larger action or situation. And clearly, if we went on to add yet further processes and participants and circumstances, we should pretty soon have things which, formally at least, would start to take on the appearance of stories. People, things, places, actions, states, and so on, would begin to interconnect and develop.

But of course all this is to stay at a merely formal level. It is also to start with very rudimentary perceptual and linguistic building blocks, as though stories were the result of the merely additive accumulation of discrete elements. None the less, it does remind us of a simple yet crucial fact: stories (like all texts) can to some extent be analysed as – and are to some extent produced by – the structured accumulation of clauses and sentences of certain kinds, in certain sequences and with certain consequences. They therefore involve developing configurations of participants and processes and circumstances. Equally significantly, with the choice and combination of every successive word, clause or sentence, each text entails a turning that was *not* taken – or might have been taken *differently*: a story untold – or half, or one-tenth's told: some *other* participants, processes and circumstances that have been marginalised or excluded – or the same participants, processes and circumstances that might have been configured differently. (As an instance of a radically transformed version of 'Dave got up late' consider 'Father got Dave up late – for the resurrection', in which an extra participant has been invoked as agent/subject and 'Dave' is now the **affected/object** of what has become a transitive verb. Moreover, the appended prepositional phrase ('for the resurrection') prompts a total review of the circumstances and, indeed the discourse, within which we are operating: suddenly this is a Christian end-of-the-world scenario and maybe a more than human 'Father'!)

But this matter of choices and combinations of participants, processes and circumstances (*present, absent* and *different*) applies to any string of words. In order to come closer to some working definition of what we mean by 'narrative' (as distinct from, say, 'drama' or 'exposition' or 'argument'), we need to sort texts (and utterances) into different categories. More importantly and more often, we need to sort different parts of the same text into different categories. We also need to recognise that the same text can be simultaneously both 'narrative' *and* 'dramatic' depending upon how we look at it, and upon the frame or layer of textuality we concentrate on. This is what we explore next.

3.1.2 Trains of thought and chains of verbal events

The following activity begins with a handful of words and phrases and finishes up with a couple of fully worked-up texts: your own and someone else's. This should assist in the active process of defining what is meant by narrative and/or drama. And it is a reminder that in fact you already know *how* to put together the building blocks of both, separately or together. Further analysis and theory can then begin to explain *what* you know and perhaps even *why*.

(1)

Use each of the following words or phrases as prompts to set off a separate train of thought. Write down each one as a chain of linguistic events no more than 20 words long. Do this in note form or fully formed sentences, as you wish, and remember that each of these items may eventually occur at the end or in the middle as well as at the beginning of a particular chain. Be adventurous!

  (i) a lovely girl

 (ii) Ekido (person, place, activity, state . . . ? – it's up to you)

(iii) they met

 (iv) travelling

  (v) until that night when

Now look closely at each of the various 'chains of linguistic events' you have produced. Out of what perceptual and linguistic materials have you forged them, and how are they linked? Putting the following questions to each in turn will help you grasp the distinctive wor(l)ds you have begun to create (see 5.2 for full checklist).

(a) **How far was your 'chain' held together** by: tightly or loosely linked clauses and sentences; items which routinely collocate as members of the same semantic field – or which, for you, have particular associations; sound-patterning and/or visual presentation?

(b) **How far do these words come across as a report *about* someone or something or an address *from* somebody *to* somebody else?** More formally, to what extent do they focus on a *spoken-about subject* (conceived as a distanced 's/he', 'they' or 'it'); and to what extent do they operate on an interactive 'I/we'–'you' axis, calling attention to the explicit or implicit presence of *speaking* and *spoken-to subjects*? If both, where and in what degrees (cf. 2.2)?

(c) **Did you use past or present (or future) tenses – or a mixture?** And are they predominantly progressive or non-progressive in aspect; and lightly or heavily **modalised?**

(d) **What specific kind of text (*genre*) might your string of words be attached to, and what larger way of seeing and saying the world (*discourse*) might it be aligned with?** For instance, could it readily be part of: a poem or song; a novel or short story; a drama or film script; a conversation (what kind?); a textbook or formal report; an advert; etc.? And is there some particular worldview it seems to offer, or some set of social and cultural interests it seems to support?

(e) **Why do you think you personally (psychologically, socially, historically) produced that particular chain of linguistic events – and not another?** What idiosyncratic memories or desires, and what more general impulses appear to have gone into its making?

Once you have put these questions to each piece of text in turn, you will be in a good position to say more precisely what kinds of text you produced and how they hold together. In particular, shadowing each of the above questions point for point, you will know:

(a) how far the cohesion of your text depends on sound-patterning, grammar or vocabulary;

(b) how far, at least formally, it tends towards narrative/report or drama/conversation;

(c) how far it is concerned with the 'telling' of what is absent (past or future tenses, retro- or prospective experience and events) or the 'showing' of what is understood to be present or constant (present tense, circumspective experience and events);

(d) what genre(s) and discourse(s) it might be conceived as growing out of or into;

(e) what personal 'voice' it is an expression of, always remembering that this 'voice' is formed through interaction and is social and historical, too.

3.1.3 Narrative and drama provisionally distinguished

All the above trains of thought do not depart from or arrive at the same points. Nor can the chains of verbal events they prompt be tied up neatly into a single ball. But they do at least help us think about narrative as one textual mode amongst many others; and about the kinds of formal feature which generally characterise the 'narrative' side of textuality. You may even find some such definition as the following to be both warranted and useful:

Narrative is typically – though by no means exclusively – the representation of events in the third person and in the past, with the emphasis on who and what is being spoken/written about rather than on who is speaking/writing and to whom.

This is rough and ready of course. And you may well (rightly) recall such apparent exceptions as 'first-person narration' (e.g. autobiography) and may even be sporting with the thought of narratives wholly in the present tense (e.g. dramatic monologues, sports commentaries, and certain kinds of textbook). However, the definition did suggest what narrative is 'typically'. And we shall quickly see that so-called 'first-person narration' is less exceptional than it initially appears, and is in many respects simply a covert form of 'third-person representation' (in that the narrating 'I' is a narrative construct too). Such refinements can be built in later, however. The above definition of narrative at least gives us a fairly firm base from which to get our initial bearings (see Figure 3.1). It may also be usefully related to models of subject/agent positions offered elsewhere in the book (cf. 2.2):

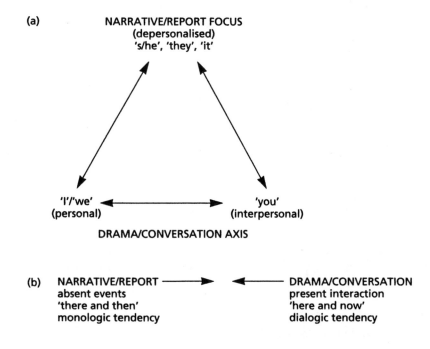

Figure 3.1 Distinctions and connections between narrative and drama

3.1.4 A 'whole' story – a story full of 'holes'

So far we have used only very brief examples to help generate the kinds of broad distinction and interconnection between 'narrative' and 'drama' plotted above. We have not tackled a text of more than a few clauses – two or three sentences at most – and have therefore little sense of the larger structural options of narrative. We have paid virtually no attention to one of the most abiding interests of narrative: the particular and often peculiar relations between *narrators* (the 'story-tellers') and *narratees* (the people for whom the story is told). And other fundamental distinctions still remain to be made, notably that between 'narrators' and 'actual authors' on the one hand, and, on the other hand, 'narratees' (the real or imagined initial addressees of the story) and 'actual readers' (e.g. you and me).

But again all these terms and concepts are most profitably approached through practice. Or at least they are if they are genuinely to mean something in 'your own terms': to be really useful to you as the actual reader *as well as* the potential re-writer of your own and other people's narratives. Here is what you do.

(2)

Take *all* the words and phrases listed in (1i)–(1v) above (p. 72) – 'a lovely girl', 'Ekido', 'they met', etc. – and fashion them into a single text of no more than 100 words. The only constraints on what you do are these:

include some narrative report as well as quoted speeches;

work in instances of *all* the principal personal pronouns ('I', 'we', 'you', 'she', 'he', 'it' and 'they'), using the oblique cases if you wish ('me', 'yours', 'her', etc.);

include instances of both past and present tenses;

give your text a title.

For the rest, the precise substance and overall shape of the text are up to you. So are the particular genre(s) and discourses you wish to recall and the peculiar 'voices' you wish to invoke.

(Tip: After a few minutes planning, write fairly freely in the first instance. Then work over your text a couple of times so as to accommodate all the required features and observe the word limit. Do this before reading on.)

Now read over the following story (Reps, 1957: 28):

Muddy road

Tanzan and Ekido were once travelling together down a muddy road. A heavy rain was still falling.

Coming around a bend, they met a lovely girl in a silk kimono and sash unable to cross the intersection.

'Come on, girl,' said Tanzan at once. Lifting her in his arms, he carried her over the mud.

Ekido did not speak again until that night when they reached a lodging temple.

Then he could no longer restrain himself. 'We monks don't go near females,' he told Tanzan, 'especially not young and lovely ones. It is dangerous. Why did you do that?'

'I left the girl there,' said Tanzan. 'Are you still carrying her?'

This text, like yours, also includes the words and phrases 'a lovely girl', 'Ekido', 'they met', etc. Also like yours, it is less than 100 words long; mixes narrative report and quoted speech; uses both past and present tenses, and one or another form of all the principal personal pronouns (here 'I', 'we', 'you' × 2, 'her' × 3, 'he' × 2, 'his', 'it', 'they' × 2). The above text is therefore in some respects comparable to yours, at least in certain items of vocabulary and certain formal features. For the rest it is likely to be extremely different. Just how different will probably be confirmed by your very different titles. (Unless, that is, you recognised and chose to recall this particular story!)

Here are some questions and suggestions to help fix the various similarities and differences between the above text and your own. Each activity has a larger issue or concept signalled in the heading.

(a) **Genres and discourses.** What *kind of text* would you say 'Muddy road' is, and what *ways of saying and seeing* does it seem to offer? Put another way, what sorts of text does it most remind you of, and whose interests does it most obviously represent? Conversely, whose interests does it under- or misrepresent? (Cf. 'dialectical discourse questions' on p. 124).

Go on to put the same questions to the text you yourself produced. How dis/similar, then, are the genres and discourses represented by 'Muddy road' and your text?

(b) **Narrative and/or drama: spoken-about, speaking and spoken-to.** Now go through both texts systematically comparing:

the relative quantities and overall distribution of narrative report and quoted speech: whose words we are offered – those of the narrator and/or the characters;

the various people and things represented by the personal pronouns: who or what is referred to or implied by the various 'I's, 'we's, 'you's, 'she/her's, 'he/him/his's, 'it(s)', 'they/them/their's – and who or what is thereby offered as speaker, spoken-to and spoken-about (cf. 2.2). Whose 'points of view' do they help us plot – or, more precisely, whose subject/agent positions are privileged?

the predominant tense used (past or present or future), and the perceptual 'distance' this sets up as normal between the reader and what is being told or shown;

the overall 'point' or 'aim' of each text; what 'end' it serves or tends towards. For instance, sometimes we find some clue as to the 'point' of a text in its title. You might therefore like to ponder why the above tale is called 'Muddy road' and whether, on reflection, this title should be understood metaphorically as well as literally. You too will have put some thought into your own title – so what was that thought? Alternatively, you might feel that the ultimate 'end' of a text is most obviously expressed at precisely that point – at 'the end'. So at what point does the above text effect closure, not just of events but of issues? What 'moral' or 'message' is being driven home by the line '"I left the girl there," said Tanzan. "Are you still carrying her?"' Is there any comparable 'closing' or 'rounding off' of events and issues in yout text? Or have you eschewed such a neat 'moral' and 'message'?

Now for the critical and ideological implications, and some counter- and alternative inferences.

(c) Re-cast the centres and margins: invert and subvert; refine and extend. Concentrate on 'Muddy road' in the first instance, then go through the same operations with your own text. That is, drawing on the analysis of formal features in (b), identify all those subject/agent positions which are in some way centred, marginalised or totally ignored. Which positions? In what ways?

Go on to consider in what ways you might challenge and change the positions offered by the base text. Do this systematically by reviewing your options, e.g.:

Redistributing or modifying speech roles: Who else might speak, be spoken to and be spoken about, or who might be doing it differently? (Do a rough draft of some possibilities.)

'Colouring' or 'angling' the narrative comments, so that a different and perhaps critical view of what Tanzan and Ekido say and do is offered. For instance, the base text's '"Come on, girl," said Tanzan at once' might have a different report clause (e.g. 'Tanzan ordered sharply'); or be recast into *indirect speech*, with the result that our view of his words and actions is subject to more overt narratorial control and manipulation (e.g. 'The old monk eagerly invited the young girl to climb into his arms').

Changing the title and/or the avowed 'point' or 'end' of the text (e.g. the last line of 'Muddy road'). What other aspects of the same situation might be thereby drawn attention to? Or what substantially different situations and evaluations might be opened up?

Transforming the genres and discourses (and perhaps media) through which the text is realised. For instance, you might 'frame' the above text by making it the pleasurable reminiscence of an aged monk; or part of a anti-religious diatribe illustrating the hypocrisy and sophistry of the male clergy; or a cautionary tale told by an old woman to a young; and so on. Or you might 'frame' the text with a preface and commentary drawing on a particular critical or analytical discourse: Marxist, feminist, deconstructionist, psychoanalytic, formalist, etc. You could even make it part of an advert, in which case the ultimate 'point' of the text would be to sell something (kimonos, perfume, cars, washing machines, plane tickets to exotic places?!).

Therefore, you might finish up – or begin – by opting for a re-realisation of the text specifically in terms of film, cartoon, puppets, opera or pop music. This could be in a medium which is only marginally – if at all – verbal. Though it would still leave you with analogous decisions concerning narrative product and narrational process.

The overall point, then, is that while texts may *imply* one set of readings and receptions, it is none the less always ultimately up to actual readers to see and say what they themselves *infer*. Implication (by the writer) and inference (by the reader) are two ends of an interpretative procedure which need not agree. Texts open up and offer to close down *differences*: but the final preferences, the most telling 'say so' and the most revealing 'see so', are up to me and you and you and you . . .

3.1.5 Ideal narratees and actual readers

All this brings us to the crucial matter of the relations between narrators and actual writers on the one hand and narratees and actual readers on the other. I shall attempt to fix the main outlines of these problems and possibilities in a diagram (Figure 3.2) which is a variation on some models offered earlier (see 2.2). This will simply sketch theoretically what the above analysis and rewriting has already demonstrated in practice.

actual writer ◄——► narrator ◄——► narrative ◄——► narratee ◄——► actual reader/s

implications ◄——► differences/preferences ◄——► inferences

Figure 3.2 **Narrational processes: implication and inference**

The 'actual writer' is the author conceived as existing *outside* the text: the living, breathing, eating, loving, defecating, dying, etc., identity who is describable in biological, psychological, social and historical terms. The '(authorial) narrator' is that version of the author (her or his views, sympathies, beliefs, etc.) offered *within* the text: the particular (self-)projection the text implies. The 'narrative', broadly conceived, comprises all those characters, descriptions and actions (including speech and thought) which are represented in the text. (Narrative therefore includes such 'characters-as-narrators' as Jane in *Jane Eyre* (see 4.4.3) and Pip in *Great Expectations*.) The 'narratee' is the person or type of person for whom the narrative is apparently intended and whom it ostensibly assumes as addressee: overtly in the 'dear reader' mode of fiction, but covertly, as a supposedly sympathetic ear and knowing mind, in all modes of writing. The narratee is therefore the narrative's implied 'ideal reader'. 'Actual reader/s' – always pointedly singular for each individual reader/reading and always potentially plural when more than one reader /reading is involved – is and are each and every one of us every time we come to terms with a particular text. Actual readers are therefore never wholly or exactly identifiable with the text's implied 'ideal reader', its narratee. Indeed, in so far as actual readers may interrogate and challenge anything and everything the text brings their way (characters, descriptions, actions; authorial narrators and what not), they may turn out to be anything from mildly sceptical to utterly '*un*ideal readers' – or simply 'readers with different ideals'. For worse and better, then, the roles of idealised 'narratees' and actual readers must be carefully distinguished if we are to maintain any active critical-historical sense. Moreover, it should be pointed out that 'actual readers' (plural) must to some extent be equated with 'actual reading*s*'; for in some sense each one of us is a slightly or a very different reader every time we read what is ostensibly 'the same text'.

In sum, actual readers are tricky customers. And, like actual writers, they have a tense, potentially changeable and experimental relation with the narrative; hence the persuasive two-way arrows in Figure 3.2. These signal a two-way and dialogic, not simply one-way and monologic, relation amongst all those engaged in the production and reproduction of the narrative's meanings and values. Indeed, 'actual readers' may be so engaged that they recognise themselves as *actual re-writers*. Consequently, the whole diagram should be reduplicated and extended to the right, with actual readers/re-writers, in their fully developed role generating texts to be read – and maybe re-written – by other actual readers in turn. The same, of course, applies to actual writers, extending indefinitely the other way, page left. And so on – to the last syllables of recorded or recordable time . . .

The two-way and, in principle, infinitely extendable arrows in the lower part of the diagram serve a parallel function. For the reading of a narrative (and, indeed any text) involves the constant renegotiation of *differences and preferences*: what participants, processes and circumstances are to be distinguished, and how they are to be valued. Actual writers, through the dialectical process of constituting parts of themselves in and through their texts, may make certain *implications*. But it is still up to actual readers to make whatever *inferences* we/they judge appropriate. In this way, making sense of narratives is as assertive and responsible an activity as making sense of any text. It's simply helpful to re-frame these distinctions so as to relate them to the dominant terms of narrative analysis.

3.1.6 'Story', 'plot' and some other useful terms

Before going further, we shall engage briefly with some other relevant terms current in narrative theory. Perhaps the simplest and most enduring distinction, in English studies at least, is that made by the novelist and critic, E. M. Forster, in his *Aspects of the Novel* (1927): his distinction between *story* and *plot*. 'Story' he defined as 'a narrative of events arranged in their time sequence'; whereas 'plot' he defined as 'a narrative of events, the emphasis falling on causality' (Forster, 1927: 82–3). And this is how he illustrated the difference:

The king died and then the queen died. (story)

The king died, and then the queen died of grief. (plot)

The latter is a plot, Forster maintains, because 'the time-sequence is preserved, but the sense of causality overshadows it'. It is the prepositional phrase 'of grief' which therefore serves to motivate the story and, in supplying it with a rationale, turn it into a plot. Otherwise, as in the former example, we are simply left with an unmotivated sequence: two events which simply happen in a certain order but we do not know why. Forster then goes on to offer a slightly more developed example of 'plot' – one 'with a mystery in it':

The queen died, no one knew why, until it was discovered that it was through grief at the death of the king.

He therefore sums up his story/plot distinction thus: 'If it is in a story we say "and then?" If it is in a plot we ask "why?"'

To translate this into our terms, we might say that he sees story as primarily concerned with *sequence* and a bare *chronology* of events ('and then?' – what happened next?); and plot as primarily concerned with *consequence* and the 'logic' or *motivation* of events ('why?' – why did it happen?).

Forster's story/plot distinction has proved durable and valuable – not least because the 'and then?/why?' distinction is both simple and memorable. Certainly it is more accessible, if less techically precise, than the following story/plot distinction offered by the formalist critic Tomaschevsky in his influential *Thematics* (1925; in Rylance,1987: 58):

> the *story* is the aggregate of motifs in their logical, causal-chronological order; the *plot* is the aggregate of those same motifs but having the relevance and the order which they had in the original work.

This makes a partly different distinction from Forster. For here there is a much stronger insistence on the difference between 'story' events conceived as though they existed extra-textually and independent of any particular telling ('in their logical causal-chronological order'), and 'plot' conceived as the configuration of events offered in a particular telling or version ('having the relevance and the order which they had in the original work'). In effect, Tomaschevsky institutes what was to become a commonplace of formalist-structuralist analyses of narrative: the distinction between the *fabula* (the extra-textual ordering of events) and the *sjuzhet* (the plotting of events in a particular story). Benveniste, Genette and other modern French structural linguists and narratologists have further reworked such distinctions so as to produce that between *histoire* (abstractable and de-personalised 'content' – the enduring 'deep structure' of what is being represented) and *discours* (the unique and untranslatable 'form' – the peculiar 'surface' realisation of a particular representation). All these distinctions have some overlap and can be easily confused. But real and substantial differences remain and any attempt at bland homogenisation must be resisted. (For further reading and references; see Prince (1987), Toolan (1988) and Wales (1989).)

Some common concerns amongst narratologists of all persuasions can be registered, however, even if these do not add up to a consensus. A preliminary summary of these may be useful at this point. This will allow us to get our theoretical bearings by drawing larger inferences from the practical experiments so far. Virtually all theorists and analysts of narrative are concerned with aspects of the following:

- the 'how' and 'why' of narratives (causality, motivation, rationale) as well as the 'who', 'what', 'when' and 'where' (the constituent times, places and persons); *consequences* as well as *sequences*; 'logic' as well as *chronology*;

- the relation between the configuration of *events in a particular telling* of a narrative (including flashback, anticipation, extension or telescoping of time, multiple plotting, narratorial framing and intervention, 'point of view', evaluation, etc.) and those events conceived as though they were *independent of any particular teller or telling* (abstractable, depersonalised, transferable – 'raw material', 'already existing');

- attempts to distinguish between *'obligatory' functions of narrative* (also called 'cardinal functions', 'nuclei' and 'kernels') on the one hand and *'optional' functions of narrative* (also called 'catalysers' and 'satellites') on the other hand (this distinction is especially problematic in that it presupposes everyone would agree what is essential in a narrative and what can be left out);

- the processes of *narrative transformation* between genres and media, and the processes of *narrative translation* between distinct languages and cultures or varieties of the same language and culture (including treatments of ostensibly 'the same material' in sources, analogues, imitations, adaptations, parodies and pastiches).

To these common concerns may be added the more specific emphases of a number of narrative and text analysts with whom I have especial sympathy and to whom I owe an especial debt. Of particular relevance are:

- *sentence as story; story as sentence*: exploring analogies between the grammatical structuring of sentences at the micro-linguistic level and narrative structuring at the macro-textual level of genre, discourse and medium (Barthes, 1970, 1977; Labov, 1972; *'dialogic' possibilities of narratives (especially novels)* as they re-present heterogeneous 'voices' and discourses in new and telling contexts (Bakhtin 1981, 1984);

— *centres and margins; gaps and silences; inclusions and exclusions*: what is initially 'centred', 'marginal' and 'excluded' in the base text – and what can therefore be de- and re-centred in a subsequent critical re-writing (Macherey, 1978; Bhabha, 1990);

— *the process of narration*: at its simplest a stronger interest in what makes related narratives different rather than in what makes different narratives similar; in this respect the approach is particularistic and post-structuralist rather than generalising and structuralist.

All this may be summed up as a commitment to exploring 'whole narratives' through the 'holes in narrative'. You cannot have the one without . . . the many. Just as you cannot grasp 'sense' without grasping – or failing to grasp – 'non/sense'. But all this is just the theory. In practice, it's always another story. And that is what we turn to next.

3.2 SENSE AND NON/SENSE IN NARRATION

Here is a very short story. Please read it a few times.

> There was an old man
> And he had a calf
> And that's half
> He took him out of the stall
> And put him on the wall
> And that's all

Obviously this is a joke, a kind of 'mock story', something and nothing, inconsequential, trivial. In short, **nonsense.** And because it is all wrapped up with rhymes and sound patterns to produce a sense of wholeness we might add that it is 'nonsense verse'. And then, after that quick and conventional gesture of categorisation, we may be inclined to leave it at that. What else is there to say? Is there any serious point in lingering longer?

My answers to those questions are, respectively, 'a lot' and emphatically 'Yes'. And my reasons are three: (a) 'nonsense' is always extremely useful and, indeed, dialectically essential when attempting to define what can be meant by 'sense'; (b) a 'mock story' is likely to prove a good way of understanding what can be meant by and expected from 'stories' in general; (c) a text which is both 'nonsense verse' and 'narrative' is an ideal vehicle for preventing any facile separation of 'narrative' from 'poetry', as though 'narrative' were virtually synonymous with 'prose fiction' and we could conveniently ignore such huge verse narratives as *The Odyssey*, *The Canterbury Tales*, *Aurora Leigh*, and *Omeros* – as well as the palpably narrative dimension of ballads, lyrics and even sonnets and epigrams. In any case a text which so briskly makes and breaks generic conventions and so artfully and openly sports with its own textuality obviously has a place in a method such as this. Making alternative kinds of 'non/sense' is the main point of most of our own textual practices.

So what precisely is 'non/sensical', 'inconsequential' and 'trivial' about this little text? Which norms of 'sense', 'consequence' and 'seriousness' might we measure it against, and how does it travesty them? More particularly, how does this text play with and against our expectations so as to produce not any old text (or gibberish – i.e. genuinely incomprehensible and unintelligible 'nonsense') but a 'mock story' as well as – if you like – a 'mock poem'? In theory such questions can be initially forbidding. In practice, fortunately, they prove quite accessible. Here, I suggest, is what you do:

(1)

Re-read the base text attentively several times, preferably aloud. Run it through your mind and over your lips to see what obstacles it encounters (or throws up) and how these are negotiated. Meanwhile,

> **identify those points at which conventional sense-making and story expectation break down and are thwarted or deflected;**

> **ask yourself how a text which threatens to fall apart actually manages to hang together.**

(Do this before reading on.)

Many people's experience of reading this text runs something like this (compare this with your own experience). The first two lines present no problems: 'There was a . . .' is a standard opening in many kinds of story; the whole first line could also come from the kind of short, humorous, versified story known as a 'limerick' (of the type 'There was an old/young man/woman from . . .'). But then the third line ('And that's half') pulls us up. Half of what? Half of the text, presumably. But this is only really confirmed later, when we get to the parallel last line: 'And that's all'. Momentarily, at this mid-point in the actual process of reading we cannot be sure. The sense seems to collapse or switch to another plane, and all we have to hang on to is the sound-link back to the first line through the rhyme 'half–calf'. Semantic sense is temporarily suspended; syntactic sense depends upon no more than the comparatively weak link of a coordinator ('And'); and only the echo of a sound persuades us that someone may still be structuring things for us. All these effects are virtually instantaneous and more or less unconsciously registered, of course. None the less it is instructive to run them through in slow motion.

And so on to the fourth line and the second half of this micro-narrative: 'He took him out of the stall'. This makes perfectly reasonable sense if we assume that what's being referred to is what the old man did with the calf. Even then, however, it is worth noting that it requires some nifty information processing to infer that the first masculine pronoun ('he') refers to 'an old man' while the second ('him'), hard on its heels, has a different referent, 'a calf'. The penultimate line ('And put him on the wall') also makes sense as a continuation of the fourth line. Or at least it does in a narrowly linguistic fashion: semantically (assumed co-reference of the two 'him's and routine collocation of 'wall' with 'stall'); syntactically (coordinated clause with ellipted agent and parallel structure – dynamic verb + 'him' + preposition + 'the' + concrete noun); and phonologically ('wall–stall' rhyme and parallelism). There is therefore a very high degree of textual *cohesion* in lines 4 and 5. However textual cohesion is not necessarily the same thing as perceptual *coherence* (see 3.1.4). A text can hold together linguistically; but that does not automatically mean that it holds up to extra-textual or supralinguistic knowledges. Cohesive words do not guarantee coherent worlds. *Why* does the old man put the calf on the wall?! What are the reasons, conditions or circumstances for him doing this? We have a *sequence* of actions. But we have not yet been supplied with a *motivation* – and we shall wait in vain for meaningful *consequences*.

'And that's all', taunts the last line. The end. Finito. *Consummatum est.* But of course this is palpably and playfully a case of an ending which refuses to carry out all the tasks conventionally required of endings. To be sure, it rounds off the text very cohesively: the careful parallelism of lines 3 and 6 ('And that's half' and 'And that's all'), as well as the final trio of 'stall–wall–all' rhymes leave us in no doubt about the text's cohesion. But at the same time and in the same gesture the text blankly refuses to close down the play of meanings it has set in motion. We are still searching for coherence – and will be left searching. Quite simply, this is a narrative which is and is not 'complete' – a tantalising and instructive case of '*non/consummatum est*'. We have a formally neat closure open to multiple interpretations, and a final statement begging umpteen questions.

Another way of seeing the problems posed by this text is in Forster's terms of 'story' and 'plot' (see 3.1.6). We might then say that this is a *'story' in search of a 'plot'*: a sequence in search of some consequences; '*and* then?'s in search of some 'why's? (NB grammatically, the text is wholly coordinated: 'And . . .' × 4); and even an old man and a calf in search of an author! Alternatively, with Tomaschevsky and other formalist critics, we might say that our base text exposes the ever-present potential for disjuncture between the plotting of events in a particular text and our attempts to relate those events meaningfully and relevantly to some extra-textual reality. In this case, then, textual cohesion is a substitute for – not a reflection or a mediation of – extratextual coherence. Word-frames and world-frames simply do not fit.

It will therefore be abundantly clear, I hope, that such 'non/sense verse' can tell us a lot about what normally passes as 'sense' – especially about the process of making (and breaking) sense in language. More particularly, it points the way to an understanding of texts as part of a self-conscious and reflexive process (i.e. metatextually), and opens up the concept and category 'story' to a peculiarly searching interrogation through 'mockery' or 'parody'. At least we now have a pretty good idea what a story *isn't* 'normally' and therefore, conversely, what it *is* and *can be* 'abnormally'. The artfully 'deviant' encourages us to identify – and challenge – the artificially 'normal'.

3.2.1 Text into film

The next thing we do with this little text is speculate how we might turn it into a film. Not only is this interesting in itself, it also helps us to explore what may and may not be transferable in narrative from one medium to another.

(2)

Analyse and discuss 'There was an old man' with a view to making it into a short film. Consider strategic and tactical matters in any order you wish; but each time you make a decision ask yourself what precisely in your reading of the text prompted that decision.

Strategic decisions	*Tactical decisions*
What kind of film?	How would you handle:
Who is it for?	time, place and figures;
What is your overall aim?	sequencing of states and actions;
+ or – sound, speech, music?	beginning, middle and end;
Black and white or colour?	narrative 'points of view' – camera
Acted or animated?	positions?
Would it be spare or lavish?	
Would it be cheap or expensive?	

(Read on only when you have made some provisional decisions.)

3.2.2 Medium specificity, metatextuality, re/presentation, in/determinacy

This section gives an overview of the kinds of problem and possibility which people most commonly encounter when attempting to turn 'There was an old man' into a film. Compare their experiences with your own. I have not followed the preceding questions slavishly, but responses to all of them figure somewhere. Instead, I have highlighted terms such as those in the above section heading to signal the larger theoretical issues in play.

The switch from words on a page to images on a screen is a radical one. It shows up many features specific to each medium. It also confirms the tendency of artefacts to draw attention, implicitly or explicitly, to the specific medium and genre in which they are constituted: to be not just textual products but also metatextual comments on the processes of textuality. They present themselves for inspection, even while they represent something else.

This shows up clearly when struggling to decide which aspects of our verbal base text will and will not 'make it' into the film, and which other aspects will have to be substantially transformed. For instance, most people decide – or assume – very early on that some version of the principal participants, processes and circumstances have got to 'make it' from one medium to the other: the old man and the calf, the stall and the wall; the actions of 'taking out' and 'putting on'. Or at least they assume that these elements have got to appear if there is to be any re/presentational or referential common ground between one version and the other (as we shall see in 3.2.5–6, this is not necessarily the case). People also quickly become aware that certain other things will have to be left out – or be radically transformed. (I shall for the moment concentrate on film as a primarily wordless medium.) The rhymes and verse form of the base text would have to be omitted, as these are purely verbal matters. And the whole of lines 3 and 6 ('And that's half', 'And that's all') could only make it into a filmic medium by being changed to suit that medium. In the base text such devices are comments *in* language *on* language and are therefore *verbally* metatextual. They explicitly refer to the preceding text deictically, with the demonstrative pronoun 'that'; and they shift into the present tense ('that'*s*'), thus producing a marked distance from the surrounding lines which are in the past tense ('was', 'had'/'took', 'put'). To be sure, such 'middle' and 'end' points can be marked equally obtrusively in film; but it must be emphasised that this would need to be done by exploiting analogous – not identical – resources and techniques. It is therefore instructive to review some specifically filmic solutions to this problem. These have included: (a) insertion of notices simply saying 'End of Part One' and 'The End/Finis', in the manner of early silent films and early commercial TV; (b) cuts to an external narrator figure who frames the story; (c) abrupt black-outs or slow fade-outs at these points; (d) the use of music or sound effects to signal the two halves (e.g. a gong or bell, as in some sport and theatre); (e) two brief shots exposing the camera(s) shooting the action (though significantly and almost inevitably *not* including a shot of the camera filming the camera that is filming!). And so on. All these are potential analogies specific to a filmic (and in some cases a theatrical) medium: what by analogy with 'appropriate technology' might be termed 'appropriate metatextuality'.

So how did *you* propose to tackle this problem? Or did you evade it by simply leaving the 'comment breaks' out? And, if so, with what effects on the structure, perceptual framing and wit of the resulting piece? Either way, you may now wish to adjust or replace your initial gestures towards the metatextual frame and, in specifically filmic terms, acknowledge the narratorial roles of the director, camera, camera crew and film editors – the film as process as well as product.

But there are other fundamental problems and possibilities opened up by the attempt at a verbal–visual transformation, and other major decisions to be made. How do we *physically present* the participants that are *represented verbally* in the base text? What do the old man, the calf, the stall and the wall actually look like? What precise appearances do they have? Where precisely are they and how do they move in relation to one another, spatially and kinetically? And how are they lit? Straight away we are obliged to confront the fact that in some respects the written or spoken word, compared with film or photography, is a highly **indeterminate** code. Put more positively, verbal language has a high degree of *generality* and requires a correspondingly high degree of *participation* from the reader/listener in order to fix meanings. Thus, in the verbal base text, we are given no more than a few short noun phrases to cue us for the principal figures and elements of the scene: 'an old man', 'a calf', 'the stall' and 'the wall'. With the exception of the single, generalised adjective 'old' (how old?) and the indefinite and definite articles ('a' and 'the' – the latter, typically, implying that we already have some acquaintance with '*the* stall' and '*the* wall'), we are given absolutely no other information about what this person, this animal and these things look like. In so far as they exist, they exist as shadowy and rudimentary outlines in the mind: highly indeterminate constructs requiring the cooperation of the reader/listener to be realised.

But in a film – or at least in the most dominant and familiar presentational kinds of film – all of this would need to change. The director and actor (assisted by location and production crew) would need to present viewers with a *particular* old man (visibly of a certain age, colour and race), dressed in *particular* clothes (visibly denoting a certain nationality and region, prosperity and perhaps personal habits and traits); an animal which could not be merely the generalised notion of 'a calf', but a very *specific* instance of one (a few hours, days or weeks old; black, white, brown, grey or parti-coloured; clean or dirty, 'sweet' or 'foul', etc.). And so on to 'the' *particular* 'stall' and 'the' *particular* 'wall': ancient or modern; mud, wood, stone, brick, breeze-block, corrugated iron or plastic; dirty and derelict or spick and span, etc. What's more, in order to turn the whole narrative situation into a plausible scene, we would need to include all sorts of other aspects of the (farm-?)yard and house (mansion, cottage, apartment?!) – as well as, of course, some indications of the time of day (or night) and the weather. And so on. The sheer number and possible permutations of visual particularities, even in as slight a scene as this, are obviously considerable. And each one of them would need to be decided upon by someone realising this text as a presentational film.

This is why we speak of film (and photography) as being predominantly highly **determinate** codes: modes of communication which are characteristically specific and particular, in part determined by the materials they present. In Peirce's terms, they are predominantly **iconic** and **indexical** (rather than, like language, 'symbolic'). They record or point to some more or less recognisable aspects of the referential world. In Saussure's terms, they offer a partly 'non-arbitrary' (i.e. necessary) relation between **signifier** and **signified.** And this, of course, is why films, photographs and images in general have a much readier international currency than newspapers and books. We can immediately see at least something of what a film or photo or painting is about, even without subtitles and captions. (How fully we 'understand' what we see, culturally, is another matter.) However, we cannot understand a verbal text at all unless we know the language in which it is written, or unless it is translated into one that we do. In this respect at least, we can recall the photo-journalist's adage, 'a picture is worth a thousand words'.

It must be added, however, that all this is to view films and photos as 'predominantly', 'characteristically' and 'typically' determinate: tied to material particulars, iconic and indexical, non-arbitrary, etc. Hence the conspicuous presence of such adverbial qualifiers in the preceding paragraph. For there are other uses and kinds of film – albeit less dominant or familiar – and there are aspects of all films – even the most meticulously presentational – which evade or ignore all or some of the paraphernalia of particularity and determinacy. Certain uses and kinds of film and certain aspects of all films avoid proliferation of material details and concentrate on the abstract, the outline, the non- or barely presentational image: the image which before and beyond being an image of something else is itself. Indeed, you may have imagined *your* film to be just such a film. And you can hardly have avoided drawing in at least some of these aspects.

Perhaps, then, you decided to go for a cinematically 'minimalist' realisation of this text: black and white, with outline, shadowy or distant figures, stylised costumes, silhouettes and sharply contrastive lighting. This is often the option people choose on further reflection and discussion. Alternatively they go for that very particular kind of film devoted to patently artificial outline and surface, the *animated film* – whether using successive stills of models or of cartoon drawings. This is a popular solution too. It also very clearly throws into relief the minimal, indeterminate and generalised (or, perhaps better, 'typicalised') features of the verbal text. Moreover, animations – especially 'shorts' – tend to be built round humorous, odd and implausible situations. They too offer kinds of amusing and maybe thought-provoking 'non/sense'. (One should here think of the seriously witty products of the animators' arts, including Eastern European and Oriental examples, and not only the popular and commercial Western staples of 'Bugs Bunny' and 'Daffy Duck'.) All these aspects of the base text are perhaps conducive to such a choice. What's more, once we get into this line of thinking, it is certainly not hard to come up with a cartoon/ animated way of overtly signalling the middle and end of the tale. Perhaps the figures briefly step out of character – and the frame – and say 'And that's half! . . . And that's all!'? Or they lift placards on which these words are written. ('Bugs Bunny', in fact, usually finishes with just such spoken and handwritten flourishes, i.e. 'That's all for now, folks!')

Such devices also remind us that analogous cinematic techniques are available too, ones which we may have forgotten if working, as we were initially, from strictly non-verbal presentational premises. Inserted stills, rapid montage or cumulative collage, freeze-frame, slowed or accelerated motion (domestic video analogies include pause, fast forward and rewind) – these are just some of the ways of fracturing the illusion of a continuous situation and a 'whole' artefact. And yet, at the same time, as in the 'non/sense verse', such techniques develop their own peculiar *dis/continuities* and expose their own '*w/holes*', even as they succeed in displacing others.

A final note on metatextuality and in/determinacy in relation to specifically *verbal* texts should perhaps be added. Words *can* be highly determinate, *can* concentrate on material particularity and physical texture and *can* be offered – and understood – as though they were the immediate and transparent presentation (not the mediated and opaque representation) of events beyond themselves. However, it must be stressed that if this natu- ralistic 'reality effect' is to be achieved you need two things: (a) a great number of words (particularly adjectives and adverbs, so as to detail the qualities, attributes and circum- stances of the represented event); and (b) the resolve to suppress every overt clue as to the agency of the writer and narrator(s), as well as every aspect of words and texts which calls attention to itself (i.e. metalanguage and metatextuality). The first requirement (lots of words) accounts for the length and detail of many a nineteenth-century 'classic realist novel'. The second requirement, however, is strictly impossible; for no work can ever entirely suppress traces of its own status as a product produced by processes. And even if writers attempt to obscure or occlude their own role as agents, it is still the right and capac- ity of every actual reader to expose the constructedness of the wor(l)ds they are offered as 'natural' or 'neutral'.

Overall, then, we can conclude that words *represent* worlds. Far less than film and photo- graphy do they *present* worlds. Words offer *absences*. Far less than film and photography do they project *presences*. In these respects at least (though not in all) language tends more towards a narrativising or 'telling' of experience than the kind of dramatising or 'showing' of experience we associate with the image, whether still or moving.

It will also be clear that cross-media adaptation is always a matter of thoroughgoing *trans- formation* – never of mere transference. For this reason the very activity of attempting to transform a text from one medium to another is always as illuminating about the base text as it is about the adapted text. Indeed, I would argue again that it is impossible fully to identify and evaluate what is going on in one medium and text *unless* we try transforming it into another. For how can we know what a text is 'in itself' unless we also know what it is not 'in something else'? How can we know a text's many actual 'selves', so to speak, without exploring its many potential 'others'?

That is what we carry on doing now, in still finer analytical detail yet with equally broad theoretical implications.

3.2.3 Verbal and visual processes: actions and states; tense and time; sequence and consequence

Moving across the verbal–visual interface proves particularly illuminating when it comes to processes. How do we realise the various actions, states, relations and perceptions in which the participants are involved? And how do we articulate and interrelate the temporal and causal dimensions of those processes: broadly, the sequences and the consequences.

At this point it will be helpful to review the descriptive frameworks for verbs (processes) presented in 5.2, pp. 195–6. Then proceed to apply them as follows.

Go through 'There was an old man' again and identify:

(a) all those verbs concerned with processes of 'being' or 'having' (the *state* verbs), and all those verbs concerned with processes of 'doing' or 'acting' (the *dynamic* verbs);

(b) the present-tense verbs, and the past-tense verbs.

Go on to ask yourself precisely how – or whether – you registered such distinctions in the initial sketch of your film version. In what ways, if any, did you project differences between general 'states' of being or having and specific 'dynamic' actions? And what, if anything, did you make of the 'past' narrative set within a 'present' narratorial frame? (Read on only when you have done this.)

It will now be clear that parts of the base text are built round very different kinds of verbal process and therefore offer very different challenges for visualisation. The first three lines and the last line are built round *state* verbs of 'being' and 'having': 'was', 'had', 's' (i.e. 'is' × 2) (in functional terms these would all be called **relational**). The fourth and fifth lines, however, are built firmly round *dynamic* verbs of 'doing' and 'acting': 'took (out of)', 'put (on)' (in functional terms, **material action-intention** processes). There is thus a clear distinction between 'being/having' and 'doing' processes, and therefore some fundamental implications for how we might realise those processes visually.

If we then add *tense* to the picture, we see that it gets slightly more complicated. For clearly there are two quite distinct tenses used over the the course of the text: past tense for the narrative in the first and second, and the fourth and fifth lines ('was', 'had', 'took', 'put'); and present tense for the metatextual comments by the narrator in the third and sixth lines (''s'× 2). If we put all these processes together (state and dynamic, past and present) along with their narrative functions (narrative and narratorial/metatextual), we come out with a patterning as in Table 3.1.

Table 3.1 Tense, narration and in/action

There *was* an old man	state	past	narrative
And he *had* a calf	state	past	narrative
And that's half	state	present	narrator
He *took* him out of the stall	dynamic	past	narrative
And *put* him on the wall	dynamic	past	narrative
And that's all	state	present	narrator

Such a diagram maybe looks overschematic. But it does at least allow us to identify very explicitly the kinds of verbal process we are dealing with *and* relate them to narrative function. It may therefore encourage us to make analytically informed and creatively considered decisions, not so much about localised tactics (on an *ad hoc* basis) but about overall strategies (from a position of knowledge, and therefore power).

How and when, therefore, in *your* film did *you* propose to articulate the past narrative states reported in the first two lines: the facts that there *was* an old man and he *had* a calf? How and when did *you* decide to modulate the narrative into and out of specific dynamic (transitive) actions: 'He *took* him out . . . And put him on . . .'? Moreover, did this take place in exactly the same 'past', the same temporal frame, as the establishing of the old man's age and his possession of the calf – or one which was subtly or markedly different? Such questions also oblige us to return to the crucial matter of the position of the narrator (director, camera, observer, viewer) with respect to the narrative s/he (or it) frames and comments upon: the succession of events to which s/he or it assigns an overt middle and an end. What state, then, did *you* present *your* 'narrator'/'observer' in? What were her, his or its *observations* – in the fullest sense of that most pregnant word: analytical, metatextual and evaluative? Or were you content to suppress any explicit reminder of the activity of narration and observation?

Here, for comparison, are some very brief sketches of how other people have tackled these possibilities. This is how they responded in practice to the above 'verb/process' brief; and how they related to the above matrix of processes and narrative strategies. For a start, most people opted to open conventionally by 'setting the scene' with some shots establishing the who, what, when and where of the situation: they wanted to get the 'state' processes in at the beginning. Often this took the form of a long shot, slowly focusing in on or panning across to the old man, the calf in the stall and the perhaps the wall. More adventurously, some chose to establish this relation by casting back to earlier moments, when the calf was born or bought – and even when the man was young, witnessing the birth of his first calf (this last done in 'flash back' as the memory of an old man). Such flexibilities remind us that 'states' can be established in a variety of temporal and perceptual frames. They always exist potentially to one side of any main action. Therefore, they can also be established at a later point or built up piecemeal as that action develops. In fact in many films the *mise-en-scène is* delayed to a greater or lesser degree, and the audience is fed information piecemeal.

For this reason, a substantial minority of other people decided to engage with the participants and their actions by jumping directly 'into the middle of things'. They plunged us straight into the dynamic processes of taking the calf out and putting it on the wall. And the circumstantial detail we were left to pick up later (from a long shot pulling out or panning round) or left to infer from the participants in action.

The options with respect to the visual presentation of 'states' and 'actions' therefore fall into four basic categories:

1   state (scene setting) + actions;

2   actions ('into the middle of things') + state;

3   concurrent development;

4   alternating development.

In this respect it is perhaps worth stressing that our base text offers an instance of just one of the possible permutations (i.e. (1)). This may be common and familiar, but it is by no means universal and necessary. Moreover, you, being actively responsible for the adaptation to another medium and maybe genre, may well feel that one of the other process-sequences may be more effective for that medium and your intended effects.

By way of conclusion here, I shall mention one ingenious suggestion made by a sub-group doing their utmost to maintain a sense of the film product as a filmic process. They suggested that a mirror be placed behind the wall on which the calf is finally placed. In this we would see the camera crew shooting the 'final' narrative shot – only to continue for a few moments while they began to remove the film canister and pack up their equipment. This, it was generally agreed, was at least one way of signalling an end to the narrative as product (as in the base text) which was not an end to the narration as process (also in the base text). This still, of course, left room for argument about when precisely the filming was to stop – and what might happen to the mirror. (Should it be shattered in shot? To reveal what behind it?) Notwithstanding such literally endless haggling about the sense and non/sense of endings, this was the best any of us could come up with.

You will certainly have come up with a different 'non/sense of an ending'. Which, on further reflection and discussion, do you prefer? (For further work on the 'non/sense' of endings, see 4.3; also Kermode, 1968.)

3.2.4 Genres and viewers, titles and trailers

In an educational exercise such as this a sense of the kind of film (*genre*) and who it is intended for (*addressees*) tends to develop gradually. It may be one of the last things you firm up. This is the exact reverse of highly commercial film production. There the potential viewers (always primarily conceived as a section of an existing or potential 'market') are a crucial factor in planning and design right from the start. So is the notion of – often the formula for – a certain kind of film, again with mass marketability and ready recognisability in mind, as well as the legal banding requirements that obtain nationally and internationally (suitable for 'minors', 'minors accompanied by an adult', 'adult' etc.). All these communicative factors are conducive to very early decisions on content, form, emphasis and appeal; and these decisions are predominatly company-based and market-led.

We, however, are engaged in more broadly educative, analytical and critical-creative processes. We can literally 'afford' to stand back and speculate about *potential* kinds of text and *potential* kinds of addressee. Our options are not in this respect narrowed or prematurely foreclosed by pressing actualities. Hence the playfully speculative, often 'impractical' and 'implausible' – sometimes ideally 'Utopian' or deliberately 'ludicrous' – aspects of many of our activities. For worse and for better, we are playing. For, to repeat, we are here primarily concerned with critical-creative education – not instrumental training. We are exploring processes of narration – not aiming at finished (or commodifiable) narrative products.

Notwithstanding, it is highly instructive to speculate in some detail how you *would* target and market your *potential* film *if* it were to be communicated as an *actual* film.

Go through the following checklist. It will help you to 'fix' what kind of product you were leading towards and with whom in mind (however implicitly). It may also suggest ways in which you might refine the rationale and point out the intended effects of that product.

Would your film be:

'broadcast' for the many, 'the masses' (which one?); and for high street distribution or peak-time TV viewing? Why/not?

'narrowcast' for the few, a 'minority' (which one?); and for film-club distribution or off-peak TV viewing? Why/not?

appealing to people of a particular age range; national, regional or racial culture; class; sex; education; cinema-going or TV-watching habits and tastes?

describable as 'thriller', 'chiller', 'domestic comedy', 'rural documentary', 'a disturbing/light-hearted/thought-provoking/sensitive study in – or spoof – of . . .'? Or something else?

practically im/possible or commercially im/plausible?

A good way of drawing together and fixing the above insights is to decide on a title and 20–30 words 'trailer' for your film. This could be as it would be advertised and described in a TV-programme or film guide. And a selected visual could be added. Do this for your own film before reading on.

Here are some titles and trailers for potential films based on the text 'There was an old man . . .'. These were put together by groups of students working to the above brief after they had already sketched provisional scenarios and in some cases written full scripts.

The wall
No, not the cartoon with Pink Floyd – but an intriguing and amusing tale of a country idiot by the Czech animator Vaclav Holub. Perhaps not enough happens for very young children. (English subtitles.)

For Auld Lang Syne
A deeply disturbing yet sensitive portrayal of senility in a Scottish Highland village. James Cameron plays the old man who finally realises he can no longer cope alone on his small-holding ['with "Angus" as the calf!' – added by a cheerfully disaffected member of the group]. (Grampian TV)

Half a Calf?! (French, untitled)
A recently rediscovered, unfinished 'short' from the French director François Truffle. Made sometime between the early 'Monsieur Hulot' farces and his later, more sombre 'comic realist' work, this flawed yet fascinating piece attempts to combine visual slapstick with documentary pathos. The situation turns on a drunken old man who, for a bet, tries to make a calf dance on a wall. Only two parts of the film remain and it is uncertain which order they should be in. Decide for yourself.

Perhaps not surprisingly, though still interestingly, hardly anyone ever conceives their film as a box-office block-buster or as the basis for a scene in a prime-time soap opera! And yet it is not absolutely impossible to imagine such a transformation. In fact you might like to spend a moment or two weighing precisely what such a transformation might entail. What 'ingredients' and maybe 'formulae' might be invoked for popular success? But then again, your adaptation might already be well on the way to *There Was an Old Man 'III'* –

The Calf's Revenge!. In any event, compare your title and trailer with those for the films advertised above. And perhaps go on to explore the consistencies and parodic possibilities of the 'trailer' genre itself.

So far our main concern has been to adapt the verbal text to a filmic or televisual medium. But we have still not, as yet, radically intervened in or de- and re-constructed the materials in the base text. More precisely, we have not yet challenged and changed the fundamental configuration of subject/agent positions in and through which that text is constituted. What other related yet alternative stories might be woven out of and into the tissue of this text? What complementary and supplementary wor(l)ds may be teased out of and into the design? What causalities and consequences might inform the existing sequences – and what alternative participants, processes and circumstances might be inferred from and into the base text's silences and margins? In short, what radically alternative 'non/senses' can we make of all this?!

3.2.5 Blowing up the text – narrative expansion and explosion

What we shall now do with this little non/sense narrative is really 'blow it up'. And we shall do this in two senses: expand it *and* explode it. (As we know from elementary physics, when working on volatile material in a confined space the first process tends to lead to the second!) Our material is the base text. Our apparatus is our analytical and critical-creative techniques. And the experiment will give us first-hand experience of a number of constitutive features of the text which only show up when it is put under pressure: when it is fissured and fractured, re-formed and transformed by bombardment with extraneous yet relatable materials. In particular, we shall be looking at:

1 what happens to traditional notions of *beginnings*, *middles* and *ends* (in modern parlance, **points of entry/opening, development** and **closure**) under the pressure of extreme forms of relativism – both *de*constructive and *re*constructive;

2 how far the standard division of narrative events into *obligatory* ('cardinal', 'kernel', 'nucleus') elements on the one side and *optional* ('catalyser', 'satellite') elements on the other stands up under the same pressure (see Toolan, 1988: 22–31);

3 the resulting ferment of *subject/agent positions* which these procedures generate within, around and beyond the gaps of the text, and how this ferment may be further cultivated by systematic inferencing procedures at the level both of micro-linguistic clausal structures and of macro-textual practices of *discourse* and *social-historical processes*.

Fortunately, all this is easier done than said.

(1)

Label the six lines of 'There was an old man' alphabetically A–F: first line A; second line B; etc.

(2)

Now ask someone else to jot down *three* **random sequences of those same letters (e.g. perhaps FECBAD, BEDFAC, CFABED).**

(3)

Referring back to the lines of the base text, use each of these sequences of letters to sketch a corresponding sequencing of events. Recast the actual words of each version as you wish; but aim to produce *three* distinct versions, each of which is textually cohesive and perceptually coherent in its own way. Be adventurous and ingenious; and perhaps use Table 3.1 to help plot the strategic possibilities of each line as a certain kind of event. For instance, a modestly modified version of the configuration FECBAD might begin 'It all ended like this: / The calf had been put on the wall / But that's only the half of it / . . .' (i.e. F/E/C . . . modified); whereas a more extravagantly transformed version of BEDFAC might begin 'Imagine you're a calf owned by someone / and suddenly you find yourself put on this high wall, out in a cold wind / when only a few moments before you'd been warm and cosy in the straw of your stall . . . (i.e. B/E/D . . . transformed).

(*An alternative 'randomising procedure'* is to write out the base text with the six lines labelled A–F, as above, then simply cut out each line separately, shuffle them 'blind' three times, and work from the configurations you produce. The main thing is to set yourself the challenge of making alternative 'sense' out of permutations of 'the same materials'.)

(4)

Now analyse what you did in each of your three versions. Generally speaking, how modestly modified or extravagantly transformed was each version? More precisely, which participants, processes and circumstances did you include or exclude; expand or contract? In simple grammatical terms, which nouns, verbs, adjectives, adverbs and connectors did you add, delete or change? And how far were your sentences linked through coordination or subordination? (See 3.1.1–2 and 5.2.)

Whatever you did, the result will have been a particular textual cohesion and a particular perceptual coherence. What were they and how were they achieved? For instance, some of the more obvious modifications in the FECBAD version above are: the use of the (existential/prop) pronoun 'It' as a conventional story opener; the thematising of the calf as the grammatical subject of a passive, past perfect verb; deleted or delayed reference to the old man; use of the qualifying connector 'But' in the third line; etc. The transformation in the BEDFAC version is still more radical and wide-ranging: total reorientation of the narratorial frame so as to address the narratee directly and urge the adoption of a specific subject position ('Imagine you're a'); focus on and focalising through the projected experience of the calf (where the narratee and the narrated figure coalesce in a compound 'you'); lavish contextualising and 'texturising' of the action and situation through the addition of adjectives ('high', 'cold', 'warm', 'cosy') and adverbial and prepositional phrases ('only a few moments before', 'in the straw of'); and, again, deletion or delay of the old man through passivisation ('owned', 'put'), accompanied by a variety of tense shifts and temporal-perceptual framings ('you find', 'you'd been'). In all these ways and more, each of these particular versions of these particular configurations of events develops its own peculiar textual cohesion and offers its own preferred coherence. You will have developed different cohesions and coherences – even if you did the same basic configurations. What were those differences? And which, on reflection, do you prefer – and why?

To conclude this activity, I should like briefly to consider one particularly interesting permutation of the base text (total inversion). This will also serve as the 'pre-text' for a bout of theorising.

(5)

Experiment with possible versions of the 'totally inverted' configuration FED-CBA. Give particular attention to three areas:

how you construct your new *beginning, middle* and *end*;

choices of verbs in terms of *tense* and *aspect*, and *dynamic* and *state* processes;

narrator's role and *metatextual* framing.

Again, the overall question is: what kind of 'sense' have you now made of the text, and how? Be as restrained or extravagant, subtle or outrageous, as you wish – but work to the configuration FEDCBA somehow. (One possible version beginning FE . . . is sketched above in (2). Perhaps use this to help set you thinking – though not as a model.)

(6)

On the basis of your experiments with a 'totally inverted version', debate the following proposition *for*, *against* and *alternative* (i.e. substituting an alternative proposition):

There is no absolutely 'natural' and 'neutral' order for beginnings, middles and endings.

(See Aristotle's *Poetics*, ch. 7; Kermode, 1968; and Marshall, 1992: ch. 6, for some very various grist to this particular mill.)

3.2.6 Preludes, interludes and postludes; complements and supplements

So far we have played around with permutations of the *present, actual* narrative events, as though they were an *internally closed* – albeit variable – system. We now consider how these narrative events may be supplemented and marginalised and even (ultimately) displaced; how they may be related to the 'open' and 'external' system of 'absent', 'potential' choices and combinations which have *not* been made, but might have been – and may still be. In other words, we are off again to other worlds. Here is what you do:

(1)

Make bold yet systematic inferences about some of the participants, process-es and circumstances that have *not* been mentioned in the base text, but which might – and in your view perhaps should – have been. Go on to weave a story round them, putting the events of the base text on the margins – not at the cen-tre – of your design. For instance, here we can identify 'old man', 'calf', 'stall' and 'wall' as the principal animate and inanimate participants. Now all we do is place each *actual reference* at the centre of a *cluster of potential inferences*. Each participant is thereby used as the cue for and clue to all those relatable participants (persons, animals and things) which our 'real world knowledge' (including cultural competence) suggests *might have* co-occurred and been

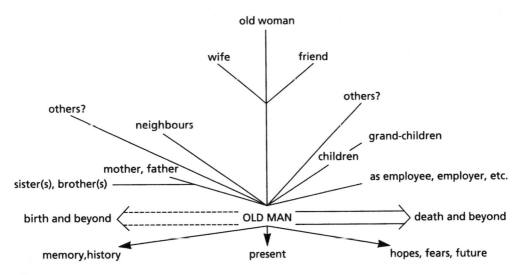

Figure 3.3 Potential participants: an inference cluster centred on 'old man'

referred to – but in the event weren't. The result is a kind of 'lexical-word association game' combined with a 'real world inference model'. And in the case of the cue 'old man' it leads to clusters something like Figure 3.3.

Notice that each of the above participants would themselves be implicated in a range of processes and circumstances. In this way we may generate stories within – and beyond – stories: wor(l)ds within – and beyond – wor(l)ds.

(2)

Now generate similar 'inference clusters' for *calf* and *stall* or *wall*. See just how many contingent animals, persons and things, as well as implicated processes and circumstances you can generate – initially by random 'brain-storming' and then by disposing the results in some kind of design that gives visible shape to the connections.

The simple, crucial point is that each of these terms represents a potential 'growth point' for whole arrays of new participants and, by extension, new processes and circumstances. For each and every *actual, present participant* is implicated in a network of *potential, absent participants*, and through them, in the words and worlds of other stories: complementary and supplementary, alternative and perhaps opposed. (Compare the modelling of 'present' and 'absent' subjects/agents in 2.1.)

Clearly, then, every *actual story* has a number of *potential stories* waiting to spring out 'hydra-headed' from under the same hat. We may think of these as 'pre-stories', 'inter-stories' and 'post-stories', depending where in the narrative (or the process of narration) they occur. Moreover, by extending an analogy with the main ways of structuring sentences, we may also think of such stories as added or embedded – 'coordinated' or 'subordinated' (cf. 3.1.4). However, as our emphasis is on the *'play' between* actual and potential narratives, it is perhaps better to hold onto a couple of existing terms and add just one coinage to the critical currency: **prelude, interlude** and **post/lude.** Here are some examples of each broad type, culled from many, more exotic and longer re-writes produced by students. I leave it to you to decide how far these are 'complements' (filling out the base story) or supplements (displacing and even replacing) it; as well as how far the fresh material should be viewed as 'coordinated' (added and of equivalent story status) or 'subordinated' (embedded and of dependent story status). As the appended extracts from the ensuing discussion show, such distinctions are helpful in principle – as long as they are handled with discrimation in practice.

Prelude (Pre-(hi)story)

Long, long ago, before there were even people or other mammals, but only earth and water and air and plants, in a tropical sea, tiny molluscs slowly settled into mud and even more slowly sedimented into rock. From this rock (which was oolitic limestone), many millions of years later – though it was now on the side of a hill in a land which was no longer tropical – some stones were cut. And from these stones was built a wall. And on that wall, one night, an old man placed a calf. Later he and the calf died. But the rocks remain . . .

Inferencing led by a Geology/English student based primarily on 'wall'. This records the 'work of people *and* of nature that went into the wall'. The old man and the calf are now not the only animate focuses: they vie for attention with the molluscs and the people who cut the stone and made the wall (notwithstanding the passivisation and formal deletion of the latter). The base plot is therefore itself 'subordinated' and 'embedded' in another plot which massively complements yet does not wholly supplement it. Indeed, it is still possible to see the presence and action of the old man and the calf as the primary focuses. They are still the most interesting figures in the landscape. Moreover, theirs is the only fully transitive, active process ('an old man placed a calf'). All the rest of the text can therefore – though need not – be construed as scene-setting and background (hence the high incidence of 'circumstance' items: the adverbial and prepositional phrases). As always, however, the precise relation between 'foreground' and 'background' is where actual readers – e.g. you and me – choose to fix it. A case of 'Molluscs and wall-builders, unite . . . !' perhaps?

Interlude

'Come down from there, you silly old bugger!' cried his daughter, 'And bring that poor creature with you!'

'And who's going to make me?' he shouted, saving anyone the trouble by falling off.

The calf promptly sat down and began to munch a tuft of grass that was growing in the cracks on top.

Inferencing from 'old man' generated a 'daughter' – and then a very specific relation between them. The high drama (and comedy) of this interlude is, of course, produced by leading with speeches which are exclamative, interrogative or both; intensification of emotion and volume in the narrative report clauses ('cried', 'he shouted'); the sudden reversal of expected granddaughter/grandfather relations ('you silly old bugger'); and the evident indifference of the calf to the old man's fall. But again, whether your overall focus is on the daughter, the old man, 'that poor creature/calf', the 'tuft of grass' – or all four, and more, in various measures at various moments – is again partly up to you: an effect of the text – but also of the way you allow yourself to be affected.

Postlude

Then the calf fell off and broke its neck. The vet and the RSPCA were called. The old man was charged with cruelty to animals, but they dropped the charge on the grounds of diminished responsibility. He was taken away to a private nursing home, where fortunately he died just before the money from the sale of his estate (including stall and wall) was spent in bills. The calf recovered but was already too old for veal, so it was sold to a neighbouring farmer who bred it for another year for beef. It was finally slaughtered and turned into pre-packed joints and dog food and bonemeal for the garden.

Next week's cautionary tale: Humpy Dumpty, eggs and salmonella.

Inferencing centred on 'calf' and developed in a decidedly modern frame: 'vet', 'RSPCA', 'veal', 'pre-packed joints', etc. The old man's plight is also contemporised (e.g. snippets of legal discourse, 'private nursing home') and put in the middle of this 'postlude' – but not necessarily at the perceptual 'centre'. The base text's trick ending is perhaps picked up in the carry forward to 'Next week's cautionary tale'. Evidently what is in store is another traditional piece of 'nonsense' adapted to point up the ills of modern factory-farming! Overall, then, this version may have begun modestly enough as a 'complement' to the base plot. But in the end it promises nothing less than a whole series of full-blown 'supplements'!

3.2.7 Summarising the story so far . . .

Some summary comments on the value of such procedures may be in order – especially for those who doubt either their effectiveness or 'academic' repectability. De- and re-constructing narrative in this way:

1 explodes actual narratives in order to open up potential narratives, thereby emphasising narration as an active, continuing process rather than the simple observation of already achieved products;

2 sharpens powers of critical inference by systematically and imaginatively scrutinising the implications of every major participant, process and circumstance in turn – turning the 'half' or 'not said' into the 'fully' or 'differently said';

3 draws attention to the fact that 'beginnings', 'middles' and 'ends' are both arbitrary and necessary, notably through types of 'prelude', 'interlude' and 'postlude';

4 challenges the notion that any one event is necessarily more 'obligatory' or more 'optional' than another by reminding the actual reader that what to one person may be viewed as 'inessential', 'minor' or (structurally) 'secondary' may for another person be a 'growth point' – a 'node' for the concerted cultivation of counter- or alternative narratives;

5 reminds each one of us (analytically, critically and creatively) that the privileged subject/agent positions are those which are 'made' as well as 'found'; and that focalising is an operation *on* the text as well as a property *of* the text;

6 finally, it is serious fun! For the results are often not only 'ludicrous' (in the sense of 'laughably implausible') but, more importantly, 'ludic' (in the sense of 'playfully serious'). And 'serious play' is the one thing that distinguishes 'education' in the broadest sense from 'training' in the narrowest.

In all these ways the narrative text is ceaselessly re-realised not as a 'whole thing' but as a kind of 'space full of holes': an arena for conflict and celebration; the negotiation of one kind of 'non/sense' with another.

That's our story anyway.

3.2.8 A postscript on history and ideology

The ideological issues raised in this chapter have been deliberately framed in general terms so as to be applicable to a wide range of texts. The value and versatility of such theoretical practices as 'non/sense', inferencing, narrative de-and re-construction, complements and supplements, etc., extend far beyond the particular text we have had in hand. However, it must also be insisted that *in any particular case* ideology is a deeply specific social and historical matter; it is implicated in very specific moments and modes of production and exchange – of meanings and values as of everything else. Some basic information on our main base text will therefore be in order. This is indicative, though hardly adequate.

This particular version of 'There was an old man' is from *Mother Goose's Melody*, printed in London in 1765 (Rhys, 1927: 153 and see pp. v–vi). Parts of the latter collection – including one version of our base text – derive from Charles Perrault's *Contes da la mère l'oye* (1697); and he in turn, like his English counterparts, drew them from much older oral traditions as well as the printed collections of 'quips and jolly jests' or 'delights and diversions' which circulated widely, first in broadsheets and then in newspapers, joke- and songbooks, from the sixteenth to nineteenth centuries (see Darnton, 1985: 17–78).

So what was the social-historical function of such collections as *Mother Goose's Melody*? A clue is there in the fact that such collections were frankly (as their names suggest) 'diversions', 'sports' and 'delights': they were 'diverting' (i.e. entertaining) in themselves, while also presumably being 'diverting' (i.e. distracting) in that they deflected people's attentions from the harsher or more routine aspects of life. Moreover, as with virtually all jokes and anecdotes (and indeed all 'fantasies' and 'fictions') we can also expect some oblique refraction of how people saw life at the time – though never of course a direct reflection of those lives. In other words, however indirectly or obscurely, such texts will have had *certain relations* to people's lives both as actually lived and as they perceived them to be lived. They will have 'diverted' *to* pleasurable experiences and *from* painful ones; and they will have picked up and refracted fragments of contemporary life in the process. They will also have depended upon, and themselves constituted, *certain notions* of 'sense' and 'nonsense'.

What those 'certain relations' may have been between 'There was an old man' and other aspects of people's lives in, say, the mid-eighteenth century in England is well beyond the scope of this book and my current competence to specify. Moreover, a history of the changing and multi-layered notions of 'sense' and 'nonsense' at the time would be as colossal as it would be fascinating (see Darnton, 1985: *passim*, for relevant fragments of this design; also Foucault, 1986: 273–90). However, some provisional questions can at least be framed here and the shape of some potential answers implied in them.

> What attitudes to *old age* prevailed at the time amongst different sections of the community: rich and poor; in town and country?

What *family and community* networks or formal institutions were available for *health care* of the old, the sick and the infirm?

How did *old men*, as distinct from *old women*, fit into these networks and institutions? And how did they figure in stereotypical (and anti- and a-stereotypical) representations of *age and gender*?

How were *animals* (e.g. 'calves') situated and viewed in the changing cultural economy? What humanistic, animistic or ecological worldviews informed that economy?

What were the formal and institutional, moral, social and political limits to 'sense' and 'nonsense' at the time? And what social sanctions and legal mechanisms were brought to bear on transgressors?

What dividing lines were imposed, traversed or being redrawn between the categories 'poetry', 'political radicalism', 'religious non-conformity', 'eccentricity' and 'madness'?

Who was allowed to voice or print what kinds of 'non/sense' where, when and for whom?

Such questions are, of course, endless. They are also endlessly fascinating in the detailed and often conflicting reports that can be culled from the historical records. Moreover, with each question the questioner is obliged to ask her or himself why s/he is asking it – like that and not otherwise. What larger ideological inferences is *s/he* drawing out of *and* feeding into the text? And how far is this 'inferencing' the result of a genuinely historical dialogue with the potential plurality of meanings of the text in its various moments of production and reproduction? Or is it a merely monologic imposition of the supposedly monolithic meaning of the reader on the text, or the text on the reader, in just one artificially isolated and privileged moment?

Analogous questions might be put to any text. And for a genuinely historical understanding of what that text in its particularity, suspended in ideological space between a contested then and there and a differently contested here and now, they *must* be put – resourcefully and often.

There is one final note on the literary-historical models of narrative and hi/story employed here. These might fairly be described as a a cross between Lukacs' (1962) attempt to map 'world-historical totalities', Macherey's (1978) attempt to pick those totalities full of 'holes', and Foucault's (1986: 76–101) projection of hi/story as a succession of factional dis/continuities. Those acquainted with the often fundamental contradictions between (and within) these writers' works will recognise that such a hybrid model is a 'non/sense' too!

But a particularly productive one, I suggest.

3.3 EXTENDED WORK-OUT: RE-VISITING *ROBINSON CRUSOE*

THE ONLY PERSON TO GET EVERYTHING DONE BY FRIDAY WAS ROBINSON CRUSOE.

> (Common notice in modern British offices)

Just about every other character who appears was a candidate to be a narrator at some point. I gave

Ichiro, the little grandson, a go as narrator for some time. One of the daughters, Noriko, was a narrator for a while; there was a character who is not in it any more who was a narrator. I tried all kinds of things.

(Kasuo Ishiguro of his *An Artist of the Floating World* (1986))

Play is the disruption of presence. . . . Play is always play of absence and presence.

(Jacques Derrida, *Structure, Sign and Play in the Discourse of the Human Sciences* (1978))

These three quotations, though far apart in other respects, help identify the three main strands in this extended project on narrative: (1) the persistent myth of Robinson Crusoe and Friday as though they were eternally locked in a white master/black slave relation; (2) the crucial yet infinitely changeable matter of who functions as the narrator(s) of a given narrative; (3) the exploration and sometimes the explosion of textual 'presences' by playing around with textual 'absences' – de- and re-constructing hi/story by drawing on materials 'around' but not yet 'in' the given story.

As we shall handle them, these three strands both intertwine and unravel in curious ways. They intertwine in so far as the choice of a specific narrator usually (though not quite always) tends to strengthen the 'presence' and power of that particular subject/agent position with respect to the action: it is then primarily his or her interests that tend to be privileged or at least 'centred'. However, in so far as we pick on different narrators from those initially chosen, we tend to *un*ravel the previous power relations in particularly revealing ways. Suddenly we realise and recognise the interests of an *under*represented figure (who may be actually present and already referred to but marginal) or of an utterly *un*represented figure (who is actually absent but whose presence may be inferred as in some sense necessary or relevant). In short, we shall both observe and ourselves engage in the processes of re-narration through different narrators. And our primary focus is the actual and potential narratives associated with what is perhaps the most famous novel in the English language – and one of the most famous novels in any language: Daniel Defoe's *Robinson Crusoe* (1719).

In order to get an overview of the intertextual and cross-cultural ground we traverse in this project, flick through it. Then concentrate on whichever part interests you in whatever order suits your purposes.

3.3.1   Prelude: Friday's re-employment agency

Just as there are many 'Hamlets' besides or beyond Shakespeare's (see 4.5), so there are many 'Crusoes' and 'Fridays' and 'desert islands'. For on closer inspection and further reflection the latter always turn out to be already 'populated'. And what they are 'populated' with is a teeming host of other figures – and their associated his/tories – besides and beyond those imagined or even imaginable by a particular early eighteenth-century English novelist.

Defoe did not write the office notice introduced above:

THE ONLY PERSON TO GET EVERYTHING DONE BY FRIDAY
WAS ROBINSON CRUSOE

Nor did he or the composers of it know that it is to function as our base text in this brief prelude. Nor will you know, till you read them, the two further versions of it I shall generate now:

(A)   THE ONLY PERSON THAT GOT EVERYTHING DONE BY FRIDAY
                       HAD A GOOD SECRETARY

(B)   IF THEY WERE GAY WOULD FRIDAY HAVE HIS DAY OF REST
                       ON ROBINSON SUNDAY

Nor did Defoe or I or you, I assume, write the graffito scrawled ironically on the initial notice by a black office worker in the office where I last spotted it: 'Yis baas!'. For clearly each of these alternative or counter-versions, miniature though they are, speaks from or for a narrative position different to that assumed or asserted in the initial notice – or for that matter in Defoe's novel. Equally clearly, none of the narrative positions mentioned (including Defoe's) is a merely formal matter of 'point of view' in a purely technical sense. Each is the expression of a specifically ideological subject/agent position in language in history (cf. 2.1). What's more, each position is now palpably engaged in an actively inter-textual and cross-cultural dialogue involving distinct – yet connected – moments in history. Consequently, if this is to be a genuine dialogue, this is also the moment at which you must come in:

(1)

Re-write the initial office notice *twice* as *you* see fit. Do this ludicrously and seriously, drawing upon as many of the initial words and ideas as you think appropriate. And do this before reading on.

(2)

Now review what those two alternative versions may reveal about you, directly or indirectly, as the author manipulating a certain kind of narrative persona or posture. What historical subject/agent positions do they explore, expose and perhaps explode? What particular personal 'voices' and social 'discourses' do they fuse and refract?

To explore more of what you make of what other people have made of Robinson Crusoe, Friday, (un)deserted islands, and much more . . . read and write on!

3.3.2 NAMING AND RE-NAMING IN DEFOE'S *ROBINSON CRUSOE*

Here is the opening of chapter 24 of Defoe's *Robinson Crusoe* (1719: 202–3), over half-way through the novel.

Read this passage over a couple of times thinking about who is represented as saying, seeing and perceiving – and who isn't but might be. Meanwhile, begin to weigh how you might intervene in and re/present this scene differently.

     (A)   I call him Friday

     1   He was a comely, handsome fellow, perfectly well made, with
            straight strong limbs, not too large, tall and well-shaped,
            and as I reckon, about twenty-six years of age. He had a
            very good countenance, not a fierce and surly aspect, but

5   seemed to have something very manly in his face, and yet he
     had all the sweetness and softness of an European in his
     countenance too, especially when he smiled. His hair was
     long and black, not curled like wool: his forehead very
     high and large; and a great vivacity and sparkling
10   sharpness in his eyes. The colour of his skin was not quite
     black, but very tawny; and yet not of an ugly yellow,
     nauseous tawny, as the Brazilians and Virginians, and other
     natives of America are; but of a bright kind of dun olive
     colour that had in it something very agreeable, though not
15   very easy to describe. His face was round and plump; his
     nose small, not flat like the Negroes', a very good mouth,
     thin lips, and his fine teeth well set, and white as ivory.
     After he had slumbered, rather than slept, about half an
     hour, he waked again, and comes out of the cave to me, for
20   I had been milking my goats, which I had in the enclosure
     just by. When he espied me, he came running to me, laying
     himself down again upon the ground, with all the possible
     signs of an humble, thankful disposition, making many an
     antic gesture to show it. At last he lays his head flat
25   upon the ground, close to my foot, and sets my other foot
     upon his head, as he had done before; and after this, made
     all the signs to me of subjection, servitude and submission
     imaginable, to let me know how he would serve me as long as
     he lived: I understood him in many things and let him know
30   I was very well pleased with him; in a little time I began
     to speak to him and teach him to speak with me; and first
     I made him know his name should be Friday, which was the
     day I saved his life; I taught him to say 'Master,' and
     then let him know that was to be my name; I likewise
40   taught him to say 'yes' and 'no' and to know the meaning of
     them; I gave him some milk in an earthen pot and let him
     see me drink it before him and sop my bread in it; and I
     gave him a cake of bread to do the like, which he quickly
     complied with, and made signs that it was very good for
45   him.

At least sketch some alternative re/presentation ('narrative' and/or 'dramatic') before
proceeding to the following suggestions and questions. These are designed to help you
revise and refine your initial intervention.

(1)

'I call him Friday' – the power of grammar. The title of this chapter consists of two
personal pronouns, an active transitive verb and a proper noun; the last is usually the
name of a day of the week but here also a person's name.

**What light do these linguistic choices and combinations throw on the
precise configuration of power relations in the text?** More actively, what might

you do to the words in this chapter heading so as to challenge and change those power relations? Perhaps extend this strategy to the title of the novel itself.

(2)

(a) See what happens if you try to re-cast the first 18 lines into a first-person, present-tense speech rather than, as it is at the moment, a third-person, past-tense narration? You will therefore begin 'I am a . . .', imagined as spoken by Friday.

What does this limited form of adaptation reveal about the pervasiveness of the dominant subject/agent position in the base text, especially with respect to the relations between 'narrator' and 'narrated', and 'observer' and 'observed' (cf. 2.1)? And what other aspects of the text would need transforming to institute a genuinely and radically different subject/agent position?

(b) Consider how you might re-construct the whole passage as an interior monologue articulated through 'Friday's' sensibility. Would your 'sub-' or 'parallel' text be written *with*, *against* or *across* the grain of Crusoe's account (i.e. *complementary*, *opposed* or *alternative* to the above 'supra-text')? Even more crucially, would this interior monologue be articulated through some variety of English (authentic or merely token 'pidgin' English, for instance)? Alternatively, as 'Friday' seems to be an Araucanian native of the Caribbean, perhaps a fully convincing re-construction of 'Friday's' thoughts and 'inner speech' would *not* be in English at all. For most Anglophone readers of this novel (e.g. me – and maybe you) such a possibility is initially more or less 'unthinkable' because 'unsayable'. And yet, some such act of radical historical imagination is absolutely necessary if we are to relativise and de-familiarise the specifically 'English' linguistic and cultural competences which underpin the wor(l)ds of the novel as Defoe conceived them (cf. 4.4).

(3)

(a) How would you script lines 18–end as for a stage or TV play or a film? Consider cues for actors, stage or set directions, and camera distances and angles. Which areas of the text give you most problems – or most room for manoeuvre? After a first draft, perhaps refine your script and point up its aesthetic and political rationale. For instance, how 'in/determinate' and 'individuated' or 'typicalised' would you like your projection of figures and scene to be (cf. 3.2.2)?

(b) Full-scale re-textualisation. Go on to consider how you would re-cast the *whole* passage for one of the following:

(i) *either* an experimental stage play for a studio theatre; *or* a West End/Broadway musical; *or* a film for general release in high-street cinemas.

(ii) a TV documentary on *either* 'the great tradition of the English novel' *or* 'representations of black slaves in white literature';

(iii) some other performance medium involving words and/or music and/or images and/or dance for a specific audience or viewers.

In each case identify the kinds of supplementary literary and historical materials you would want to draw upon in order to work this part of Defoe's text into your design. And firm up the precise rationale that would inform your particular 'factional' version of hi/story (cf. 1.2.4).

3.3.3 Tournier's *Other Island* and Friday as 'other'

Here is how Michel Tournier re-made Friday's first encounter with Crusoe in *Friday or The Other Island* (*Vendredi, ou les limbes du Pacifique*) (1967: 117).

See what you in turn make of this passage both by comparison with Defoe ((A) ll. 21–30) and in itself.

> (B) Crouched in a clump of tree-fern, a naked and panic-stricken black man pressed his forehead to the ground, while with one hand he groped for the foot of a bearded and armed white man, clad in goatskin and a bonnet of fur, accoutred with the trappings of three thousand years of western civilisation, and sought to place it on his neck.

(1)

Go on to consider the precise differences – and distances – between the narrators, the narrated events and 'ideal readers' in the versions by Defoe and Tournier. In particular, consider the different effects of first- and third-person narration, not just in terms of formal perspective but also sympathy and moral evaluation. Basically, whose 'side' are *ideal readers* invited to be on? And how far are you, as an actual reader, prepared to take 'sides' in this way? (cf. 3.1.5).

(2)

Now re-tell Tournier's account using *either* Friday *or* Crusoe as a first-person narrator. Again, go on to reflect what changes in perspective, sympathy and evaluation this may entail.

Here is a slightly later passage from Tournier's *Friday or The Other Island* (pp. 119–20). It appears in an extract from Crusoe's 'Journal' account of this same first meeting.

Read this extract over weighing the differences in emphasis between Tournier's and Defoe's representations of their first-person narrators. Again, consider whose 'side' the 'ideal reader' seems to be invited to be on; and how far you, as an actual reader, are prepared to take sides.

> (C) So many bitter disappointments during the past few days, and so many mortifying setbacks to my pride! God has sent me a companion, but by some freak of the Divine wisdom He has elected to choose one from the lowest substratum of
> 5   humanity. Not only is the man coloured, a coastal Araucanian, but he is clearly not of pure blood. Everything about him points to the half-caste, a South-American Indian crossed with Negro. If he had even attained the age of reason and were capable of appreciating his own
> 10   insignificance in face of the civilisation I represent!

> But I should be suprised if he is more than fifteen years
> old, bearing in mind the extreme precocity of these
> inferior races, and his childishness moves him to impertinent
> laughter when I seek to instruct him.   [. . .]
>
> 15   I had to find a name for the newcomer. I did not choose
> to give him a Christian name until he was worthy of that
> dignity. A savage is not wholly a human being. Nor could I
> in decency give him an invented name, although this would
> perhaps have been the sensible solution. I think I have
> 20   solved the problem with some elegance in giving him the
> name of the day on which I saved him – Friday. It is the
> name neither of a person nor of a common object but
> somewhat between the two, that of a half-living, half-
> abstract entity, a name strongly stressing his temporal
> 25   character, fortuitous and as it were episodic.

Reading the above passages, it is perhaps tempting for modern 'liberal' readers (including myself) to resolve the differences between Defoe's and Tournier's versions in favour of the latter. After all, few people now would want to associate themselves with an openly racist position. Notice, however, that such a preference would depend upon reading Defoe and Tournier in two distinct ways. For one thing we would need to read Defoe's representation of Crusoe as straightforwardly approving, with an implicit identification between the positions of actual author and first-person narrator – hence 'racist'. Conversely, we would need to read Tournier's representation of Crusoe as ironically critical, with an implicit distance between actual author and first-person narrator – hence 'anti-racist'.

There are problems about such reading strategies, however. And they have to do with such tricky matters as: (1) gauging distances and differences between actual authors and fictional narrators – as well as both of them and actual readers (cf. 3.1.5); (2) the specific problem of assuming or detecting 'irony' in a work; (3) the general problem of reading a story historically, as part of a dialogue between its initial moment of production and its current moment of re-production. The following activities are designed to tackle these problems and to temper any tendency to make snap preferences.

(1)

(a) Re-read Defoe's account of the meeting between Crusoe and Friday (A) as heavily ironic, projecting a clear sense of critical distance between Defoe and Crusoe.

(b) Re-read Tournier's account (B) of the same meeting as straightforwardly approving, projecting a strong sense of identification between Tournier and Crusoe.

(Note: The point of this exercise is not to suggest that these latter readings are better; nor that all readings are as good as one another; nor that all texts can be read ironically or straightforwardly. Rather, it is to insist that what we prefer to read ironically – or quite simply what we *prefer* to read – will depend upon what positions we *infer* the writer to be taking up with respect to her or his fictions.)

This next activity is a further exercise in historical imagination and, if you wish, historical role play. It is a way of putting oneself 'at the bar of history' – rather than affecting to stand in supreme judgement.

(2)

Take on the role of 'Defoe's advocate'. Argue with all the imaginative resources and historical knowledges at your disposal that

Defoe's Crusoe is being morally responsible, compassionate, and a fount of civilised values.

That is, put yourself in the position of a capable and confident eighteenth-century English man sure that the Western imperial nation of which he is a member is generally 'a good thing' (see standard reference books and 3.4 for reading).

(3)

Conversely, turn on Tournier. Drawing on some rather different imaginative resources and historical knowledges, argue that

Tournier's Crusoe is being set up as a rather easy target. Tournier is being wise with the benefit of historical hindsight.

You might even point to symptoms of distinctly French 1960s – rather than English eighteenth-century – anxieties about its post/colonial legacy (e.g. in Algeria and Morocco; also see Fanon extract in 1.3.2).

(4)

Go on to develop a full-scale trial or debate *for* and *against* first Defoe then Tournier. Also consider how you might articulate some *alternative* position, different from and perhaps preferable to the accounts offered by *both* these writers. How, and through whom, might this position be voiced?

Here is a final extract from Tournier's *Friday or The Other Island*. It occurs towards the close of the novel (pp. 155–6).

Read over this passage considering in what discourses the relationship between Friday and Crusoe is now being constituted. How 'modern' do you feel these to be? (The 'explosion' referred to is Friday's accidental blowing up of the gun-powder kegs which represent the foundation of 'civilized law and order' on the island.)

(D) Friday's freedom, as Robinson discovered in the days that followed, was something more than a mere negation of the order that the explosion had destroyed [. . .] for [. . .] there was an underlying wholeness, an implicit principle, at the heart of Friday's way of life. Friday never worked in any real sense of the word. Unconcerned with past or future, he lived wholly in the moment. [. . .] But the truth was that the relationship between them now extended beyond either of these poles [master and servant]. Robinson now observed Friday with a passionate interest in his every act and in the effect of his actions upon himself, where they were producing an astonishing metamorphosis.

The first thing to be affected was Robinson's appearance. He gave up shaving his skull and let his hair grow in tangled locks that grew daily more luxuriant. [. . .] A glance in the mirror even told him that, by a perfectly explicable phenomenon of mimicry, there was now a perceptible resemblance between his face and that of his companion. For years he had been both Friday's master and his father. Now in a matter of days he had become his brother and he was not even sure of being the elder brother. His body was also changed.

This consummation of the process whereby Friday shifts from being, as it were, Crusoe's 'other' to an indistinguishable part of his 'self' is both subtle and richly suggestive. It seems that there is a dissolution of differences based upon colour, other aspects of physical appearance, rank, age and perhaps even gender. There seems to be a general dissolution of subject/agent positions, notably in the actual and symbolic 'mirroring' going on in this scene (see Marshall, 1992: 80–119 for a fine analysis).

At the same time, however, we may also observe that Tournier's figure of Friday serves as a very specific 'other' to his Crusoe. We might even be inclined to concur with a contemporary reviewer's characterisation of *The Other Island* as 'A reinterpretation of the events of Robinson Crusoe in the light of Freud, Jung, Sartre . . . with just a dash of the Club Mediterannée' (from *The Times*, quoted on the back cover of the 1974 King Penguin edition). To this one might add 'as well as a twist of the post/colonial conscience of a late 1960s French intellectual'. My final question – and suggestion – then, is this:

(5)

What other 'self–other' relations have been *under-* or *un*represented in Tournier's version? Project some differences that have *not* been explored so far. Obviously any full critique, as with Defoe, would require reading the novel as a whole. However, even on the basis of the above extracts, it is still possible to gesture towards – and perhaps sketch – some opposed or supplementary subject/agent positions. To do this systematically, use may be made of the 'mobile and flexible triangle' (Figure 2.4); the inferencing procedures in 3.2.6; and the 'dialectical discourse questions' in 4.1.

3.3.4 Coetzee's *Foe* and writing as a wo/man

Another novel which offers a very different critique of Defoe's *Robinson Crusoe* is J.M. Coetzee's *Foe* (1986). Coetzee is a white South African and his title is a pun on Defoe's name, both reinstating what was in fact the novelist's original name and drawing attention to what is the potential enemy ('foe') embedded within it.

We look at Coetzee's *Foe* because it opens up a number of aspects of the 'Crusoe' myth untouched by Tournier; and because it does so through more challengingly (post-) modernist writing strategies. Again, then, what is offered is an alternative modelling and systematic re-construction of a classic story. As you read over what this writer has done with these materials, you might therefore like to ponder what you, in turn, might do with other materials of your own choosing. For that, finally, is what you are invited to do at the close of this section – on as grand or as miniature a scale as you wish.

Another strong reason for looking at Coetzee's version is that there is a marked gender dimension to it. In fact, he introduces another shipwrecked figure, Sue Barton, to the island. And it is primarily the attempt to tell 'her' story which the novel addresses. Much of the time, therefore, we follow her efforts to get what she proposes as the 'true account' told by the novelist Daniel Foe (passage (E) below). Foe, however, remains an evasive figure whom we never actually see. Meanwhile, we are invited to piece together what may – or may not – have happened on the island prior to Sue Barton's arrival. Much of this revolves around enigmatic and to some extent contradictory fragments of a history concerning Friday. Friday himself is here physically mute because of the cutting out of his tongue. But we, with Sue, are never absolutely sure whether this was done on the island by Cruso or by slave traders earlier. The novel breaks down – and open – at the end when Barton and Friday come into direct contact with a supra-narrator figure whom we may identify as some version of Coetzee and/or (De)Foe (passage (F)).

Read over the following passage observing how it positions both a new narrator and a new narrative in dynamic relation to an established fictional frame. (At this point in the novel, about a third of the way through (pp. 66–7), Sue Barton is waiting for Daniel Foe in his study; she is waiting for him to record her hitherto unwritten story. Foe never shows up.)

(E)   'How much of my life consists in waiting! In Bahia I did
        little but wait, though what I was waiting for I sometimes
        did not know. On the island I waited all the time for
        rescue. Here I wait for you to appear, or for the book to be
5   written that will set me free of Cruso and Friday.
        'I sat at your bureau this morning (it is afternoon now,
        I sit at the same bureau, I have sat here all day) and took
        out a clean sheet of paper and dipped pen in ink – your
        pen, your ink, I know, but somehow the pen becomes mine
10   while I write with it, as though growing out of my hand –
        and wrote at the head: "The Female Castaway. Being a True
        Account of a Year Spent on a Desert Island. With Many
        Strange Circumstances Never Hitherto Related." Then I made
        a list of all the strange circumstances of the year I could
15   remember: the mutiny and murder on the Portuguese ship,
        Cruso's castle, Cruso himself with his lion's mane and ape-
        skin clothes, his voiceless slave Friday, the vast terraces
        they had built, all bare of growth, the terrible storm that
        tore   the   roof   off   our   house   and   heaped   the
20   beaches with dying fish. Dubiously I thought: Are these
        enough strange circumstances to make a story of? How long
        before   I   am   driven   to   invent   new   and   stranger
        circumstances: the   salvage   of   tools   and   muskets   from
        Cruso's ship; the building of a boat, or at least a skiff,
25   an adventure to sail to the mainland; a landing by cannibals
        on the island, followed by a skirmish and many bloody
        deaths;   and,   at   last,   the   coming   of   a   golden-haired
        stranger   with   a   sack   of   corn,   and   the   planting   of   the
        terraces? Alas, will the day arrive when we can ever make
30   a story without strange circumstances?'

This passage is complexly layered, both textually and intertextually. It draws attention with artful simplicity to a number of fundamental aspects of the narrational process of the novel: the physical materials (paper, pen, ink); the capacity to write and read; an author and/or a narrator (who may or may not be directly implicated in the events narrated); a character who may also be a narrator; and the narrated 'events' themselves (which may be in varying degrees supposedly 'true' or 'invented', 'factual' or 'fictional'). Stepping even further back from the narrative to the overall act of narration, there is also the presence of an actual author to be inferred (Coetzee himself); as well as specific interactions among a range of variously 'implied' and 'actual' readers – most immediately, you and me. (An additional, specifically intertextual irony in this passage arises from the fact that everything Sue claims to be 'a True Account' does *not* occur in Defoe's version, whereas everything she fears may be 'invent(ed)' actually *does* occur there. One fiction is offered as the counterfactual inversion of the other.) The following activities are designed to unpick and re-weave this design.

(1)

Use the diagram of the narration process (Figure 3.2, p. 78) to help label each constituent role as it seems to you to operate in this passage. Go on to consider what particular configuration of power relations the passage seems to underwrite in terms of, say, gender, race and occupation? Who is writing whom?

(2)

Now consider how the narrative relations described in (1) might be reconstructed so as to re-distribute power to different subjects – and perhaps realise some of them as more active agents in their own right/write. Who else might be represented as writing – or speaking or in some other way 'signalling' – whom? What alternative recentrings are still available in terms of gender, race and occupation? Sketch or draft some possibilities.

(3)

Writing as a wo/man? Coetzee was a man in his mid-forties when he wrote this. And yet, with the exception of a few pages at the close of the novel (see passage (F)), his narrator is a somewhat younger woman. To this end, all the novel except for the last section is represented as spoken by Sue Barton, and is presented in inverted commas (as in passage (E)). All this prompts some tricky questions, both analytical and theoretical, to do with gender and writing. For instance:

(a) Would you have known from the writing in front of you that the author (Coetzee) is a man personating a woman (Sue Barton)? Is there any aspect of its 'style' or 'content' that leads you to this conclusion? (Perhaps add in a reading of passage (F) here.) More theoretically – and contentiously – is there anything that stops a man who is 'male by sex' being 'feminine by gender' – or at least capable of recreating an 'authentic feminine' from within 'himself'? In other words, what are the **theoretical** and **practical** limits – if any – to any and all of us writing as a 'man' and/or a 'woman'? (For relevant reading, see Cameron, 1990: 33–56, 160–5; Belsey and Moore, 1989: 81–132.) Fix these questions by applying them to a range of male and female writers, including yourself.

(b) Go on to re-write passage (E) in ways which might be considered more markedly – perhaps stereotypically – 'masculine' or 'feminine'. Attach a commentary explicating the problems and possibilities encountered.

We now turn to the very last passage in Coetzee's *Foe* (pp. 157–8). It is an enigmatic 'underwater' and/or 'dream' sequence and therefore requires especially attentive re-reading. But the effort is well worthwhile. As you read, try to identify the various configurations of subject/agent positions into which the narrative is being sedimented. Who is 'signalling' what to whom, when and where and how? And where – and how – do you, an actual reader, stand in all this?

In short, see what sense you make of this text – and what sense it makes of you. (Note: the 'I' here seems to be some version of Coetzee and/or (De)Foe. At any rate the 'I' is no longer Sue Barton; for she figures *in* the scene, and the previously ubiquitous inverted commas signalling her speech have disappeared too.)

(F)   Sand rises in slow flurries around my feet. There are no
        swarms of gay little fish. I enter the hole. [. . .]
            I come to a bulkhead and a stairway. The door at the head
        of the stairway is closed; but when I put a shoulder to it
5   and push, the wall of water yields and I can enter.
            It is not a country bath-house. In the black space of
        this cabin the water is still and dead, the same water as
        yesterday, as last year, as three hundred years ago. Susan
        Barton and her dead captain, fat as pigs in their white
10   nightclothes, their limbs extending stiffly from their
        trunks, their hands puckered from long immersion, held out
        in blessing, float like stars against the low roof. I crawl
        beneath them.
            In the last corner, under the transoms, half buried in
15   sand, his knees drawn up, his hands between his thighs, I
        come to Friday.
            I tug his woolly hair, finger the chain about his throat.
        'Friday,' I say, I try to say, kneeling over him, sinking
        hands and knees into the ooze, 'what is this ship?'
20   But this is not a place of words. Each syllable, as it
        comes out, is caught and filled with water and diffused.
        This is a place where bodies are their own signs. It is the
        home of Friday.
            He turns and turns till he lies at full length, his face
25   to my face. The skin is tight across his bones, his lips
        are drawn back. I pass a fingernail across his teeth,
        trying to find a way in.
            His mouth opens. From inside him comes a slow stream,
        without breath, without interruption. It flows up through
30   his body and out upon me; it passes through the cabin,
        through the wreck; washing the cliffs and shores of the
        island, it runs northward and southward to the ends of the
        earth. Soft and cold, dark and unending, it beats against
        my eyelids, against the skin of my face.

Before considering the more detailed questions and suggestions that follow, make sure you have made some provisional sense of this passage for yourself.

(1)

Who do *you* take the 'I' to be? Coetzee and/or (De)Foe and/or someone else? And how far are you prepared to identify yourself with this first-person position? If not, with whom or what?

(2)

'But this is not a place of words . . . This is a place where bodies are their own signs. It is the home of Friday.' This reconstruction of the mute Friday can be seen as a glorious celebration of a pre- or post-verbal phase, an escape from 'logocentrism' to a semiotic space beyond words where 'bodies are their own signs' (cf. Kristeva, 1980; 1984). Coetzee is perhaps even signalling to us that he is well acquainted with contemporary psychoanalytical semiotics. However, this reconstruction can also be seen as an evasion: an idly intellectual and politically irresponsible gesture towards a 'Utopia' ('Dystopia'?) in which the historically powerless remain dispossessed of the power of words. Their state is thus still in effect 'unspeakable' because it remains 'unspoken'.

How do *you* see (hear, touch . . .) Friday at this point? And are you going to concentrate on the *intra*-textual subject/agent relations: narrator–narrated, observer–observed, figures and scenes, etc.? And/or are you going to turn your attention to the *extra*-textual subject/agent positions: perhaps the acutely ambiguous position of privileged South African whites such as Coetzee, however liberal or radical, during the early 1980s (before the beginnings of the formal dissolution of apartheid)? or perhaps yourself in your own racial configuration, then or now; or some others – in distinct yet related hi/stories – in still other times and places . . .? (For instance, see next section and Gates (1987) for some early slave narratives by women and men who were themselves slaves.)

3.3.5 Pre-texts and post-texts: Aphra Behn's to ours

Possible questions cutting across and around, before and after, all the above 'Robinson Crusoe' narratives are of course endless. They are also, strictly, without absolute beginnings. None the less, it is important and, indeed, imperative, to try to put answers to some of those questions. To be sure, cross- and multicultural hi/stories are complexly and contentiously intra-, inter- and extra-textual in scope. They are inescapably 'factional' too. For they are written in many more things than ink: blood, sweat, landscapes and economic and political systems, for instance.

The following extracts from a range of texts pre- and post-dating those above are therefore offered as no more than gobbets from a constantly metamorphosing body of cross- and multicultural hi/stories. They are in 'English' and have to do with 'Literature' because those are the main institutional subject/agent positions within which the present text works (see 4.4). Other distinct yet connected hi/stories, in other distinct yet connected discourses and materials – from reggae to architecture and the world banking system – would draw on other parts of the same, changing body. Your body and my body, for instance.

As you read through and round these passages, weigh at least two kinds of possibility:

(a) **what activities you might design to encourage other people (and incidentally yourself) to explore these texts critically and creatively, interpersonally and intertextually;**

(b) **how these texts might contribute to a large-scale re-textualisation of the 'Robinson Crusoe' story (or any connected hi/story you choose)** (cf. 1.2.4; 2.6).

The narrator is a young white woman who is the daughter of a man appointed to be Lieutenant General of (British) Surinam, later (Dutch) Guyana. Behn was herself probably in Surinam round 1664:

(G)   I ought to tell you that the Christians never buy any slaves but they give 'em some name of their own, their native names being very likely barbarous and hard to pronounce; so that Mr Trefry gave Oroonoko that of Caesar, which name will live in that country as long as that (scarce more) glorious one of the great Roman; for 'tis most evident, he wanted [lacked] no part of the personal courage of that Caesar, and acted things as memorable, had they been done in some part of the world replenished with people and historians that might have given him his due. But his misfortune was to fall in an obscure world, that afforded a female pen to celebrate his fame; though I doubt not but that it had lived from others' endeavors, if the Dutch, who immediately after his time took that country, had not killed, banished, and dispersed all those that were capable of giving the world this great man's life, much better than I have done.

(From Aphra Behn, *Oroonoko, or The Royal Slave* (1688), complete in Abrams, 1993, vol. 1: 1864–910; here p. 1889)

The following extract is from Woodes Rogers' account of his first encounter with the castaway *Andrew Selkirk*, when the latter was picked up from an otherwise uninhabited island 400 miles west of Chile ((1709), in Carey, 1987: 205–8). Selkirk is recognised as a factual source for Defoe's fictional Crusoe.

(H)   Our pinnace return'd from the shore, and brought abundance of craw-fish with a man cloth'd in goat-skins, who looked wilder than the first owners of them. He had been on the island four years and four months, being left there by Captain Stradling in the *Cinque-Ports*. His name was Alexander Selkirk, a Scotchman, who had been master of the *Cinque-Ports* [. . .] The reason of his being left there was a difference betwixt him and his captain [. . .] At his first coming on board us, he had so much forgot his language for want of use, that we could scarce understand him, for he seemed to speak his words by halves.

The next extract is from *The Interesting Narrative of the Life of Olaudah Equiano or Gustavus Vassa the African, Written by Himself* ((1789; 2nd edn 1814; complete in Gates 1987: 1–182, here pp. 51–2). Equiano/Vassa was a Nigerian Igbo prince who was kidnapped as a child by black slavers and sold into European slavery in the 'New World'. His master at this point was the commander of an English ship based in London.

(I)   It was now between two and three years since I first came to England, [. . .] I could now speak English tolerably well, and perfectly understood everything that was said. I not only felt myself quite easy with these new countrymen, but relished their society and manners. I no longer looked upon them as spirits, but as men superior to us; and therefore I had the stronger desire to resemble them, to imbibe their spirit, and imitate their manners. I therefore embraced every occasion of improvement; and every new thing that I observed I treasured up in my memory. I had long wished to be able to read and write; and for this purpose took every opportunity to gain instruction, but had made as yet very little progress. However, when I went to London with my master, I had soon an opportunity of improving myself, which I gladly embraced.

Johann Wyss' sequel to Robinson Crusoe, *The Swiss Family Robinson*, was first published in 1814 and many times thereafter. It was adapted into a successful commercial film by the Disney Studios in 1960. Here is the opening of the novel (1894 edn), narrated by the father:

(J) The tempest had lasted six days, and, far from abating, now redoubled in fury. Driven out of our course to the south-west, it was impossible to tell in what parts we were. Our vessel had lost her masts, and leaked from end to end.
'Children,' I said to my four boys, who clung weeping to their mother, 'God can still save us if it be His will: if He has decreed otherwise we must submit. At the worst, we shall only quit this world to be united in the better one.'
My wife dried her tears, and, following my example, assumed an enforced calmness, to inspire the children with courage and resignation.

Here are extracts from the back-cover blurbs of two books offering very different modern versions of the 'Robinson Crusoe' story. The first summarises and advertises Lucy Irvine's autobiography *Castaway* (1984; adapted as a film starring Amanda Donohoe and Oliver Reed by Cannon films in 1986). The second summarises and advertises Jane Gardam's novel *Crusoe's Daughter* (Abacus, 1986).

(K)(a)'WRITER SEEKS "WIFE" FOR A YEAR ON A TROPICAL ISLAND'
The opportunity to escape from it all was irresistible. Lucy Irvine answered the advertisement – and found herself alone on a remote desert island with a 'husband' she hardly knew.
Uncompromisingly candid and sometimes shocking, *Castaway* is her compulsive account of a desert island dream that threatened to turn into a nightmare of illness, thirst and hatred.
Blazing with emotion, painful self-knowledge and the seductive, if cruel, beauty of an untouched Eden, it is the unputdownable story of a man and a woman locked, once again, in the eternal battle.

(b) In 1904, when she was six, Polly Flint went to live with her two holy aunts at the yellow house by the marsh – so close to the sea that it seemed to toss like a ship, so isolated that she might have been marooned on an island. And there she stayed for eighty-one years while the century raged around her, while lamplight and Victorian order became chaos and nuclear dread. *CRUSOE'S DAUGHTER*, ambitious, serious and wholly original, is her story.

FURTHER RE-WRITING AND READING

A. Chains of verbal events (cf. 3.1.1–4)

Experiment freely with the potential of random simple sentences, phrases and words. Add extra participants, processes and circumstances before, during and after the text as you see fit. Go on to categorise these verbal events 'narrative-report' and/or 'drama-conversation', using the criteria in 3.1.3.

B. 'Consequences' (cf. 3.1.4)

Here, in the words of a Victorian parlour-game book, is what you do:

This game requires paper and pencils. And each player is to write according to the directions of the leader. The first player is told to write one or more terms descriptive of a gentleman. He does so, and then folds down the paper so as to conceal what is written, and hands it to the next player, who, after receiving the order, writes, folds the paper down as before, and passes it on to the next, and so on until the directions are exhausted. The leader then reads the contents of the sheet aloud, which from its inconsistencies and absurdities will cause much amusement.

And here are the directions:

Begin by writing a term descriptive of a gentleman. (write – fold down – pass on)

A gentleman's name; someone you know or some distinguished person. (write – etc.)

An adjective descriptive of a lady

A lady's name

Mention a place and describe it.

Write down some date or period of time when an event might happen.

Put a speech into the gentleman's mouth.

Make the lady reply.

Tell what the consequences were.

And what the world said of it.

(Parlour Games for the Young (1857); in Augarde, 1984: 192–5)

And here is an example of the kind of result experienced then according to 'Uncle George', the pseudonymous author:

The handsome and modest Napoleon, met the graceful and accomplished Miss Norton, at Brighton, that fashionable place of resort, on the 10th of November, 1890. He said, 'Dear lady, my respect for you is unbounded,' and she replied, 'Yes, I am very fond of it.' The consequences were, that they were united in matrimony, and the world said, 'It is so very silly.'

Now play the game yourself with friends. To get the most out of it for our present purposes, I suggest you play it twice in two distinct ways: one 'translated'; the other radically 'transformed'.

Game 1: Translate the instructions from a Victorian educated middle-class idiom into one with which you are more familiar and feel easier. However, keep the same sequence of instructions as in the base text (man, then woman, then 'what the world said', etc.); but notice the shifts in personal 'voice' and social 'discourse' your translation entails. Go on to identify and label each line in so far as it can be aligned with a contemporary discourse, comparing these with those discourses you perceive in the sample Victorian version above. What different (or similar) ways of saying and seeing are entailed?

Game 2: Now transform the instructions so as to lay the foundations for a differently articulated male–female encounter. Consider such things as changing the order (who initiates and who responds), and who or what might now be put in the 'what the world said' slot – or whether you even want such an act of publicly sanctioned closure for your mini-narrative! Also consider whether you want or need a single 'leader' issuing 'directions'. Is there a practicable alternative? If so what?

C. More whole stories full of holes (cf. 3.1.2; 3.1.4)

(a) **Identify a (very) short story, fable or anecdote** which includes instances of: direct speech and narrative report; a range of personal pronouns; more than one verb tense. (Many will fit the bill.)

(b) **Select half a dozen words or phrases which you consider in some way interesting, and perhaps strategic.** Present these items to a group of colleagues and invite them to produce some kind of story in line with the brief in 3.1.2.

(c) **Compare the tales they produce with the initial tale** in terms of genre and discourse, 'centres' and 'margins', 'presences' and 'absences', etc. (see 3.1.4).

D. Un/ideal narratees and actual readers (cf. 3.1.5)

Think of two narratives (novels, short stories, films, etc.): (a) one that you like; (b) the other that you dislike. Attempt what for you will seem to be very perverse readings, perhaps in the form of reviews or trailers (cf. 3.2.4). Read (a) as an *unideal narratee*, someone totally antipathetic to its concerns and strategies; and (b) as an *ideal narratee*, someone totally in sympathy and harmony with every aspect of its content and form.

E. Interactive hi/stories (cf. 3.2.5–6)

There is a significant range of textual genres variously called *interactive story-books, counter-factual (hi)-story games, programmed learning* and, more narrowly, *simulations* – all of which are devoted to interactive learning and/or entertainment. Modern hi-tech versions include interactive computer games and even 'virtual reality' adventures.

Here is a simple example of the kind of 'Decide now!' and 'What next?' formula which regularly punctuates interactive story-books. This one is from Allen Sharp's *The Story-Trails Book of Science Fiction* (1987: story 2):

> I now had to decide whether to spend the night by the fire (if so, turn to *12), or take the boat and begin the journey to the other world (if so, turn to *10).

A more adult and formally educationally oriented example is Guerrier and Richards' *State of Emergency: A Programmed Entertainment* (1969). In this cross between novel and multiple-choice game we, the readers, are asked 'Could you govern Lakoto?' (Lakoto is the made-up name of a newly independent African state, until recently under British rule.) And the particular subject/agent position we are offered is that of the newly elected Prime Minister: 'You are at his shoulder. You can choose between the courses of action open to him.'

In order to explore such strategies for critical-creative purposes here is what I suggest you do:

(1)

Take an existing 'classic' narrative and identify three events which you consider to be crucial to the development of its plot: one at the beginning; another around the middle; a third at the end. At each of these points list what you consider to be three options: one for the characters involved; a second for the narrator(s); a third for the author. (In other words, what goes on in a narrative is not just a matter of 'character re/actions' but also of narratorial perspectives and authorial control.)

(2)

Go on to sketch the likely consequences and implications if a set of options that were *not* actually explored in the base text were to be explored by you in an alternative text.

Again try to plot changes in so far as they operate at all three levels: character re/action; narratorial perspective; and authorial control.

(3)

Comment upon what this exercise shows about the relation between the formal properties of the base text and the reproduction of meanings in a variety of historical moments (cf. 3.3.5). What are the historical differences exposed? And where – aesthetically, morally and politically – do you locate your preferences?

(4)

Finally, design a board-game, a computer game, or a role-play activity in which you encourage other people to explore the base text in as creative and critical a way as possible.

F.   More narrative non/sense: examples and exercises

Examples

Here are some pieces of text for practising the strategies applied to 'There was an old man . . .' in 3.2. The first six are 'whole texts' and in that sense (very) short stories in their own right. The last is the beginning of a novel. The various operations you might go through with *each* of these narratives are summarised afterwards. At some point, you might also like to explore ways in which *all* of these texts might be framed within a single narrative and/or drama. They have been chosen with this possibility in mind (cf. 2.6 and 1.2.4).

One last point. Don't underestimate the fascinatingly complex resources of such short, apparently simple – even trivial – materials. A text is as long, as complex and as significant as we make it.

To get us in the right non/sensical frames of mind, the first three pieces are from the same collection as 'There was an old man', *Mother Goose's Melody* (1765) (Rhys 1927: 151, 167, 159).

(1)
Little Betty Winckle she had a pig,
It was a little pig not very big;
When he was alive he liv'd in clover,
But now he's dead and that's all over;
Johnny Winckle he
Sat down and cry'd,
Betty Winckle she
Laid down and dy'd;
So there was an end of one, two, and three,
Johnny Winckle he,
Betty Winckle she,
And Piggy Wiggie.

(2)
Robin and Richard
    Were two pretty men,
They lay in bed
    'Till the clock struck ten:
Then up starts Robin
    And looks at the sky –

Oh! brother Richard,
    The sun's very high:
You go before
    With the bottle and bag,
And I will come after
    On little Jack nag.

(3)
There was an old man
In a velvet coat,
He kiss'd a maid
And gave her a groat;
The groat it was crack'd
And would not go,
Ah, old man, do you serve me so?

(4)
            Sea Chest
There was a woman loved a man
as the man loved the sea.
Her thoughts of him were the same
as his thoughts of the sea.
They made an old sea chest for their belongings
together.

                           (Carl Sandburg, *Good Morning America* (1928))

(5)
        A frowsy woman
        Bending down
        To do her washing
        In a stream
That mirrors banks aglow
With blossoming plum!

            (Mumei, *Escaped as a Bird, Verses from A Japanese Leprosy Hospital* (undated),
                    trans. L. Erikson, London: The Leprosy Mission)

(6)
A Woman in widow's weeds was weeping upon a grave. 'Console yourself, madam,' said a Sympathetic Stranger. 'Heaven's mercies are infinite. There is another man somewhere, beside your husband, with whom you can still be happy.'
'There was,' she sobbed – 'there was, but this is his grave.'
    (Ambrose Bierce, *Fantastic Fables* (1899), analysed in detail by Sergei Eisenstein in *The Film Sense* (1942), and further discussed by Stephen Heath in Bennett *et al.* (1981: 221–2))

(7)
He was an old man who fished alone in a skiff in the Gulf Stream and he had gone eighty-four days now without taking a fish. In the first forty days without a fish the boy's parents had told him that the old man was now definitely and finally *salao*, which is the worst form of unlucky, and the boy had gone at their orders in another boat which caught three good fish the first week. It made the boy sad to see the old man come in each day with his skiff empty and he always went down to help him carry either the coiled lines or the gaff and the harpoon and the sail that was furled around the mast. The sail was patched with flour sacks and, furled, it looked like the flag of permanent defeat.

    The old man was thin and gaunt with deep wrinkles in the back of his neck. The brown blotches of the benevolent skin cancer the sun brings from its reflection on the tropic sea were on his cheeks. The blotches ran well down the sides of his face and his hands had the deep-creased scars from handling heavy fish on the cords. But none of these scars were fresh. They were as old as erosions in a fishless desert.

    Everything about him was old except his eyes and they were the same colour as the sea and were cheerful and undefeated.

                    (opening page of Ernest Hemingway's *The Old Man and the Sea* (1952) 1976: 5)

Exercises

Here is a review of the steps taken with the non/sense verse narrative 'There was an old man'. Try retracing them with the each of the above narratives, returning to the appropriate sections for further explanation and illustration. For the rest, feel free to revise and vary these strategies as your material demands and you see fit.

(1)

Consider how you would turn the text into a film (cf. 3.2.1–4). Make larger *strategic decisions* on genre, audience, aims, emphases, etc.; and *tactical decisions* on handling of persons, time, scene, sequencing, plot, etc. Consider the theoretical implications of your decisions in terms of *in/ determinacy, re/presentation*, and *metatextuality* (3.2.2), refining and perhaps re-directing your practice accordingly.

Formulate a line-by-line or clause-by-clause break-down of the text in terms of: *dynamic* or *state* verbs; *past or present tenses*; and *narrative-narrator* functions. Use all these analytical observations to help make considered decisions on individual shots and sequences of shots, as well as overall decisions about (meta)textual cohesion and perceptual in/coherence. Finally, 'fix' the *genres, aims* and intended *audiences* of your film by deciding on a *title* and drafting a sample *trailer* or *review*.

(2)

Consider how you might expand (and perhaps explode) each of the above narratives (cf. 3.1.6 and 3.2.5–6). That is, gradually 'blow up' the base text into something slightly or very different. You might do this by:

assigning a different letter to each line, sentence or clause, then developing a different (perhaps randomised or inverted) textual cohesion and perceptual coherence (cf. 3.2.5);

selecting specific participants, processes and circumstances as prompts for a number of 'inference clusters' (cf. 3.2.6);

exploring alternative textual 'centres' and marginalised or excluded subject/agent positions (cf. 1.2);

developing such insights (and 'outsights') into full-blown preludes, interludes and postludes, and sustained complements and supplements (cf. 3.2.6);

finally – or perhaps first – getting to know about the base text's various moments of production and reproduction: by and for whom, when, where, how and why (cf. 3.2.8).

G. Re-casting a classic novel (cf. 3.3)

Use similar strategies to those used by Tournier, Coetzee and others to re-write Defoe's *Robinson Crusoe* so as to re-write part of another 'classic novel' of your own choosing. Of course, exactly the same processes of de- and re-construction will work with lesser-known works. But one advantage of choosing a 'classic' text is that other versions (adaptations, children's versions, films, plays, etc.) are already available for comparison and perhaps stimulation. A wide range of reviews and criticism also exists and can be fed into the mix. (This was a possibility we did not have space to explore with the 'Crusoe' materials; but cf. 'Re-producing *Hamlet*', 4.5.) Indeed, very well-known texts often turn up in 'popular culture' as allusions in adverts, newspapers, comedy shows, pop songs, etc.

Once you have identified a likely base text, simply ask yourself the following questions:

What aspects of this text do I wish to challenge and change?

What alternative 'centres' do I wish to identify?

What strategies of de- and re-construction am I going to employ to achieve these ends?

Everything else can be worked in through processes of reflection and research, trial and error, analysis and discussion. And when confronted by a particularly fascinating or frustrating problem, turn to such writers as Tournier or Coetzee above (or Stoppard, Marowitz, etc., below) to see how they engaged with similar – yet inevitably different – problems. Experiment can thus be both tempered and inspired by example.

Stimulating brief *introductions to narrative* are Stubbs in Carter and Burton (1982: 57–85) and Rosen (1985); and for reference see Prince (1987). Fuller studies are: Toolan (1988), Rimmon-Kenan (1983), Bal (1985), Ricoeur (1984) and Reid (1992). For critical-creative work on *narration as process* (predictions, alternative summaries, group re-tellings, etc.) see Carter and Long (1987: 5–19), Brumfit and Carter (1986: 110–32), Collie and Slater (1987: 93–162) and Stibbs (1991). Distinctions and connections between narration in *prose fiction and film*, are treated in: Chatman (1978), Cohan and Shires (1988) and Giddings *et al.* (1990). For film narrative in general see Metz (1974: 16–28, 185–227), Bordwell (1985); also Bordwell and Thompson (1990); and for televisual narrative, see Kozloff in Allen (1987: 42–73) and Fiske (1987: 128–48). *Point of view* is given its classic literary-critical formulation in Booth (1961), and a more radical textual-ideological orientation in Simpson (1993); also see Bal (1985: 100–15) on 'focalisation' as well as the work on *subject/agents* referred to in 2.8. Other narrative theorists and analysts who have been especially influential in the formation of the present approach are: Labov (1972), Barthes (1977: 79–124) and Bakhtin (see the practice in 4.4 and the references in 4.6).

Work relevant to the exploration of *non/sense in narration* in 3.2 includes: Hughes and Brecht (1978) on conundrums; Hutcheon (1985) and Nash (1992: 83–98) on *parody*; Waugh (1984) on metatextuality; and McHale in Toolan (1992: 6–39) on 'non/sense' verse. More specifically Bakhtinian arguments for 'travestying' and 'transgression' can be found in Stallybrass and White (1986), and Glazener in Hirschkop and Shepherd (1988: 109–29). Further work on versions of the 'Crusoe and Friday' story and their cultural ramifications might start with Davis (1983), Marshall (1992: 49–146) and Brantlinger (1990).

4 Dialogue, discourse and dramatic intervention

4.1 PRELIMINARY DEFINITIONS

In dialogue a person not only shows himself outwardly, but he becomes for the first time that which he is, not only for others but for himself as well. To be means to communicate dialogically.

(Mikhail Bakhtin, *Problems of Dostoevsky's Poetics* (1984))

Dramatic worlds are hypothetical ('as if') constructs, that is they are recognised by the audience as counter-factual (i.e. non-real) states of affairs, but are embodied *as if* in progress in the actual here and now . . . drama . . . cannot be understood unless some notion of hypothetical worlds – realised or abandoned in the course of the drama – is applied . . . the possible worlds of the drama have to be 'supplemented' by the spectator on the basis of his or her knowledge and hypothesizing before they are fully constituted.

(Keir Elam, *The Semiotics of Theatre and Drama* (1980))

For the smallest social unit is not the single person but two people. In life too we develop one another.

(Bertolt Brecht, *A Short Organum for the Theatre* (1948))

Some preliminary definitions of the terms in the title of this chapter will indicate where we are going. That is, if you agree to go there too.

Dialogue in a loose sense means simply *conversation*. More narrowly conceived, it means a kind of *negotiation* between people with different interests (e.g. 'political dialogue'); and, in yet another specialised sense, it means the kind of *quoted or scripted conversation* found in novels and plays (e.g. 'a piece of dialogue'). But much broader senses are also current. Dialogue may also be conceived as just about any exchange and transformation of words, spoken, written or otherwise recorded: we 'enter into a dialogue' with any message as soon as we actively respond to it, most obviously by producing other words, but also by silences, changes in posture, gesture, eye movement as well as other more or less involuntary and invisible changes in physiology (e.g. pulse rate, in extreme cases releases of adrenalin, etc.). Still more broadly, it is quite common to talk of 'dialogues' with history or the environment, between computers, and among animals and plants – in fact between anything and anything else across any conceivable interface.

All of these usages have something in common, however.

Dialogue always entails interaction: two- or many-way processes of exchange and transformation – whether of information, people or anything else.

In these respects, dialogue may be usefully distinguished from 'monologue'.

Monologue is the one-way transfer of information, with the assumption that the information is substantially unchanged and that all the receiver can do is react – not interact or pro-act.

It is these last meanings of dialogue and monologue we shall be working with in this chapter. And that 'we' should be stressed. For this chapter – like the rest of the book – can only really work if it too is conceived and conducted as a dialogue. That means it is also up to you to come to your own terms with these terms and to interact with and act upon – not simply react to – the materials presented. Moreover, sometimes this means drawing on materials and initiating responses of your own. Certainly, I shall attempt to put words into your mouth and your mind. But it is still up to you whether you chew and digest them or spit them out, and then choose others more to your aesthetic and political 'taste'. (A specialised meaning of **dialogic**, after Bakhtin, is offered in 4.4.1).

At this point it is useful to introduce another term and concept often linked, and sometimes confused, with dialogue: 'dialectic'.

Dialectic in its most common classical sense means the *opposition of one idea to another to produce a new idea*. **Thesis** is set against **antithesis** so as to generate a third proposition which is not merely the sum or 'mean' of the other two but a genuinely new proposition in its own right – the **synthesis**. The proposition the thinker or investigator initially had in mind as the imagined or likely outcome is termed the **hypothesis**. 'Dialectical materialism' as a historical model and a philosophical and politico-economic method is principally (though by no mean exclusively) associated with Marx. It is concerned with the constant collisions, coalescences and transformations which characterise the fundamental processes of life – including social and political life. More philosophically, proponents of dialectical materialism are committed both to observing and promoting the process whereby every 'truth' or 'fact' which is claimed to be single, universal and immutable is challenged and changed through systematic **negation** (from Latin *negare* 'to say no'). The result of such 'saying no' or 'speaking against' is always to produce, or at least imply, an alternative 'yes': some act of 'speaking for', the 'posited positive' informing the act of negation. However, this alternative 'truth' or 'fact' may itself then reify into something supposedly single, universal and immutable – and therefore itself need challenging and changing in turn. And so on.

Extreme forms of dialectic lead to ceaseless scepticism; scientifically, to the development of methodologies premised on 'doubt' and the need to 'prove through progressive disproof' (e.g. Popper); and, politically, to a belief in permanent revolution. For Marxists, dialectic is inextricably linked to the 'dialectic of history' conceived in terms of class conflict. But feminists, black, gay, Green and disabled-rights activists also explore what they see as the dominant oppressing ideology dialectically, through negation: opposition to dominant practices accompanied by proposals to revalue 'muted' practices. They may also aspire to a complete remodelling of social and natural relations on alternative lines and to alternative ends.

A crucial distinguishing feature of all kinds of dialecticians, and indeed of all critical thinkers, is the degree to which they are prepared to turn the dialectical 'gainsaying' apparatus on their own premises and procedures: how far they are really prepared to 'negate the negation' and thereby 'posit a positive' which may be very different from the 'hypothesis' they first envisaged and maybe hoped for. For, Marxisms and feminisms and black consciousnesses, etc. are plural too, constituted through their own internal differences as well as their variously shared or distinct differences from certain 'external' conditions. In short, good dialectic ceaselessly de- and re-constructs itself. It is reflexive as well as reflective. The cultivation of a dialectical outlook and method is therefore essential for the construction of a genuinely analytical, critical and creative consciousness. (But of course, you may not agree. In which case we agree! See pp. 182–3 for references.)

Clearly, then, there is much potential overlap in the uses of the words 'dialogue' and 'dialectic'. They both involve some sense of opposition, exchange and transformation; and indeed the two words are intimately related. Both use the prefix *dia-*, from Greek meaning 'across' (note: *not* meaning just 'two', and therefore *not* binary); while the '-logue' bit of 'dialogue' comes from Greek *logos* (meaning both 'word' and 'knowledge') and the 'lect' bit of 'dialectic' from a Latinised Greek form meaning 'reading' (cf. '*lect*ure', '*lect*ern'). Such etymological closeness has ensured that the two terms have tended to be used both in harness and even interchangeably. For my part, I try to use 'dialogue' and 'dialogic' when referring to a primarily *verbal* exchange or transformation, and 'dialectic' when referring to the more narrowly logical method of negating and positing through the successive formations of hypothesis, thesis, antithesis and synthesis. However, it is impossible to be completely consistent in these matters – not least because we are here exploring a dialectical method in and on language between ourselves (i.e. dialogically)! (See Israel (1979) and Sharratt (1982) for some theoretical and practical grappling with the problems and possibilities.)

Discourse was introduced earlier. Several levels of meanings may be usefully distinguished. 'Discourse' can mean:

1 a *formal speech* or *treatise* (now archaic, e.g. Descartes' *Discourse on Method*);

2 *conversation* in particular or *dialogue* in general (meanings for which I prefer precisely those terms);

3 stretches of text above the level of the sentence, extending to matters of *intertextuality* and *genre* (again, where possible, I use such terms);

4 *communicative practices* expressing the *interests* and characteristic 'ways of seeing and saying' of a particular socio-historical group or institution; these are always definable in terms of relative *power* or *powerlessness*.

It is these last two meanings ((3) and (4)) of discourse we are primarily concerned with here: how we make sense of collections of relatable texts, and the ways in which texts are implicated in specific social and historical relations. It is therefore not primarily the formal, isolated, narrowly 'linguistic' features and effects of texts that engage us, but the specific interactions among persons and places that those texts represent or prompt.

A single line from the British national anthem will serve as illustration: 'God save our gracious Queen'. Formally, we may say such things as the following: that this line is marked as a directive and 'subjunctive' (i.e. 'Let/May God save'); that it includes the first-person plural pronominal adjective ('our'); exhibits passing alliteration ('*G*od/*g*racious'); and that it shows signs of elevated vocabulary (e.g. 'gracious' not, say, 'nice'). But clearly none of this on its own gets us very far. For one thing, it fails to take into account the cumulative features and effects of the rest of the text: the line 'Happy and glorious, long to reign over us', for instance, employs similar resources of grammar, vocabulary and sound-patterning. Nor is there any recognition that both the form and content of such a *national anthem* (with equal emphasis on both terms) is in part an intertextual construct, relatable by genre to other instances of hymns specially designed to celebrate monarchs, religions and states. What's more, we must also notice that the line 'God save our gracious Queen' represents the interweaving of a number of distinct ways of seeing and saying; that it is constituted from the interplay of a number of discourses. These range from discourses on *religion* ('God'); *monarchy* ('Queen'); group identity – here *nationalism/patriotism* ('our') through to those implicated in *gender* ('Queen' again) and social decorum ('gracious'; a term also tinged with notions of religious 'grace'). Most obviously, our sense of these discourses is cued by the presence of particular items which we associate with distinct areas of activity. More generally and pervasively, because we usually meet these words in specific types of context and on particular occasions, we are likely to associate them with the formal, ritualised openings and closings of certain kinds of British event (sporting, theatrical, etc.). In all these ways, textual *and* contextual, according to usage *and* users, the opening words of this national anthem constitute a very particular and to some extent peculiar configuration of discourses. That is, these are discourses both relatable to and distinct from the words (and occasions and contexts) of other national anthems: French, (East/West) German, American, Soviet/Russian, South African, Zimbabwean, etc. What's more, as all these examples confirm, discourses are constituted in history. As geopolitical boundaries and economic and cultural spheres of influence are re-drawn, so are the discourses in and through which they are communicated. In this respect we may note that following the American Declaration of Independence the *tune* of the British national anthem was retained – but now beginning with the words 'My Country [i.e. America] 'tis of thee . . .' rather than 'God save [someone else's] King/Queen . . .'. Clearly, then, specific configurations of discourses arise, change and disappear with the historical conditions which support them. And no geopolitical configuration lasts forever.

But even this is only a part of the picture. Just as every word or phrase displaces another that might have been used, so every configuration of discourses displaces another, slightly or very different, which might have come into play. For clearly there are many *other* ways in which people might – and do – celebrate the openings and closings of events in Britain. And there are many who would resist using or refuse to use the words of the British national anthem, along with the particular configurations of religion, monarchy, nationalism, gender and social decorum that it offers. Moslems, Buddhists, atheists, materialists, republicans, socialists, anarchists, internationalists, feminists, gays, and many others – all might (and often do) have different songs to sing and different occasions to celebrate.

Try recasting the opening lines of the British national anthem (or any other) drawing on discourses which are opposed or alternative. How might these words be modified or replaced by other, dissident or disinterested, groups – celebrating the opening or closure of what other social events? Go on to consider what such an experiment reveals about the the nature and functions of discourse. (Incidentally, there already are versions of 'God save the Queen' by the early 'punk' group The Sex Pistols as well as by the rock group Queen. The former version was banned by the BBC and the latter referred to the band themselves – not the monarch.)

The activity just suggested is both a risky and hilarious business. It all depends who, when and where you are – and what attitudes you hold or are expected to hold. That is precisely what makes discourses such a persuasive and pervasive matter, and a grasp of their operations so crucial. Moreover, it is precisely those ways of saying and seeing that are assumed to be 'natural', 'neutral', 'true', 'real' and 'factual' – or asserted as 'proper', 'respectable', 'official', etc. – that present the most problems. Challenging and changing the words of a national anthem is for some people as 'unthinkable' – because 'unsayable' and 'unseeable' – as for others it is 'heretical' or 'blasphemous' to question the meanings or change the letters of holy writ; or 'irrational' to doubt the current wisdom in economics; or 'unscientific' to reject the current formulas of wave-particle physics. And so in all these areas it is precisely the domain of the 'natural*ised*', the 'real*ised*' and the 'factual*ised*' (as well as the 'sanct*ified*' and 'object*ified*') where the addition of those verbalised forms is so necessary if we are even to begin unpicking discourses. For only then can we begin asking questions about agency and process, preferences and alternatives: who says? How? When? Where? Why? And who else might have said and seen this differently?

In sum, then, we may conclude that:

Discourse = variety + power/lessness

Whose power (or powerlessness) is, in the nature of things, itself a matter of consensus and conflict. And that is why the 'discourse' questions we put to every text have to be dialectical in structure. They entail forms of negation and require as much attention to the heterodox, the marginalised and the muted, as to the orthodox, the centrally privileged and the noisily dominant.

Dialectical discourse questions

Whose Wor(l)ds are being represented – and whose wor(l)ds are thereby being mis-, under- or unrepresented?

Whose interests (economic, political, cultural, aesthetic) are (not) being served?

What preferences are being expressed – and what others are thereby being suppressed, oppressed or repressed? And do I/we prefer others?

We must remember, too, that even what is ostensibly 'the same word' may have different meanings and effects depending on who is using it, when, where and how. Struggles over discourse therefore occur *within* words not just *between* them. 'God' and 'queen', for instance, have many more potential meanings than are bounded by the British national anthem, as have 'save' and 'gracious'. Many different social groups appropriate such terms to their own ends and understand subtly or markedly different things by them. For instance, it is very unlikely to imagine, say, present Moslem or past Roman deities going out of their way to 'save' the British Queen; and the world is full of gay, rose, and beauty 'queens' – as well as 'queens' of pop – who have precious little in common with past, present or future female British monarchs. Indeed, it is the very multiaccentuality of ostensibly 'the same words' that is so important in the formation of discourses which are always inherently multiplex and unstable. So is the capacity of each and every language user, consciously or unconsciously, to inflect and weight 'the same words' slightly or very differently with every use. Discourse in discourse is perpetually re-made not permanently given.

Drama comes from a Greek word meaning simply to 'act' or 'perform', and this is the main sense which is favoured here. It is also both conventional and convenient, at least initially, to distinguish 'drama' (the activity of 'showing' and 'presenting') from *narrative* (the activity of 'telling' and 'representing'). Furthermore, as observed elsewhere (see 3.1.3), while drama tends typically to offer present interaction on an 'I/we'–'you' axis, narrative tends typically to report absent events in the past tense and the third person (focused on 's/he' and 'they'). These basic distinctions prove serviceable. They can also be quite easily refined so as to incorporate such patently 'dramatic-narrative' hybrids as 'dramatic monologue' and 'autobiography'. But there is a still further twist to the 'story of drama' that will be given in this chapter. It had perhaps even better be called 'the way drama tells stories'. Its chief expositor and exponent is Bertolt Brecht; though arguably all dramatists – and indeed all conversationalists – do it all the time at least to some extent. This is the simple fact that people who talk to one another (on an immediate and present 'I/we'–'you' axis) also invariably talk *about* someone or something (on a more remote and absent 's/he/they/it' axis; see 2.2). Moreover, even when the participants speak *about themselves*, it is always inevitably not as speaking subjects but as spoken-to or spoken-about 'objects': 'me, my and mine' – not 'I'; 'us, our and ours' – not 'we'; and so on. In other words, every conversation has a narrative side to it: whether telling of others or telling of oneself. Put yet another way, there is a greater or lesser degree of 'objectification' or 'depersonalisation' in every dialogue. Conversely, we may say that every act of narration, even if concentrated apparently exclusively on third-person report, has an implicit or understood relation between the person who narrates (the narrator) and the person who is narrated to (the 'narratee') (see 3.1.5). We must therefore learn to see drama and conversation as always partly and potentially narrational acts – and narrative as always partly and potentially a proto-dramatic act. Moreover, whether and precisely how we choose to see which when, will depend as much on what we (as actual readers or listeners) are looking out for as on what is 'in' the text or utterance in question. The difference between 'drama' and 'narrative' therefore becomes not so much a property of the text as a product of the relations between the text and specific readers/audiences.

Take the example of one person uttering the words 'I love you' to another person. From one point of view this is wholly *dramatic*: it is patently rooted in an immediate 'I'–'you' situation and the verb is formally marked as 'present'. However, also notice that the speaker is in a sense reporting on and therefore *narrating* what she or he perceives to be the romantic or sexual state of affairs: talking *about* as well as talking *from* and *to*. Consequently, simply by the act of 'going verbal' and '*expressing*' the speaker is in effect objectifying and *re*presenting something – not just showing and presenting it. We may therefore say that the activity of saying 'I love you' is a compound of two acts: one dramatic; the other narrative. Through these words the 'I' and 'you' directly interrelate (i.e. interact); but at the same time they also indirectly 'interrelate' (i.e. 'tell one another stories'). The words may confirm a closeness between the participants; but they also establish a distance. Dialectically speaking, they both draw together and push apart.

The dramatic–narrative duality of all language acts is explored through experiment throughout this chapter – and in some measure throughout the book (e.g. 2.4–5). For the moment, it will be sufficient to signal Brecht's particular interest in the narrational dimensions of drama; and more especially his insistence that good 'acting' and 'performing' (i.e. good 'drama') should set up a critical distance between the actor and her or his role, and that this critical distance should be extended to the audience, who would then be persuaded not only to *feel* and *empathise* with the characters depicted but also to *judge* and *evaluate* the courses of action open to them.

Brecht's belief in the narrational aspects of drama went hand in hand with his belief that the theatre should instruct through entertainment. Thus in the very first numbered section of 'A Short Organum for the Theatre' (Brecht, 1964: 180) he affirms:

> 'Theatre' consists in this: in making live representation of reported or invented happenings between human beings, and doing so with a view to entertainment.

And he expressly added later (ibid.: section 12, p. 183) 'And according to Aristotle – and we agree there – narrative is the soul of drama.'

What all this means in terms of the actor's relations to the character s/he plays and the audience's relations to both is spelt out at length in section 5.2. And there, as throughout the Organum (and indeed throughout Brecht's writings on and in the theatre), it is above all the critically and politically empowering aspects of overtly 'narrativised drama' that he draws attention to. Here he is talking of the need to challenge the 'illusions that the player is identical with the character, or the performance with the actual event' (ibid.: 195):

> We shall find that this has meant scrapping yet another illusion: that everybody behaves like the character concerned. '"I am doing this" has become "I did this," and now "he did this" has got to become "he did this – when he might have done something else."'

Quite emphatically for Brecht, then, the capacity to shift from a first-person, *present progressive* perspective ('I *am doing* this') to a first-person, *past perfective* perspective ('I *did* this') was of signal importance. For what it signalled was the ability to distance and narrativise – not simply experience – the self. The same process is at work in the re-presentation of 'others', third persons. Then the value of such a perspective is to increase the audience's sense of choices open to that figure, to see her or his actions with the benefit not only of hindsight but also of critical foresight: '"he did this" has got to become "he did this – *when he might have done something else*."' In this way total identification with a character, either by actor or audience, is blocked. For, as Brecht insists time and again in his writings, *total* identification is ultimately totally paralysing: it inhibits the full exercise both of the creative imagination and the critical faculty. Wholly to 'be' the figure closes off the possibility of 'becoming' someone else – of taking an alternative course of action, of making an alternative world. What Brecht was after, then, was not simply 'experience' (empathy) but *experiment* (the exploration and testing of hypotheses). He therefore concludes the above section with the following highly influential injunction (ibid.: 195):

> [In the theatre] there should be something approaching experimental conditions: that is, that a counter-experiment should now and then be conceivable. In short, this is a way of treating society as though all its actions were performed as experiments.

It is just such 'experimental conditions' leading to dramatic 'counter-experiments' that we set up in this chapter. And for us, as for Brecht, the most pressing consideration will be 's/he did this – *when s/he might have done something else*'. And our most searching strategies will involve what might be called the 'othering of the self' (by narrativising and thereby critically distancing the 'I' who speaks) and, conversely, the 'selfing of the other' (re)-dramatising the previously merely reported figures so that s/he or they may speak in her/his/their own rights, as fully dialogic 'I's and 'we's and 'you's. In other words, we shall *experiment with conversations and plays as potentially ongoing and genuinely dialogic processes – not simply experience them as finished and apparently monologic products*.

In all these respects, Keir Elam's observation earlier (1980: 12) on the fundamentally 'hypothetical' and 'counter-factual' status of 'dramatic worlds' is of crucial importance.

That leaves just one further distinction about 'drama' and some final words about 'dramatic intervention'. It is useful to distinguish between what may be termed (genuine) drama on the one hand and (mere) ritual on the other. (The bracketed adjectives are there to signal my preferences without forcing them.) These terms may be defined as follows:

Drama generates new and previously unforeseen meanings and values through conflict and celebration. It is historically dialectical and fundamentally dialogic.

Ritual confirms existing and predetermined meanings and values through mock conflict and spectacle. Whatever it may initially appear, it is always in effect logically monolithic, anti-historical and fundamentally monologic.

Dramatic intervention may be defined as the activity of challenging and changing whatever is, was or has threatened to become 'ritualistic' – either in 'the utterance/ performance itself' or in the gradually habitualised response to that utterance/performance. That is, sometimes it is a matter or intervening in texts which have always served a ritual function; and sometimes of intervening in texts which have come to serve a ritual function. Most adverts and religious services belong to the former category; many classic dramas (including plays by Shakespeare, Ibsen and Beckett) tend to be pressed into the latter. To experience these texts and experiment with this 'drama/ritual' distinction for yourself, read and write on!

More pointedly, in every sense, *act*!

4.2 ASSERTIVENESS AND NON/COOPERATIVE PRINCIPLES

The first thing we shall do is challenge some of the received wisdom of mainstream 'speech act' and 'discourse' theory. This will itself act as a kind of practical-theoretical prelude to the dramatic interventions which follow. First some information, and then an invitation to engage in a dialogic critique and a dialectical negation of that information.

Following the work of Grice (1975), it is conventional to approach dialogue in general and conversation in particular with an eye to what he termed the **cooperative principle** (also called 'conversational maxims'; see Wales, 1989: 95–6). Basically, this principle assumes or asserts that normal, effective and successful communication relies upon a substantial degree of cooperation amongst the participants. To this end Grice proposes four 'maxims' (here designated in brackets) which must be observed for successful communication to occur. Speakers, he claims, should:

1 give adequate information – neither too little nor too much (*quantity*);

2 not tell lies (*quality*);

3 be relevant (*relation*);

4 avoid obscurity (*manner*).

To these may be added a fifth maxim proposed by Leech (1983); speakers should also:

5 be polite (*'politeness principle'*).

Accidental failure to observe these maxims 'violates' the cooperative principle, according to Grice. More deliberate and concerted attempts to resist or refuse this principle he refers to as 'flouting' it.

Now, as a kind of 'ideal world' model of what effective successful communication might or should be these criteria are fine. As personal and social aspirations, there is nothing to criticise and everything to commend in communicative activity which aims to be informative, truthful, relevant, clear and polite. Moreover, Grice arguably intended neither more nor less than this; for philosophers are pre-eminently concerned with the mapping of ideal worlds and, here, idealised communicative practices. Indeed, Grice himself, like many subsequent pragmatic linguists (including Leech), shows himself to be healthily aware of the persistently 'this-worldly' obverse of his idealised 'other world': he (and they) characteristically spend much more time and energy working over the countless and infinitely graded instances of the ways in which actual language users accidentally 'violate' or deliberately 'flout' those very principles people are ideally supposed to aspire to. In fact, it is virtually impossible to point to a 'real-world' utterance – let alone a lengthy, full-scale interaction – where all or possibly any of the above maxims is fully and faithfully observed. As a result, then, it may seem at least worth exploring the grounds for a set of counter- or alternative premises which are not especially 'cooperative' at all. Let's start with some simple, sceptical questions addressed to each of the above 'maxims' in turn.

1 What *is* an 'adequate quantity of information' – 'adequate' to whom, when, where and for what purposes? And *who* is to say when 'enough is enough'?

2 Can we ever, in the strictly superhuman words of the legal witness's oath, 'tell the whole truth and nothing but the truth'? That is, can we ever wholly avoid telling partial, half or nine-tenths truths? or, conversely, ever wholly avoid telling 'lies' – if not as acts of deliberate commission then as acts of accidental omission?

3 What – and whose – terms of reference are we to use to define the relevance or otherwise of this or that (but not that) and the other (but not that other)? And can we ever really assume an absolutely undifferentiated and equal ('free'?) relation amongst all the parties to an exchange – whether of words, goods, money, labour, or anything else?

4 Similarly, avoiding obscurity is fine if all addressers know exactly what they want to say before they say it, and they also know precisely how much or how little their addressees already know – or need to know. But does your experience of communication in general, and, say, teaching and learning in particular, really convince you that understanding is simply about the transference of transparently clear and unproblematic ideas? Or is it rather about the transformation of frequently opaque and contentious materials?

5 Finally, with the best will and manners in the world, should anyone really be 'polite' (and presumably 'patient' and 'reasonable') if somebody else is persistently and systematically ignoring you and your interests; and if they then add insult to injury by insisting that to point this fact out is 'rude' (and presumably 'impatient' and 'unreasonable')?

But of course there is more to all this than mere individual will or whim and intellectual sophistry. For there are also strong social and political reasons for resisting the imposition of an 'ideal-world' model of communication on actual historical relations and economic conditions. At root is the problem of how far you and I, in our respective world-historical positions, find it expedient or desirable to espouse a view of human interaction based on *consensus* and/or on *conflict*. Do you or I feel denied certain rights? or excluded from certain forms of legitimate expression or power? Is 'the system' – however and wherever that term be understood (economically, politically, educationally, etc.) – really serving your or my interests? In any case is this a 'system' which is humanly and ecologically sustainable, and in everybody's and everything's interests?

Re-write the above five maxims so as to encourage somebody who is relatively powerless to be *non*-cooperative and *non*-polite in ways which are personally and politically productive. Put more positively, set down the ground rules for an *assertiveness principle*. This may be done by critiqueing the words of the base text closely, through dialectical negation and dialogic negotiation. Or you may generate a quite independent, alternative set of formulations. Either way, do this before reading on.

Here, for comparison, are my own preferred negations and negotiations of the above 'cooperative principles'. Though it should be added straightaway that these are themselves the product of repeated negations and negotiations with students and colleagues over the years. They are therefore preferred but, like every other formulation, provisional.

Assertiveness Principles

Do not cooperate with every word, text or speech you meet.

Violate and transgress all the maxims where you see due cause and occasion.

More particularly and positively:

1 Ask for more – or different – information.

2 Expect to be told partial truths – there are no others.

3 Ask relevant to whom, and with what different relations in play?

4 Look for all the obscurities and contradictions that must have been ignored so as to achieve total clarity and consistency. Explore the 'holes' in the 'wholes'.

5 Be forthright and assertive. And then – if your real interests are still being ignored – get cross and get organised!

But of course you may not agree with any or all of these counter- or alternative maxims. In which case we at least agree in practice – even if we appear to disagree in theory!

(For references to the debate on 'cooperative principles' in relation to political models of 'ideal-' and 'real-' world models of consensus and conflict, see pp. 182–3).

4.3 PLOTTING ALTERNATIVE OUTCOMES IN CONVERSATION AND DRAMA

This section provides practice in exploring alternative outcomes in dialogue both on and off the stage (or on and off the screen). It also introduces the strategy of treating a transcript of 'ordinary conversation' as though it were a play or film script involving constructed (and therefore reconstructable) roles, exchanges and plots. We then go on to treat the ends of finished play and film scripts as though they were parts of continuing (and therefore differently extendable) conversations. This is also an opportunity to deepen and broaden a working knowledge of 'discourse acts', both through performance and analysis. As usual, you the audience have a crucial role to play. As active participant.

4.3.1 Daughter–father dialogue at home

Here is part of an interaction between a 10-year-old girl and a 40-year-old man. They are daughter and father. She is leaning against the doorway of a room. He is working at a word-processor with his back to the door.

Read over these exchanges a few times, preferably aloud and with other people. Meanwhile, try to gauge the personal and power relations in play, and how exactly they are being displayed. Also begin to think about possible outcomes: what might be said and done next?

> GIRL: Dad! Can we go to the park now?
> MAN: In a minute.
> GIRL: You said in a minute five minutes ago. [*Pause*] We've got our wellies on . . .
> MAN: Alright, alright. Just a couple more minutes now – when I've finished this.
> GIRL: How long will that be? Ten minutes?!

Try the following experiments. They will help you settle on a preferred interpretation and performance, before finalising a sense of what may happen next.

(1)

Experiment freely yet systematically with a wide range of vocal and interpersonal dynamics

(2)

Go on to identify the various kinds of 'move' which constitute each 'turn' taken by the two participants. For instance, 'turn 1' (Girl: 'Dad! Can we go to the park now?') consists of a *summons* or an *elicitation* (summoning or seeking to engage the attention of 'Dad!'); and this is followed by an *interrogative* ('Can we go to the park now?'). Also consider who the 'we' might refer to: daughter + father; daughter + someone else (see turn 3); or all three.

Go through the other turns and the moves which make them up with such resources in mind. In particular, notice who is using structures which are grammatically or formally marked as *declarative, interrogative, directive* and *exclamative*; and consider what more subtle and indirect acts of threat, promise, entreaty, apology, etc., might be built into the actual delivery.

(3)

Consider the various ways in which 'time' is signalled by the two participants, and how it functions as a topic of conversation – and bone of contention.

(4)

On the basis of this combination of experiment and analysis, settle on a final preferred version of this part of the interaction. Perform this out loud.

Before hypothesising about 'what happens next' in this interaction, it may help to summarise what seems to be going on so far. *Dialogically*, there is clearly a patterning of various kinds and degrees of statement and question, each one working off the other. There is also a passing back and forth of specific verbal items (i.e. 'minute' and 'now'), each time with their meanings oriented in different ways. Close inspection also reveals that there are many subtle modulations – modalisations, to be precise – among the various verb forms, especially in choice of auxiliaries and shifts in tense ('Can we . . .' 'You said', 'when I've finished', etc.) along with routine yet significant manipulations of personal pronouns ('we', 'you', 'I'). Each one of these shifts or switches signals an attempt to establish a point of temporal and attitudinal purchase on which to move the conversation. *Dialectically*, what we are presented with is none other than an argument about time. And, as usual in conversation, this is realised through a mixture of logical manoeuvres, interpersonal relations and situational constraints. On the one side we have the question from the daughter ('Can we go to the park *now*?'), the 'now' implying an extension of an earlier stage of the argument and maybe a promise made by the father. This is then countered by the father's studiously vague and patently colloquial phrase 'In a minute'. As the daughter is quick to point out, this is evidently a turn of phrase which the father used before – and again conspicuously *without* reference to 'clock time': 'You said in a minute five minutes ago.' What's more, this mixture of reproachful quotation and metalinguistic shrewdness is backed up by an appeal to empirical evidence: 'We've got our wellies on'! Then back comes yet further evidence of the father's merely expedient, chronometrically highly irregular and evidently infinitely extendable time-keeping ('Just *a couple more minutes now – when* I've finished this'). Small wonder, then, that the daughter fills the yawning 'time gap' that opens up with the derisory precision of 'How long will that be? *Ten minutes*?!'

In short, dialectically – as well as in a Bakhtinian sense 'dialogically' (see 4.4) – the girl has proved her point. Vague gestures towards merely expedient, colloquial time have been vanquished by the combined force of the logic of mechanical 'clock time' and the dialogic of parodic quotation.

But of course, winning an argument does not always mean carrying the day. A series of exchanges is only part of an overall interaction. And the outcome of exchanges of all kinds is often more a matter of real power than of abstract 'reason' or 'truth'.

So what might have been the outcome in the above interaction? What happened next? Here is a way of exploring the options systematically.

(5)

(a) Develop and script *three* alternative outcomes for the above conversation according to what you see as: (i) most desirable for the daughter; (ii) most desirable for the father; (iii) some compromise – or wholly alternative – solution. (Pick up from the girl's turn: 'How long will that be? Ten minutes?!' Be as resourcefully 'alternative' in (iii) as you wish, perhaps even adding other figures or 'unforeseen' events.)

(b) Once you have drafted these three alternatives, decide which you consider: (i) most likely; (ii) most desirable from *your* point of view (as partial observer); (iii) most 'dramatic'. In each case say why. Read on only when you have done all this.

Here, for comparison, is a transcript of what actually happened next in the above interaction:

> MAN: Oh, alright then. Go and see if Sophie's ready. And while you're doing that . . .
>
> GIRL: We're all ready. I just said.
>
> GIRL 2 [*enters carrying men's wellies*]: Here you are, Dad. It's stopped raining anyway. You've been ages.
>
> MAN: [*Pause*] Let me just store this then . . . (He does, and switches off the word-processor)
>
> [*They go*]

(c) Compare this version with each of your versions. Which one(s) is it most like and in what respects? Go on to consider how predictable or unexpected was this particular outcome on the basis of *your* preferred reading of the earlier part of the interaction.

(d) Conclude with three or four general observations on what you have learnt about the natures and structures of 'dialogue' in the course of these experiments. For instance, how far does this experience lead you to align yourself with a 'cooperative' and/or 'non-cooperative' view of conversational and interpersonal dynamics? For instance, was your projected outcome more or less *conflictual* and/or *consensual* than that projected above? And who in each case might have *asserted* themselves in different ways and to different ends? (cf. 4.2).

For my part, there is one very important lesson to be learnt from the above interaction: don't try to keep on writing about speech acts if you have promised your daughters to go to the park with them!

(Note: the above 'transcript' was pieced together by us afterwards from memory. And as we couldn't altogether agree upon that either (am I really such a bully?), perhaps the whole thing should best be considered a 'tran/script', a 'real life made-up drama' – a typical instance of 'faction', in fact!)

4.3.2 The non/sense of endings in Beckett and Ibsen

We now turn to the endings of a couple of 'classic' plays: Ibsen's *A Doll's House* (1879–80) and Beckett's *Waiting for Godot* (1956). As with similar exercises on narrative (see 3.2.6–7), we shall treat these endings as in a sense neither more nor less than 'turning points': closing moves that might have turned out differently; points of closure that might have made alternative sense both of what we know preceded them and what we inevitably speculate as succeeding them. In short, we shall experiment with turning these plays to different ends. Moreover, our aim is both dialectical and historical. For we can only understand the peculiar trajectories that each play followed in its initial moments of production, there and then, by plotting it against altered trajectories that we ourselves press it into following in our own moments of re-production, here and now. Both these moments, notice, are plural. There is never just one moment of production or reproduction – but rather an interconnected series stretching before and after and between. Moments of re/production.

Incidentally, the title of this section is an affectionately parodic allusion to the title of a finely critical and philosophical book by Frank Kermode, *The Sense of an Ending* (1968). His subject is (modernist) 'fiction' not 'drama'. But Kermode shows as well as any deconstructionist that the 'sense of an ending' is deeply dependent on the kind of 'nonsense' that it thereby cuts out. We too shall try to grasp the dialectical 'non/sense of endings' – differing the plays as well as playing the differences.

Re-building A Doll's House?

Below are two very different endings to *A Doll's House* – both written by Ibsen. They were written for different performances in different theatres with different audiences in different countries – but by the same man. (More on this shortly.)

Read over these alternative endings a couple of times, preferably out loud and with other people. Meanwhile, begin to build up a sense of their main differences, weighing which ending you prefer and why.

The immediate situation is this. Torvald Helmer, a lawyer, and his wife, Nora, are a married middle-class couple with children; and they are here reaching the climax in a long-term crisis in their relationship. This has been immediately precipitated by the revelation that Nora once forged her dying father's signature on a letter applying for a secret loan. The loan had, in fact, paid for Torvald's convalescence following a near-fatal illness. Torvald, however, takes a highly legalistic and moralistic view of the deception, and Nora takes this as a sign that there has never been any real understanding in their marriage: that in effect they have always been 'strangers'. She decides to leave.

So, notice differences and begin to think about preferences.

ENDING 1

HELMER: This is the end, then! Nora, will you never think of me any more?
NORA: Yes, of course. I shall often think of you and the children and this house.
HELMER: May I write to you, Nora?
NORA: No. Never. You mustn't do that.
HELMER: But at least you must let me send you –
NORA: Nothing. Nothing.
HELMER: But if you should need help – ?
NORA: I tell you, no. I don't accept things from strangers.
HELMER: Nora – can I never be anything but a stranger to you?
NORA [*picks up her bag*]: Oh, Torvald! Then the miracle of miracles would have to happen.
HELMER: The miracle of miracles!
NORA: You and I would both have to change so much that – Oh, Torvald, I don't believe in miracles any longer.
HELMER: But I want to believe in them. Tell me. We should have to change so much that – !

NORA: That life together between us two could become a marriage. Goodbye.

[*She goes out through the hall*]

HELMER [*sinks down on a chair by the door and buries his face in his hands*]: Nora! Nora! (*Looks round and gets up.*) Empty! She's gone! (*A hope strikes him.*) The miracle of miracles – ?

[*The street door is slammed shut downstairs*]

(Ibsen, 1984: 103–4)

ENDING 2

Read as above up until the penultimate speech, then:

NORA: That our life together could become a real marriage. Good-bye. [*She starts to go*]

HELMER: Go then! [*He seizes her arm*] But first you shall see your children for the last time.

NORA: Let me go! I will not see them. I cannot!

HELMER [*dragging her to the door on the left*]: You shall see them! [*He opens the door and says softly*] Look – there they are sleeping peacefully and without a care. Tomorrow, when they wake and call for their mother, they will be . . . motherless!

NORA [*trembling*]: Motherless!

HELMER: As you once were.

NORA: Motherless! [*After an inner struggle, she lets her bag fall, and says*] Ah, though it is a sin against myself, I cannot leave them! [*She sinks almost to the ground by the door*] [*The curtain falls*]

(Ibsen, 1965: 334, n.11)

Here are some suggestions for refining a sense of the differences generated within each text as well as between them. These techniques have already been used in 4.3.1.

(1)

First try to grasp each ending in and on its own terms. What different ends is each working towards: personal and interpersonal, moral and political? Conversely, what alternative options are thereby being closed off in each case?

(2)

(a) Experiment with the vocal and interpersonal dynamics of each text in turn. What potential differences might be exploited in performance with respect to: intonation, stress, pitch, pace and voice quality, position, gesture and movement? And what patterns of initiation and response do you discern in terms of pro-action and reaction?

(b) Follow this up with a detailed analysis of the distinctive discourse structures of each interaction. Who makes what *moves* and how within each *turn* in the exchanges? Who questions, states, commands or exclaims most? What *indirect discourse acts* may also be entailed (e.g. grammatically declarative utterances that perhaps function as directives or, more subtly, entreaties, threats, promises and bribes, etc.)? How far are the meanings of *repeatedly exchanged items transformed* in the process (e.g. 'miracles', 'mother(less)')? When and how are speech acts reinforced or counterpointed by *other kinds of physical act* (e.g. grasping arm, slamming door)?

(c) **When you have explored as many of the above variables as is practicable, settle for one preferred 'performance' for each ending.** (This 'performance' may be in your head, on the page or on a stage.)

As a result of the above activities, you will have quite a firm grasp of how you, here and now, understand and interpret these two very different endings. You probably have some firm preferences too. It is time, therefore, to begin to re-construct these endings through some acts of historical imagination. How was each ending received in its initial moment of production in the late nineteenth century? And what do we thereby learn about our own moments of re-production in the late twentieth century and beyond? Obviously, there can be no single, stable answer to such questions. I shall therefore simply try to frame them so that the critical-historical issues are opened up through dialogue rather than closed down once and for all.

(3)

Which of the following *contexts* do you reckon goes with which *ending*? (For example, does Context A go with Ending 1 or Ending 2?)

Context A
One ending was written in 1880 by Ibsen, under financial duress, for a production in Germany, so as not to cause a scandal. This ending Ibsen himself later described as a 'barbaric outrage'.

Context B
The other ending caused a public scandal and very hostile reviews when it was first performed and printed in Norway in 1879. This was Ibsen's expressly preferred ending.

Decide on your own preferred matching of 'Context' with 'Ending' before reading on. Have you gone for A1 and B2, or B1 and A2? And why?

Now put the following further questions to yourself. They are designed to interrogate critical assumptions rather more than historical knowledge.

(a) What do your choices imply about Ibsen's moral outlook?

(b) What do your choices imply about the moral outlook of certain kinds of nineteenth-century theatre audiences? (Which kinds?)

(c) Which ending would now be more accepted – and perhaps even expected? (In what kinds of play or film?)

Do this before reading on.

The 'answer' to the overall con/text question (3), perhaps not surprisingly, is: B1 and A2. However, as we are here chiefly concerned with processes of inference rather than with the 'facts' as such, this is not so important. What is important is that we should be aware of the critical-historical gaps between various moments of production and re-production. For we are always involved in a variable dialogue with the past, especially in matters of relative value (aesthetic, moral and political). The past is never simply found and fixed, once and for all. It is ceaselessly renegotiated and revalued by a series of presents. The next two activities are designed to develop just such critical-historical dialogues. They involve reading a version of the whole of Ibsen's play. Meyer's translation (Ibsen, 1984) is recommended.

(4)

Read the following passage from Ibsen's 'Notes for the modern tragedy' (1878) and debate the proposition which follows it. These notes include a provisional sketch of *A Doll's House* and were written before Ibsen actually wrote either of the above endings. (For a full text, see Cole, 1961: 151–5.)

> The wife in the play ends by having no idea of what is right or wrong; natural feelings on the one hand and belief in authority on the other have altogether bewildered her.
>
> A woman cannot be herself in the society of the present day, which is an exclusively masculine society, with laws framed by men and with a judicial system that judges feminine conduct from a masculine point of view. . . .
>
> Spiritual conflicts. Oppressed and bewildered by the belief in authority, she loses faith in her moral right and ability to bring up her children. Bitterness. A mother in modern society, like certain insects who go away and die when she has done her duty in the propagation of the race. Love of life, of home, of husband and children and family.

Now debate the following proposition *for*, *against* and *alternative* (i.e. by substituting a slightly or very different proposition):

Modern wives and husbands have not moved out of the 'doll's house': they have simply refurnished it.

(5)

While reading *A Doll's House*, speculate about alternative endings to those presented above. What different options do you feel might have been explored then? And which ones would you prefer to see now? For instance, you may find that you wish to draw in and maybe intervene with one of Ibsen's other characters so far not mentioned at all: Dr Rank, the family physician and friend; Krögstad, another lawyer and the 'villain of the piece'; Mrs Linde, who fell – or was pushed – on to hard times; or even the relatively marginal, background figures, Helen the maid and the three children (these last variously off or on stage in the above endings but silent). All or any of these figures might make a dramatic intervention – or serve as ritual chorus. It is for you to decide which, and then investigate how far such changes were real contemporary options or anachronistic wishful thinking. (For general contextualisation, see Angela Holdsworth's *Out of the Doll's House* (1988, esp. chs 1,5 and 6); Bernard Shaw's *Still After the Doll's House: A Sequel to Sir Walter Besant's Sequel to Henrik Ibsen's Play* (1890) supplies yet more grist to the factional mill. In a preface added much later (1931), Shaw characterised Besant's sequel as 'written . . . in the sincere belief that he [Besant] was vindicating that [Victorian] morality triumphantly against a most misguided Norwegian heretic'. Shaw vigorously supported the 'heresy' and his 'sequel to the sequel' shows a much stronger, more independent Nora, on her own territory, meeting Krögstad at a later date; for all of which see Shaw (1944: 187–201). A more recent 'postlude' is Elfriede Jelinek's *Nora* (1994), in which Nora leaves only to become first a factory worker and then the boss's plaything.)

Earlier we considered the fact that people both do and do not cooperate in conversation (see 4.2). This was dialectically termed an 'un/cooperative principle' and, more positively, an 'assertiveness principle'. It was expressly related to communication models based on 'conflict' as well as 'consensus'. What's more, it was argued that accidental failure or deliberate distortion in the exchange of information are not simply matters of the individual whim or will of one of the parties; rather, they are the result of structural imbalances in the power relations *among* the participants. Different discourses are based on perceptibly different – and sometimes opposed – interests.

We have just seen an instance of an acute communicative imbalance in *A Doll's House*. Nora and Torvald are speaking from different social positions within marriage and they are represented as variously resolving or dissolving those positions in the two alternative endings: resolved convergently within marriage (Ending 2) or dissolved divergently beyond marriage (Ending 1). Either way, the play is clearly not premised on a notion of complete cooperation between free and equal partners. Moreover, Ending 2 only offers a 'cooperative' and 'happily-ever-after' conclusion if we are prepared to wrench 'cooperation' so as to include, say, 'physical coercion' and 'emotional blackmail'. We would also need to turn a blindly optimistic eye to the virtually certain spiritual and psychological damage Nora does to herself by consenting to stay on ('Ah, though it is a sin against myself'). No. The play is substantially about mis- (or 'missed'), under- and non-understanding – just as we may talk of mis-, under- and non-representation. The unsaid or unsayable is as important as what is said. What is finally done up still leaves a lot undone.

Waiting for who, what, when, where, how and why?

> Back soon – Godot.
>
> (Graffito in London theatre toilet)

Significantly, the last two sentences in the previous section could apply just as well to so-called 'absurdist' drama (such as Becket's *Waiting for Godot* – the subject of the present section) as to so-called 'naturalistic' drama (such as Ibsen's *A Doll's House* – the subject of the last). This should serve as a warning to us. 'Absurdist' drama does not have a monopoly on 'breakdowns in communication'. What's more, as we have just witnessed in the differences within and between the alternative endings of Ibsen's supposedly 'naturalistic' play, there are many more kinds of sense and nonsense than two. Indeed, any alternative ending you yourself realised will have offered some distinctive kind of 'non/sense' all of its own. So, in a different vein, will some 'endings' by Beckett and you in the next section.

Here is the English version of the ending of Beckett's *Waiting for Godot* (1955; the play was first written by Beckett in French and performed as *En attendant Godot* in 1953).

Read the end of the play through a couple of times, if possible aloud and with others. Meanwhile, note the various ways in which Estragon and Vladimir both do and do not cooperate. Also begin to think how you might intervene so as to change the outcome of this interaction.

The scene for the first half of the play is 'A country road. A tree. Evening'; and that for the second half is 'Next day. Same time. Same place'. The only difference is that the tree, which was previously utterly bare, has put forth a single leaf. The two figures speaking here are variously 'tramps' and/or 'clowns'. They are still waiting for someone (or something) called 'Godot'.

VLADIMIR: . . . Everything's dead but the tree.

ESTRAGON [*looking at the tree*]: What is it?

VLADIMIR: It's the tree.

ESTRAGON: Yes, but what kind?

VLADIMIR: I don't know. A willow.

    [*Estragon draws Vladimir towards the tree. They stand motionless before it. Silence*]

ESTRAGON: Why don't we hang ourselves?

VLADIMIR: With what?

ESTRAGON: You haven't got a bit of rope?

VLADIMIR: No.

ESTRAGON: Then we can't.

    [*Silence*]

VLADIMIR: Let's go.

ESTRAGON: Wait, there's my belt.

VLADIMIR: It's too short.

ESTRAGON: You could hang on to my legs.

VLADIMIR: And who'd hang on to mine?

ESTRAGON: True.

VLADIMIR: Show all the same. [*Estragon loosens the cord that holds up his trousers which, much too big for him, fall about his ankles. They look at the cord*] It might do at a pinch. But is it strong enough?

ESTRAGON: We'll soon see. Here.

    [*They each take an end of the cord and pull. It breaks. They almost fall*]

VLADIMIR: Not worth a curse.

    [*Silence*]

ESTRAGON: You say we have to come back tomorrow?

VLADIMIR: Yes.

ESTRAGON: Then we can bring a good bit of rope.

VLADIMIR: Yes

    [*Silence*]

ESTRAGON: Didi.

VLADIMIR: Yes.

ESTRAGON: I can't go on like this.

VLADIMIR: That's what you think.

ESTRAGON: If we parted? That might be better for us.

VLADIMIR: We'll hang ourselves tomorrow. [*Pause*] Unless Godot comes.

ESTRAGON: And if he comes?

VLADIMIR: We'll be saved.

    [*Vladimir takes off his hat, peers inside it , feels about inside it, shakes it, knocks on the crown, puts it on again*]

ESTRAGON: Well? Shall we go?

VLADIMIR: Pull on your trousers.

ESTRAGON: What?

VLADIMIR: Pull on your trousers.

ESTRAGON: You want me to pull off my trousers?

VLADIMIR: Pull *on* your trousers.

ESTRAGON [*realizing his trousers are down*]: True.

    [*He pulls up his trousers*]

VLADIMIR: Well? Shall we go?

ESTRAGON: Yes, let's go.
   [*They do not move*]
   [*Curtain*]

Here are some detailed suggestions to help gauge precisely how these figures are (not) cooperating and precisely what they are (not) doing. All this is by way of prelude to our dramatic intervention.

(1)

Experiment systematically with vocal, gestural and interpersonal dynamics in the usual way (see 4.3.1 and previous section). In particular, look out for:

responses which do or do not match *initiations*;

ir/relevances – depending on whose and which *frames of reference* are applied;

words which do not match *other actions*;

communication which somehow repeatedly does not – and yet persistently does – 'succeed';

effects which might be 'comic' and/or 'tragic', depending how they were played.

Once you have blended these analytical and theoretical observations with a mixture of experiment and experience, settle on your own preferred performance. What particular version of the above interaction, with what overall meanings and effects, do you propose?

Now we begin to engage more pro-actively with the above script, moving through interpretation to intervention.

(2)

Start with one or two small-scale exchanges that you find particularly intriguing or irritating. Weigh what else might have been said by way of response or initiation and try some of the alternatives out. Run the consequent dialogue out as far as you wish, in whatever direction or dimension it tends. Then return to the base text to gauge more precisely where it was – and was not – going. To what 'ends' was it (not) being shaped?

For instance, take the initial exchanges about the tree: 'Everything's dead but the tree . . . Why don't we hang ourselves?' For each of the observations, questions and answers actually offered there is an array of implicitly excluded alternatives. 'Everything's dead but the tree' therefore *might have been* 'This tree's the only thing alive'; or 'At least this tree's alive'; or 'Look, a leaf!'; or even 'Lucky for dogs there's a tree here'; and so on. Once we grasp this, we also grasp what is specific about the observation that is actually put in play: its peculiar 'thisness' – its peculiar blend of 'non/sense'.

Or take the exchange immediately following. Estragon, '(looking at the tree)', asks 'What is it?', to which Vladimir's replies 'It's the tree.' Evidently the sheer obviousness of this statement is not what Estragon was looking for ('Yes, but what kind?', he continues). Estragon was, in Bakhtin's words, waiting for 'the word that it [the address] anticipates' (Bakhtin, 1981: 280). He therefore eventually elicits from Vladimir what seems to be the required answer ('I don't know. A willow'). Though even then the initial gesture of ignorance – or carelessness – does not inspire confidence in the identification. Notice, too, that if Vladimir had been totally in tune with what subsequently turns out to have been on Estragon's mind the former's first response might have been something like 'It's something we could hang ourselves on' (not 'It's the tree'). For clearly, it turns out, the motivation behind Estragon's question, the frame of preference behind his frame of reference, is the thought of suicide. 'Why don't we hang ourselves?' he eventually reveals, as they both stand motionless and silent before the tree. In *this* case we might even now see that Vladimir's apparent obtuseness is rather a helpful, healthful and 'saving' kind of mis/understanding. Perhaps he is deflecting the other's morbid thoughts. He is *not* co-operating – but in a peculiarly friendly way!

Go through similar kinds of hypothesising (of alternative moves) and analysing (of actual moves) for all the topics broached in the interaction. These include the possibilities of hanging; the looked-for arrival of Godot; the clowning around with the pulling on/off of the trousers; and so on, up to the final split speech/act of saying but not doing ('Yes, let's go. *They do not move*'). In fact, that last piece of in/action and non/sense is so crucial and famous that we shall devote the whole of the following section to it. However, before seeing what kinds of alternative 'non/sense' other people have made of it, make some of your own script some alternative outcomes now.

(3)

***What if* Estragon and Vladimir finally did move?** Or if they said they were going to stay and did stay? Or if they finally said they were going to stay but actually left? . . . Or if something else entirely happened? Some such alternatives are likely to be put in play in our minds, if only because the sound of two people so audibly saying they are going to do something and then so visibly not doing it is striking.

Here are some alternative endings offered by students, not all of whom were acquainted with the rest of the play. The gist of their critical inferences on the nature of Beckett's ending follows.

> *Initiation*   VLADIMIR: Well? Shall we go?
> *Responses*   (a) ESTRAGON: You stay if you want. I'm off on my own [*He goes*]
>   (b) ESTRAGON: Yeah, the play's over. [*Looks out at audience*] Let's all go to the bar.
>   (c) ESTRAGON (*continues*):   . . . and do a course in Modern Drama to find out what we're all about?! [*Pulls university prospectus from pocket*]
>   (d) [*ESTRAGON passes VLADIMIR the battered cider bottle and they drink*]
>   (e) [*Enter LUCKY and POZZO as happy lovers, hand in hand and in full health*]
>   (f) [*Back projection of: (i) country road full of refugees in Yugoslavia (or Africa, or the Middle East); OR (ii) a giant logo of the GODOT MINING CORPORATION (Get Ore Dug On Time)*]

Critical inferences

(a) At least Beckett's pair finally stay together – so the play may not be that 'tragic'. Conversely, perhaps one of them making a break could be seen as a token of hope?

(b) There is clearly a limit to the 'modernist' reflexivity of the play's theatricality: it does not really extend to the audience and the theatre bar (i.e. the usual social 'ending' of the evening).

(c) The play is now a highly institutionalised 'classic' complete with copious commentaries and 'answers'.

(d) Beckett's tramps/clowns are clearly theatrical constructs; they have little to do with actual contemporary vagrancy – at least in late twentieth-century British cities.

(e) This re-invokes two other male characters from earlier in the play. However, these now offer an image of a positive, overtly homosexual relationship, rather than, as in Beckett, one of a destructive dependence and (perhaps) covertly homosexual relationship.

(f) Some provocative counter- or complementary images:

(i) What price existential *Angst* and inaction in a world recurrently full of really displaced persons? *or*

(ii) Maybe the modern 'Mr Godot' is not an ineffable existential idea, a sublimated deity or the return of the theatrically repressed, after all – but simply a multinational corporation and large-scale un/employer?

Each of these alternative endings offers its own kind of revealing 'non/sense'. And one of the main things it reveals is the peculiar kind of 'non/sense' offered by Beckett's actual ending. We may be left with no final 'answers' as to what the play is about. But we are certainly left with some provocative questions and some very productive lines of enquiry: theatrical; aesthetic; psychological; sexual; social; moral; and political. What's more, because such questions are framed both dialogically and dialectically, we are assured that such answers as arise will be genuinely historical. For, by trying to 're-tie the ends' of the base text in our own here and now, we inevitably experience the tension of trying to 'untie the ends' left loose or tight or cut short by the initial author, there and then.

Waiting for who, what, when, where, how and why . . . ?

Beckett is – and is not – saying. You too. Differently

4.4 CROSS-CULTURAL DIALOGUES WITH AND WITHIN 'ENG. LIT.'

We open this section by looking at the re-presentation of speech, thought and action in instances of the literary genre known as 'the English novel'. We shall both observe and ourselves engage in a series of dialogues with/in a number of 'classic' English novels by Trollope, Austen, Brontë and Rhys. 'With/in' because the dialogue 'in' a text cannot be wholly divorced from the writer's and reader's dialogue 'with' that text (cf. 2.2 and 3.1.5).

At the same time we shall observe and engage in snatches of a larger dialogue between these novels and the changing institutions and practices known as 'English Language and Literature' – 'Eng. Lang. & Lit.' for short. This dialogue revolves round a number of fundamental questions. Should we speak of 'English Language' (upper case and singular) as a monolithic, enduring entity with a common source which functions as a common resource for broadly consensual ends? Or should we rather speak of 'english languages' – even 'languages only partly english' – (lower case and plural) as ceaselessly shifting collections of discourses, constantly subject to the pressures of internal and external differentiation? For instance, does the English – do the englishes – used by eighth-, fourteenth- and twentieth-century users of the language(s), and by English, Malawian and Barbadian users, has/have more or less in common? How similar/different are they: one language or many?

Similarly with 'Eng. Lit.' Do we speak of 'English Literature' (again upper case and singular) with the assumption or assertion that there is a single, already known, inherently privileged body of 'classic, canonical, literary' texts, with the emphasis falling equally on all three terms (i.e. old and traditionally revered writings)? Or do we speak of diverse 'literatures' – and 'oratures' – wholly or partly in one of the englishes referred to above: works in which some form of english language is a component but which may also include all sorts of live performance and recorded audio-visual dimensions which are neither wholly verbal nor exclusively 'english'?

To engage in this dialogue and to help frame answers to these questions, we shall draw on the work of such writers and performers as Felix Mnthali, Amryl Johnson and Merle Collins. Initially we shall move in reaction to – and away from – the linguistic, literary and socio-historical 'centres' offered by Trollope, Austen and Brontë. But gradually, using Rhys' work as a bridge, we shall begin to perceive other 'centres' in their own rights/writes, performing in their own spaces and times. This movement, however, is perhaps better conceived as a variable oscillation between shifting polarities than as a linear progression. For if such a process of de- and re-centring is to be genuinely dialogic, at each point we must ask ourselves some further fundamental questions. Where do you and I stand in all this? How close together and how far apart? What English/englishes do we ourselves characteristically hear and speak, read and write? Which varieties of language – and which other languages – do we routinely have access to and familiarity with? And which varieties and languages, to us, are correspondingly 'strange', 'exotic' and perhaps 'alien' – in a word 'other'? In addition, what kinds of 'literature', 'orature' and other audio-visual activities do we most set store by – officially and unofficially, at work and play, inside and outside our designated area of study? Overall, then, what precise kinds of dialogue with 'English' and 'Language' and 'Literature' are you and I severally engaged in? Where are we coming from and going to with these subjects? More pointedly and actively, *where do we want to take them and ourselves as subjects* – not just as the passive *subjects* of linguistic, literary and historical processes, but also as *agents* re-making both them and ourselves through those processes?

For all these reasons, each of the following subsections has the tag '. . . and you' (in my case read 'and me'). For where on earth would this particular dialogue be without us?!

4.4.1 Trollope, Bakhtin and you

First a passage from a novel; then some activity; and finally some relevant theory. The passage is from chapter 10 of Anthony Trollope's *Barchester Towers* (1857). At this point in the novel guests are arriving at the mansion of Bishop and Mrs Proudie of Barchester. All are Church of England clerics and their relations. They include: Mr Slope, the bishop's personal assistant; Dr Stanhope (the prebendary) and his wife; and their disabled daughter Madeline (whose married surname is Vesey Neroni).

(I)

Read through the passage a couple of times so as to familiarise yourself with its general manner and matter. As you do so, ask yourself two questions:

(a) How would you *identify* the piece in terms of broad *genre*, *language* and *subject matter*? How may it be categorised?

(b) How far do you *identify with* the manner and matter of the piece? How much do you have in common with the ways in which the narrator and the characters talk, think and act? In what ways does it 'interest' you?

> A thundering rap at the front door interrupted the conversation. Mrs Proudie stood up and shook herself gently, and touched her cap on each side as she looked in the mirror. Each of her girls stood on tiptoe, and rearranged the bows on their bosoms; and Mr Slope rushed up stairs three steps at a time.
>
> 'But who is it, Netta?' whispered the bishop to his youngest daughter.
>
> 'La Signora Madeline Vesey Neroni,' whispered back the daughter; 'and mind you don't let anyone sit upon the sofa.'
>
> 'La Signora Madeline Vicinironi!' muttered, to himself, the bewildered prelate. Had he been told that the Begum of Oude was to be there, or Queen Pomara of the Western Isles, he could not have been more astonished. La Signora Madeline Vicinoroni, who, having no legs to stand on, had bespoken a sofa in his drawing-room! – who could she be? He however could now make no further inquiry, as Dr and Mrs Stanhope were announced. They had been sent on out of the way a little before the time, in order that the signora might have plenty of time to get herself conveniently packed into the carriage.
>
> The bishop was all smiles for the prebendary's wife, and the bishop's wife was all smiles for the prebendary. Mr Slope was presented, and was delighted to make the acquaintance of one of whom he had heard so much. The doctor bowed very low, and then looked as though he could not return the compliment as regarded Mr Slope, of whom, indeed, he had heard nothing. The doctor, in spite of his long absence, knew an English gentleman when he saw him.
>
> And then the guests came in shoals: Mr and Mrs Quiverful and their three grown daughters. Mr and Mrs Chadwick and their daughters. The burly chancellor and his wife and clerical son from Oxford. [. . .] Then came the archdeacon and his wife, with their eldest daughter Griselda, a slim pale retiring girl of seventeen, who kept close to her mother, and looked out on the world with quiet watchful eyes, one who gave promise of much beauty when time should have ripened it.

You will now have some provisional ideas as to *what* this text is (its *identity*). You will also have some preliminary sense as to how you relate to it (how far you *identify with* it). The following questions and suggestions will help firm up these ideas. They are also designed as a systematic work-out with novelistic discourse in general: exploring the kinds of dialogue we both observe and ourselves become engaged in. The same method is used on other novels later.

(II)

Read the whole passage out loud asking yourself how 'easily' and 'naturally' the various voices and discourses flow though your mind and from your lips. How similar to or different from your own characteristic voices and discourses are they?

(III)

Mark up the text so as to distinguish the speech and thought of characters from those of the narrator(s), also noting areas of overlap. If a different colour or underlining is used for each, the result is a sense of *visible structure*.

(IV)

Experiment reading the passage out loud using a variety of voices for different portions of the text. The aim is to transform the 'visible structures' identified in (III) into 'audible structures'. For instance, all the passages of *direct speech* might be read by one person (or in one voice) and all the passages of *reported speech* and *free indirect speech* be read by another. Particularly revealing effects are achieved by reading 'free indirect speech' in two overlapping voices (those of narrator and character). Alternatively, the speeches of the various characters may be spoken by various voices and the narrator spoken by just one; though again there will be interesting options with respect to who speaks the passages of free indirect speech and how.

(V)

Who is represented as speaking, thinking and acting in what ways? And how far does this behaviour conform to – or resist – expected or dominant patterns based on gender, class, age, race, region, education, etc.? The socio-historical question 'Expected by whom, when and where?' necessarily arises at this point; so does the ideological one 'Dominant for – or dominating – whom?' Try to sustain a dialogue between the moments of the text 'there and then' and 'here and now' so as to avoid a simplistically monolithic answer.

(VI)

What evaluations of persons, events and issues are *implied* by the narrator? And how are we, as *ideal narratees* there and then, being encouraged to respond? (cf. 3.1.5). This means 'listening attentively' to the text in order to discern what values it is asserting or assuming in its own historical moment. Unless we do this, the next step will be an arbitrary imposition by the reader on the text – a mere monologue.

(VII)

What *inferences* do you, as an *actual reader* here and now, make? And how far do these seem to be at odds with what was expected of *ideal narratees* there and then? (cf. 3.1.5 and 4.2). This means identifying those assumptions or assertions of the narrator (or author) which we wish to challenge – the questions the text inadvertently prompts rather than those it openly addresses. Unless we do this *assertively*, the previous step will have been an arbitrary imposition by the text on the reader – a mere monologue.

(VIII)

Go on to pose the *dialectical discourse questions* (see 4.1, p. 124):

Whose wor(l)ds are being represented? And whose wor(l)ds are thereby being mis-, under- or unrepresented, etc. Consider the kinds of supplementary information and material you feel you would need in order to develop a more fully historical and contextual dialogue with this text (cf. 1.2 and 2.5.2).

(IX)

Consider ways in which you might *intervene* in this text so as to change its discursive strategies and perhaps challenge its ideological positions (see 5.3 for a review of strategies).

At least outline your responses to each of the above questions and suggestions before reading on.

Here, for comparison and by way of illustration, is an outline of the ways in which I respond to activities **(I)–(IX)** with respect to the Trollope passage. See how far we agree and differ.

(Ia) *Identity*: The *genre* I broadly recognise as a nineteenth-century novel of manners. The *language* is a rather formal yet also conversational kind of English which would now be regarded as 'mannered': to me it breathes a kind of upper-middle-class ease or gentrified politeness. The *subject matter* is basically the social etiquette of the clergy and, incidentally, what it it is to be disabled, 'foreign' and 'English' – all quite playfully treated.

(Ib) *Identify with?* Taken as a whole, this is not the kind of language and behaviour I routinely engage in myself; though I recognise some aspects of it still in the behaviour of, say, some Oxford dons and the British upper middle classes. I am not normally concerned with clerical matters, and I suspect I have slightly different views of disability, 'foreigners' and 'an English gentleman'. Though for the moment, like Trollope, I am not saying anything more explicitly.

(II) *Reading out loud*: My experience of this is necessarily complex. In one sense the passage slips 'easily' and 'naturally' through the mind and from the tongue; for I am a practised – if not especially skilled – reader of such things. At the same time I recognise that this is not wholly 'my' voice saying these things in these ways. These are not quite or at all my 'discourses': my characteristic ways of saying and seeing and being. In the act of reading 'I' (the 'I-who-reads') feel myself to be caught between a 'here-now' and a 'there-then', between what I my 'self' would normally say and what I, ventriloquising for 'others', am being made to say. In short, I experience an internal as well as an external dialogue. Moreover, I should stress that this is experienced not merely in the abstract, but as a kind of tension in the mind and on the lips. It is a materially psychological and physiological tension. In the very activity of reading I partially come to be (i.e., become) someone and something else. The passage informs me with its words. But I lend it my mind and voice. Yes, a dialogue. But not a total acquiescence. (All this may sound obvious. However, if we do not grasp the fundamentally 'dialogic' processes of verbal reception and reproduction we shall get nowhere. Nor shall we recognise ourselves to be agents negotiating – as well as subjects pressured by – another's words in history. See the reference to Bakhtin later in this section, and those to 'reception theory' in 5.1.)

(III) Marking up the text's *visible structures*: The first paragraph consists of reported discourse; the second and the third each consist of direct discourse accompanied by report clauses; and the fourth paragraphs and fifth paragraphs move fluidly between reported discourse and free in/direct discourse (i.e., sometimes 'said' as though through both characters and narrator). All these differences and overlaps may be underlined or coloured in a variety of ways. (In fact, the situation is further complicated by the fact that some figures in the text are both observed and observers: the women in the first paragraph look at themselves; Griselda in the last paragraph looks out at others; see (V)–(VII) below.)

(IV) Realising the *audible structures* in performance: This is strictly a matter of group experiment. However, experience of how this passage is handled by various groups confirms the fact that the text is complexly multivocal. Not only is it built up from a variety of dialogues among characters within the larger monologic frame supplied by the narrator. It also involves dialogues between the narrator and the characters and between the narrator and implied readers. There is therefore a potential for 'voices' to speak simultaneously as well as by turns (especially in the last paragraph). The resulting polyphony may be variously harmonious or cacophonous – in or out of 'tune' – depending on the perceived tensions between speakers.

(V) *Representations of gender, age, class, etc.*: Take the first paragraph. The passage opens with a 'thundering rap at the front door', but the reactions from Mrs Proudie, her daughters and Mr Slope are very different. (Re-read the opening.) Clearly, these differences are based on social expectations to do with 'gender' and 'age' and 'class'. For if we invert and permutate these reactions (e.g. with Mrs Proudie rushing 'up stairs three at a time' and Mr Slope touching his cap, looking in the mirror and rearranging the bows on his bosom) they become revealingly ludicrous.

Take the second and third paragraphs – the whispered exchange between the bishop and his youngest daughter. (Re-read it.) This consists of a qualified question and a familiar elicitation from the bishop ('But who is it, Netta?') followed by a precise answer and admonition from the daughter ('La Signora . . . and mind you don't let any one sit upon the sofa'). On the one hand, we are reminded of the older man's status as 'bishop'; on the other hand we are treated to a glimpse of the relationship between an imperious 'youngest daughter' and her father. His question prompts not only an answer but also a command. The balance of power in this particular exchange is therefore subtly – and amusingly – vexed (cf. 4.3.1). For a fuller sense of the kinds of value judgement in play, we must take the next steps and the next paragraphs.

(VI) and (VII) *Ideal narratees* and *Actual readers*: What of 'the Begum of Oude' or 'Queen Pomara of the Western Isles' – or for that matter Italians and the fun of mangling their names ('Vesey Neroni/Vicinironi')? On the one hand, as ideal narratees, we are clearly invited to register the wonder, exoticism and sheer implausibility of these names. On the other hand, as actual readers, we may choose to ask who really was a 'Begum'? and where and what precisely were 'the Western Isles'? and what of actual Italy and Italians in the 1840s – as distinct from the fanciful and fashionable invocation of them in the discourse of an English novelist or the brain of a bemused bishop? It is therefore at this point that we begin to ask questions and make comments the narrator does *not* appear to invite – but which the text may none the less prompt. Or at least we do if we feel so prompted (maybe because we come from India, the Western Isles or Italy) or if we so choose (because we value a critical-historical sense).

Other questions, more or less obvious, more or less awkward, may arise as we read on. Just what attitudes to disability, perhaps especially female disability, underlie the references to Madeline Vesey Neroni? For she, the astonished bishop muses, '*having no legs to stand on*, had bespoken a sofa in his drawing-room!' and earlier had apparently taken time 'to get herself conveniently *packed* into the carriage'. ('Why "packed"?' we may ask, if we are so minded – and will certainly ask if we are disabled or know a disabled person well.)

Similarly, the doctor, at the close of another passage in which narrator's and characters' perspectives are subtly blended, is indirectly reported as saying '[he] knew *an English gentleman* when he saw him'. We may therefore wonder about the precise assumptions informing what 'an English gentleman' was supposed to look and behave like, and how we should value 'him'. Are we being invited to view such a phenomenon as admirable – or silly? Greet it with patriotic and socially superior pride – or be irritated at it as a symptom of deeply ingrained nationalism and class-consciousness? Now, I have little doubt that, though playfully ironic about the immediate situation, Trollope was assuming in both himself and his ideal narratees a casual and generally admiring compliance with what 'an English gentleman' was. However, that does not prevent us, as actual readers, from making alternative inferences. We may still prefer to recognise other differences as constitutive. Authors may imply; but it is still the task of the reader to infer. And implication and inference may not meet. Indeed, they can never exactly coincide. They are in dialogue.

At the same time, however, we should not underestimate Trollope's own sense of the slippages and imbalances of dialogue. The whole passage in which the bishop and his wife exchange courtesies with the prebendary and his wife is a delicate ironic exposure of just such mis/understandings. Notice, too, the way in which the finely regulated blend of ritualistic words and gestures is shown to break down: 'The doctor bowed very low, and then looked as though he could not return the compliment as regarded Mr Slope, of whom, indeed, he had heard nothing.' Moreover, the whole issue of whose words, actions and thoughts are here being perceived through whose eyes and mind is fascinatingly complex. Following the passage through sentence by sentence and clause by clause, we see that the 'point of view' shifts from one party to the other, with the narrator as a kind of benignly indulgent, all-pervading presence.

Even so, it would be unwise to take an uncritical, wholly 'naturalised' view of this narrator, as though his perceptions and knowledges were the only ones available. Ours are too. So, in a curious way, are those of his characters. Consequently, when we get to the description of the archdeacon's eldest daughter, 'Griselda', we may want to add an observation not made by the text but none the less prompted by it. Again the situation is complex. For the most part we observe the girl from the outside ('a slim pale retiring girl of seventeen . . . one who gave promise of much beauty . . .'), and as such we may say that she is framed as an object of the observer's evaluative (male?) gaze. At the same time, in passing, we are given a glimpse of her observing others, as it were 'from the inside': '[she] looked out on the world with quiet watchful eyes'. In other words, there is an observer within an observation, a potential story within a story. The narrator is in dialogue with the characters and, by extension, the creator with his creations. What's more, we, as actual readers, are in dialogue with all of them. If we know the story of 'patient Griselda' (in Chaucer, for instance), we cannot but be aware that Trollope's Griselda substantially conforms to type. She is, we may say, in part an intertextual construct. Trollope is therefore reinscribing – we might even say 'being written by' – a set of discourses compounding notions of 'daughter', 'female beauty' and 'restraint' which may fairly be termed dominant and patriarchal. At the same time, however, we should recognise that the narrator at least nods to the existence of an alternative position: one which is literally 'muted' but none the less watchful ('(she) looked out on the world with *quiet watchful* eyes'). The narrator is in dialogue with and to some extent subject to the enquiring gaze of his characters; just as he and they are in dialogue with us and subject to our enquiring gaze.

(VIII) *Dialectical discourse questions*: In effect, these simply oblige us to develop the above analytical dialogue into larger inferences. General lines of enquiry we now know we need to follow up include early and mid-nineteenth-century representations of: clerics, families, disability, 'foreigners' and the 'English gentleman' – all set against other historical versions of how representatives of these groups lived in practice. We may also infer we need detailed information on the communicative and commercial relations among authors, publishers, libraries and actual readers in 1857 (as well as some sense of who did not read the mainly middle-class magazines in which Trollope was serialised); and so on (cf. 1.2.2).

(IX) *Interventions*: *What if* the Begum of Oude or Queen Pomara of the Western Isles really arrived? (From an exotic Western European opera – or from an actual non-European place?)

What if some other version of 'La Signora Vesey Neroni' offered an account of the very variable facilities for the severely disabled in the mid-nineteenth century – depending on class and status? *What if* Trollope's Griselda told us what she saw when she 'looked out on the world with quiet watchful eyes'? *What if* this were translated into Italian and you, as translator and editor, had to grapple with the supposed 'exoticism' of your routine language (eg 'La Signora') or had to gloss for a modern readership what exactly was meant then and there by 'an English gentleman' or 'Oxford'? *What if* you were asked to do (a) a literary appreciation of this passage; (b) a Marxist-feminist-deconstructionist-post-colonial critique of it?

In fact, it all comes down to just one hypothetical question:

What if *you* decide the kind of critical-creative dialogue *you* want to develop with this text? Moreover, once you decide, the hypothesis becomes fact – and your very own synthesis.

For my part, I should like to close on an openly theoretical note. Here is a passage from Bakhtin's *Discourse in the Novel* (1981: 324). This is the destination I had in mind when we set out. However, if you engaged in the above dialogues attentively and assertively you will have arrived some time ago – and may now be some way further on. Some of my own responses and questions to Bakhtin follow. You may have others.

Heteroglossia once incorporated into the novel (whatever the form for its incorporation) is *another's speech in another's language*, serving to express authorial intentions but in a refracted way. Such speech constitutes a special type of *double-voiced discourse*. It serves two speakers at the same time and expresses simultaneously two different intentions: the direct intention of the character who is speaking, and the refracted intention of the author. In such discourse there are two voices, two meanings and two expressions. And all the while these two voices are dialogically interrelated, they – as it were – know about each other (just as two exchanges in a dialogue know of each other and are structured in this mutual knowledge of each other); it is as if they actually hold a conversation with each other. Double-voiced discourse is always internally dialogised. Examples of this would be comic, ironic or parodic discourse, the refracting discourse of a narrator, refracting discourse in the language of a character and finally the discourse of a whole incorporated genre – all these discourses are double-voiced and internally dialogised. A potential dialogue is embedded in them, one as yet unfolded.

It may be added that what Bakhtin says of 'double-voiced discourse' *in* the novel also applies to the reader's dialogue *with* the novel. Many of the preceding activities are designed to explore precisely this internal–external dynamic. We are engaged in dialogues *with/in* the novel and *with/in* 'Eng. Lang. & Lit.'. However, perhaps we should more properly speak of plural dialogues and '*multivoiced* discourses', rather than, as Bakhtin does, just '*two* intentions' and '*double*-voiced discourse'. The prefix 'dia-' in *dia*logue and *dia*lectic meant 'across' or 'through' – not 'two' (see 4.1). We must therefore use these methods to get 'through' – and beyond – binary thinking. None the less, Bakhtin certainly helps point the way forward.

4.4.2 Austen, Antigua, Africa and you

We now apply the same procedures to a different text. We also consider some counter- and alternative texts, so as to invoke some counter- and alternative voices and discourses.

Here is a passage from chapter 3 of Jane Austen's *Mansfield Park* (1814). The novel is set in the prosperous country house of Sir Thomas and Lady Bertram and their family in contemporary Northhamptonshire. At this point, quite early on in the novel, speculation about the financial status and conduct of a female neighbour is temporarily interrupted by other concerns.

Read the passage through a couple of times to get your initial bearings.

These opinions had hardly been canvassed a year, before another event arose of such importance in the family, as might fairly claim some place in the thoughts and conversation of the ladies. Sir Thomas found it expedient to go to Antigua himself, for the better arrangement of his affairs, and he took his eldest son with him, in the hope of detaching him from some bad connections at home. They left England with the possibility of being nearly a twelvemonth absent.

The necessity of the measure in a pecuniary light, and the hope of its utility to his son, reconciled Sir Thomas to the effort of quitting the rest of his family, and of leaving his daughters to the direction of others at their present most interesting time of life. He could not think Lady Bertram quite equal to supply his place with them, or rather to perform what should have been her own; but in Mrs. Norris's watchful attention, and in Edmund's judgement, he had sufficient confidence to make himself go without fears for their conduct.

Lady Bertram did not at all like to have her husband leave her; but she was undisturbed by any alarm for his safety, or solicitude for his comfort, being one of those persons who think nothing can be dangerous, or difficult, or fatiguing to anybody but themselves.

(Note: We hear nothing else of affairs in Antigua until Sir Thomas and his son return fifteen chapters later (chapter 18), and then only that 'His [Sir Thomas'] business in Antigua had been prosperously rapid'. For the rest, there is virtually no reference to the place and none to its people. They are omitted. None the less, it appears that much of the prosperity of Mansfield Park rests upon the family's business interests in the people and produce of Antigua. The above passage and the precise nature and shape of this omission are the dual focuses of the first part of this section.)

First of all, go through activities (I)–(IX), as for the passage from Trollope (4.4.1, pp. 143–5). That is: (I) how do you *identify* (i.e. label and categorise) this piece of writing, and how far do you *identify with* (i.e. relate to) its figures and concerns? (II) How far do its 'voices' and 'discourses' chime or clash with your own? And so on, all the way through to the *dialectical discourse questions* (VIII) and ideas for *intervention* (IX).

(Note: The following modifications are suggested for steps (III) and (IV): *'visible' and 'audible' structures*. There is no direct speech from the characters in this instance, so the method of marking up the 'visible' and 'audible' structures of the text needs modifying slightly. When reading the passage you will have been aware of a variable and sometimes critical distance between the narrator and the characters. You can therefore mark up different parts in so far as perceptions seem to be *observed by* and/or *observed of* characters (cf. 2.1). The second paragraph, for example, could all be quite easily conceived as an indirect representation of Sir Thomas' thoughts and speech. This can be confirmed if we simply shift the third person masculine references ('he', 'his' 'Sir Thomas'') to first person ('I', 'me','my') and the past tense to the present (e.g. 'reconciled' to 'reconcile'). The whole paragraph is thus readily revealed as a covert version of his speech and thought. Now try the same substitution trick with Lady Bertram in the third paragraph (thus beginning '*I do* not at all like . . .'). This starts plausibly enough from her 'point of view' but then gradually shifts to that of an external and overtly judgemental narrator ('being one of those persons . . .'). In this way, as suggested, we can mark up different portions of the text in so far as they seem to be *observed by* and/or *observed of* characters. The resulting text can then be used as a script for experimenting with performances using different voices. As with the Trollope passage, the parts where character *and* narrator seem to be represented simultaneously offer peculiarly fascinating possibilities in performance. If two voices are used at once (for narrator *and* character), we are treated to a highly dramatic realisation of Bakhtin's 'double-voiced discourse' (see p. 149). Alternatively, you may use a partially re-scripted version, drawing on the kinds of pronoun and tense substitutions outlined above. Either way, the main thing is to attempt to explore the *internally dialogic* dynamics of the text by tracing its *visible* and *audible* structures.)

Now read the following poem by the Malawian writer Felix Mnthali. It offers one possible response to Jane Austen's work (from 'Echoes from Ibadan' (1961); in Moore and Beier, 1984: 139).

The Stranglehold of English Lit.
(for Molara Ogundipe-Leslie)

Those questions, sister,
those questions
                stand
                stab
                jab
        and gore
too close to the centre!

For if we had asked
why Jane Austen's people
carouse all day
and do no work

would Europe in Africa
have stood
the test of time?
and would she still maul
the flowers of our youth
in the south?
Would she?

Your elegance of deceit
Jane Austen
lulled the sons and daughters
of the dispossessed
into a calf-love
with irony and satire
around imaginary people.

While history went on mocking
the victims of branding irons
and sugar-plantations
that made Jane Austen's people
wealthy beyond compare!

Eng. Lit., my sister,
was more than a cruel joke –
it was the heart
of alien conquest.
How could questions be asked
at Makerere and Ibadan,
Dakar and Fort Hare –
with Jane Austen
at the centre?
How could they be answered?

The poem is dialogic in a variety of directions and dimensions. It offers itself as part of a dialogue with Jane Austen and, by extension, part of a dialogue between 'Africa' and 'Europe'. At the same time, it presents a writer who is himself responding to 'those questions' from '[my] sister'. It is also, clearly, a text dedicated to the promotion of centres of interest alternative to the 'cruel joke' of 'Eng. Lit.'. We too, therefore, shall explore these questions and arrive at our own alternative 'centres' through dialogue. Here are some suggestions as to how this may be done.

(1)

The poem is cast in the form of a response to 'those questions' asked by 'my sister'. (She is presumably the Molara Ogundipe-Leslie named in the dedication; though whether she is a 'sister' by blood or collective association is uncertain.)

What were 'those questions' from 'my sister', do you think? Try drafting them. (Suggestion: Work back from Mnthali's response asking yourself how far he appears to be elaborating an expected answer or countering an awkward question.)

(2)

How far do you feel yourself to be included in or excluded from the dialogue between the poet and his 'sister'. And with whom or what do you most closely identify: Mnthali, Ogundipe-Leslie or Austen? Africa or Europe? While answering, weigh such determinants as race, sex, education, general culture and history, 'literary tastes', etc. How absolutely 'determin*ed*' do you reckon yourself to be by these criteria – as someone *subject* to social-historical processes? Conversely, how '*self-determining*' do you reckon yourself to be – as an active *agent* in those processes? (These questions are impossible to answer in the abstract. But they are none the less essential to ask.)

(3)

Now ask how far you feel yourself to be included in or excluded from the various dialogues between Jane Austen's narrator, her characters and her assumed readers? (Cf. the 'identify with' question above, 4.4.1 (Ib). Again weigh social and historical self/determinants when gauging your sense of inclusion or exclusion.)

(4)

'Mansfield Park' is the made-up name of a place in early nineteenth-century rural England. 'Ibadan' (mentioned in the poem and in the name of the collection from which it comes) is the real name of a city in modern Nigeria. **Which place is more 'real' to you? (In what sense?) And which place do you think you would feel more 'at home' in?** Consider what your responses to these questions tell you about your own perceptual 'centres' (geographical, historical and cultural) – and where you reckon your 'roots' to be.

(a) **In what words might Mnthali have commented specifically upon the above passage from *Mansfield Park*?** (Draft 30 words.)

(b) **In what words might Austen have commented upon Mnthali's poem?** (Draft 30 words.)

(c) **Drawing on the comments you drafted in (a) and (b), develop an imagi-**

nary exchange between your versions of 'Austen' and 'Mnthali'. Perhaps develop this through further reading and discussion into a full-scale interaction.

(5)

Mnthali writes of 'The Stranglehold of English Lit.'. And yet he does so in a language, a style and a poetic genre modelled substantially on quite polished 'standard modern English' linguistic and literary usages. This observation applies to the spellings, vocabulary choice, idioms, sentence structures and visual presentation. Only in the violently staccato lines 'stand / stab / jab / and gore' do we perhaps get a taste of some other discourse. In such a post/colonial perspective, there are at least two questions that arise:

(a) **How far is Mnthali himself complicit in maintaining 'the stranglehold of English Lit.' that he is apparently striving to shake off?**

(b) **How might Mnthali (a trilingual Malawian) need to write – or speak – for whom, where and when if he were to undo this 'stranglehold' completely? And would he then be accessible or even comprehensible to you or me?**

(Note: Felix Mnthali, b. 1933, Northern Malawi, studied at Malawi and Cambridge universities before returning to Malawi (via Ibadan university 1960–1) to become Head of the Department of English, thereafter moving to Botswana; see Moore and Beier, 1984: 298.)

(6)

There are of course converses to the questions in (5):

(a) **How knowledgeable about and complicit in the conditions of the contemporary slave trade was Jane Austen?**

(b) **And how much could such conditions 'reasonably' be expected to figure in her novels?**

Some provisional answers to these highly involved yet important questions may be found elsewhere (e.g. Armstrong, 1988: 38ff.; Said in Mulhern, 1992: 97–113 and Said, 1993: 100–16). And of course that 'reasonably' in (b) can be debated with varying degrees of heat and light. For present purposes, however, the main thing is that such questions be asked both vigorously and with discrimination. To this end, here is a tenth 'dialogic' activity to add to the nine already listed above (pp. 143–5).

(X)

Wherever and however possible, explore the base text through dialogues across cultures as well as dialogues across histories. This is crucial if we are even to attempt to locate texts in any 'global' or 'world-historical' frame of reference. More practically, and with an eye to the sheer plurality of such frames of reference, it is also crucial if we are to observe – and ourselves engage in – successive acts of de- and re-centring. Moreover, even if counter- or alternative texts do not already exist (and often they do), we ourselves are still at liberty to make some.

We continue this cross-cultural, historical dialogue in another direction and another dimension in the next section.

4.4.3 *Jane Eyre, Wide Sargasso Sea* and you

We now look at two more texts, both novels, which are palpably in cross-cultural and historical dialogue. Again, we ourselves shall engage with them dialogically, through a range of performance techniques and dramatically interventive procedures. This section also acts as a bridge to the next, in which post-colonial voices and discourses come into their own.

The first extract is from the middle of Charlotte Brontë's *Jane Eyre* (1847), chapter 20. At the point we enter the novel, the orphan Jane Eyre has become a governess in the household of Edward Rochester at Thornfield Hall. Rochester speaks first. Jane is the 'I'.

Read the passage through a couple of times, beginning to think about the kinds of dialogue it sets in motion, and how these might be explored through analysis, performance and critical-creative intervention.

'Sit,' he said; 'the bench is long enough for two. You don't hesitate to take a place at my side, do you? Is that wrong, Jane?'

I answered him by assuming it: to refuse would, I felt, have been unwise.

'Now, my little friend, [. . .] I'll put a case to you, which you must endeavour to suppose your own: but first, look at me, and tell me you are at ease, and not fearing that I err in detaining you, or that you err in staying.'

'No, sir: I am content.'

'Well then, Jane, call to aid your fancy: suppose you were no longer a girl well reared and disciplined, but a wild boy indulged from childhood upwards; imagine yourself in a remote foreign land; conceive that you there commit a capital error, no matter of what nature or from what motives, but one whose consequences must follow you through life and taint all your existence. Mind, I don't say a *crime*; I am not speaking of shedding of blood or any other guilty act, which might make the perpetrator amenable to the law; my word is *error*. [. . .] Heart-weary and soul-withered, you come home after years of solitary banishment: you make a new acquaintance – how or where no matter: you find in this stranger much of the good and bright qualities you have sought for twenty years, and never before encountered; and they are all fresh, healthy, without soil and taint. Such society revives, regenerates: you feel better days come back – higher wishes, purer feelings; you desire to recommence your life, and to spend what remains to you of days in a way more worthy of an immortal being. To attain this end, are you justified in over-leaping an obstacle of custom – a mere conventional impediment which neither your conscience sanctifies nor your judgement approves?'

He paused for an answer: and what was I to say? Oh, for some good spirit to suggest a judicious and satisfactory response! [. . .]

Again Mr Rochester propounded his query –

'Is the wandering and sinful, but now rest-seeking and repentant, man justified in daring the world's opinion, in order to attach to him for ever this gentle, gracious genial stranger, thereby securing his own peace of mind and regeneration of life?'

'Sir,' I answered, 'a wanderer's repose or a sinner's reformation should never depend on a fellow-creature. Men and women die; philosophers falter in wisdom, and Christians in goodness: if any one you know has suffered and erred, let him look higher than his equals for strength to amend and solace to heal.'

'But the instrument – the instrument! God, who does the work, ordains the instrument. I have myself – I tell it you without parable – been a worldly dissipated, restless man; and I believe I have found the instrument for my cure in – '

He paused: [. . .]

Follow steps (I)–(VIII) (4.4.1) so as to get your initial bearings. Also draw on the reviews of discourse acts and strategies in 4.3 to examine in detail just how the power relations among these two characters are realised. Then consider how you might intervene in this text so as to challenge and change the existing relations (ie, step (IX), p. 145).

Here are some further cues to help knit the reading and re-writing of this passage into the concerns of this chapter and the book as a whole.

(1)

Consider *discourse* as an effect not only of language but also of *social interaction in context.* Therefore, consider:

(a) *participant relations* (here male employer and female employee);

(b) *context* (the arbour and bench – pastoral and property);

(c) *actions and/as words* (e.g. 'Sit,'; 'he paused').

(2)

Consider Rochester as the architect of a rigged dialectic. For instance, notice that he offers Jane a hypothetical world ('fancy: suppose . . . imagine . . . a wild boy . . .') and a hypothetical problem couched in terms of spiritualised thesis and antithesis ('Heart-weary and soul withered . . . higher wishes, purer feelings'). He then asks her to supply the 'synthesis'; but does so in the form of a heavily rhetorical question geared for a certain kind of response ('To attain this end, are you justified in overleaping . . .?'). How, then, might these exchanges be re-framed so as to explore a genuinely open, non-predetermined dialectic? What other hypotheses could be brought forward and by whom?

(3)

Consider the functions of the personal pronouns (especially 'I' and 'you'), and the complex range of subject/agent positions which they offer to the ideal narratee. With whom do you, as an *actual reader*, align yourself most firmly – and why? Try out the 'mobile triangle of subject positions' to assist in this (see 2.2, fig. 2.4).

(4)

A crucial 'turning-point' and an alternative response. Jane *and* the reader are left with an acute dilemma at one point: 'He paused for an answer: and what was I to say?' How 'assertive' – or evasive – do you find her answer to be? What else *might she* have said at this point? And what *would you* have preferred her to say? Perhaps develop this into a very different interaction with a very different outcome, gauging the tensions between 'her' and 'you'. (cf. 3.3.3 and 4.3).

The 'capital error' which Rochester said he made 'in a remote foreign land' was to marry a Creole woman. Once they came to live in England she went 'mad' and, even as Rochester speaks, is secretly locked up in a part of Thornfield Hall. These are the events Rochester is going such a roundabout way to conceal/reveal.

What follows is a passage from Jean Rhys' *Wide Sargasso Sea* (1966). This is a novel devoted to telling the story of the 'mad' Mrs Rochester ('Antoinette') before she came to England and before the action of Brontë's *Jane Eyre*. This is therefore an interesting instance of one novel written *after* another but with the aim of charting fictional events *before* those previously represented – not so much a sequel as a *pre*quel. It is also a highly instructive example of intertextuality as critical-creative intervention, knitting elements of auto/biography with elements of colonial history (Rhys was herself half Creole and born in Dominica, coming to England at age 16).

Familiarise yourself thoroughly with the following passage. It is complex and offers many voices and perspectives, and is well worth the effort (Rhys, 1966: 85). Bear in mind that Antoinette, Rochester's wife, is a Creole woman and that the 'I' who narrates is a recently married Edward Rochester. They are in Jamaica in the late eighteenth century. Christophine, a black serving woman and friend of the family, has just been telling off Antoinette's black maid for singing a song in Jamaican patois that appears to slight her mistress.

> 'She worthless and good for nothing,' said Christophine with contempt. 'She creep and crawl like centipede.'
> She kissed Antoinette on the cheek. Then she looked at me, shook her head, and muttered in patois before she went out.
> 'Did you hear what that girl was singing?' Antoinette said.
> 'I don't always understand what they say or sing.' Or anything else.
> 'It was a song about a white cockroach. That's me. That's what they call all of us who were here before their own people in Africa sold them to the slave traders. And I've heard English women call us white niggers. So between you I often wonder who I am and where is my country and where do I belong and why was I ever born at all. Will you go now please. I must dress like Christophine said.'
> After I had waited half an hour I knocked at her door. There was no answer so I asked Baptiste to bring me something to eat. He was sitting under the Seville orange tree at the end of the veranda. He served the food with such a mournful expression that I thought these people are very vulnerable. How old was I when I learned to hide what I felt? A very small boy. Six, five, even earlier. It was necessary, I was told, and that view I have always accepted. If these mountains challenge me, or Baptiste's face, or Antoinette's eyes, they are mistaken, melodramatic, unreal (England must be quite unreal and like a dream she said).

Re-trace steps (I)–(VIII) (4.4.1, pp. 143–5) so as to explore the particular configuration of voices and discourses in play. Attempts at variously differentiated dramatic readings (steps (III) and (IV)) are especially rewarding. So rich is the interplay – and overlay – of voices and thoughts. Do this before reading on.

Here are some specific cues for further analysis, discussion and experiment.

(1)

'I don't always understand what they say or sing.' Or anything else. Edward is here presented in dialogue not only with Antoinette but also with himself. And in the last paragraph he proceeds from observing Baptiste's 'mournful expression' to the general observation that 'these people are very vulnerable'. This in turn prompts him to the inner enquiry: 'How old was I when I learned to hide what I felt?' Consider this as a representation of that dialogue between 'self' and 'other', 'personal' and 'public' wor(l)ds described by Vygotsky in terms of 'inner' and 'outer voices' (see Vygotsky 1934, and 5.1). How, on balance, does Edward resolve the dialogue here: preferring what view of himself in relation to others? And what view of him do you think we are being encouraged to form by the narrator behind him (i.e. Jean Rhys)? Does she seem to approve or disapprove?

(2)

'So between you I often wonder who I am and where is my country . . .'. Antoinette's identity crisis is presented not so much as 'personal' as the result of external pressures from contending social – here primarily racial – groups. On one side the black maid taunts her with 'a song about a white cockroach'; on another side 'I've heard English women call us white niggers.' Both sides use the word 'white' – but they refract it differently. It is as though the one colour has many shades of meaning, depending who is using it and with what aim.

(3)

'Patois'? The only trace of the native language variety that we get here is in Christophine's speech. And then it is characterised solely by ellipsis of the verb 'to be' ('She worthless . . .') and by the uninflected third-person verbs ('She cree*p* and craw*l*'). For the rest we are simply told that Christophine 'muttered in patois before she went out'. However, we are not told precisely what she muttered. Nor, even if we were told – and especially if it were accurately represented – would many of us be likely to understand it instantly. For the fact is that many of us habitually use other varieties of English ('other englishes') and therefore, like Edward, would not 'always understand what they say or sing'. In short, Rhys' text is here written through the wor(l)ds of 'standard English'. Other voices and discourses are referred to, and are even marginal presences. But they are framed by and on the edges of a certain 'wor(l)d order': a certain way of organising words; and, in this case, through Edward, a certain way of ordering the world. We might therefore say that *Wide Sargasso Sea* offers us a dialogue 'within' a certain version of the English language; just as the novel as a sequel/prequel to *Jane Eyre* offers an extended dialogue with/in 'English literature'. Extended, yes. Ruptured and re-made, maybe not.

At the close of the above passage there is a contest between 'unrealities'. Edward is shown resisting 'these mountains . . . Baptiste's face, or Antoinette's eyes' as 'mistaken, melo-dramatic, unreal'. But the last words (bracketed) are those of Antoinette reverberating in Edward's mind: '(England must be quite unreal and like a dream she said).' Competing unrealities, yes. But not, as yet, an alternative reality. We now extend this dialogue still further: up to and beyond breaking point; up to and beyond the point where 'Eng.' and 'Lang.' and 'Lit.' break down – and where other wor(l)ds and other realities begin to break through.

4.4.4 Conversations across cultures: Johnson and Collins

In this section we look more closely at and listen more attentively to differences within an expanded 'English' – or expanding 'englishes' – depending precisely how we conceive it/them. And as usual, we, as interested language users, have crucial roles to play too.

Here is an extract from Amryl Johnson's 'Conqueror of a forbidden landscape' (1985, in Allnutt *et al.* 1988: 47–8). A boy, Leroy, is bathing in the river close to where his mother, Miss Millie, and her friend Miss Agnes (the boy's teacher) seem to be washing.

Read over this passage tracing the play of words across the page. Meanwhile, begin to think how you personally relate to the various wor(l)ds being represented, and how you might realise them in performance with and for other people.

He could bask along the stream
keep himself cool
shelter and be lost
inside the caves

Slide into a curve

          Boy, yuh ehn hah no shame?!!

slide to

          Miss Millie!

slip further

          Yes Miss Agnes!

deeper into

          Is so you bringin' up yuh son?

the sweet

          De boy eyein' up meh tut-tuts

gentle

          Leroy!

waters

          How he get to be so dam' fresh-up?

where no

          boy is cut-arse fuh yuh

one could reach
him
He loved her
loved Miss Agnes
through sleepless nights
haunted classroom hours
tortured tongue-tied indecision
to offer his feelings

(1)

Where, then, do you see yourself in relation to the various words and worlds on offer? Consider such variables as sex, gender, age, and race, as well as broad linguistic and cultural competences – both in yourself and as figured in the text.

(2)

How do you propose actually reading and perhaps performing the materials in the two columns? Clearly they offer us quite distinct – albeit interconnected – experiences. The left-hand column focuses on the boy Leroy in a lyrical narrative mode and a standard literary variety of English; while the right-hand column focuses on the dramatic exchanges between the two women and is in a colloquial Trinidadian variety. However, do you read *across* from column to column, interleaving snatches of narrative with snatches of conversation (as the lineation seems to invite)? Or do you read straight *down* one column (Leroy/narrative) and then straight down the other (women/drama)? Moreover, in performance would you use one, two three, or more voices – simultaneously or by turns?

After due analysis, experiment and discussion (perhaps also retracing steps (I)–(VIII) on pp. 143–5), decide what suits you and the text best. Resolve the potentially infinite play of its – and your own – differences into a few provisional preferences.

Here are some further activities to help draw on relevant terms and techniques featured elsewhere in the book. In effect, this is a reminder that drama and narrative are intimately interconnected modes, and that cross-cultural dialogues readily turn into (or grow out of) cross-cultural hi/stories. In any event, we are dealing with processes and practices of cultural re/presentation which are potentially visual and, indeed, musical as well as verbal. Hence the multimedia emphasis of this follow-up activity (cf. 3.2).

(3)

How might you transform this text into a short film (or song, or dance, etc.)? More particularly, consider:

who and what might be *observed* how and by whom (notice that both parts of the poem feature observing and observed subjects);

how *interiorised* or *exteriorised* the various speeches, thoughts and actions might be;

how highly *determinate* the setting of this 'forbidden landscape' might be;

what *temporal, spatial and perceptual frames* you would set up, and in what ways you would overlap or alternate them. (Look particularly at the ranges of verbal tense and modality in the two columns; and see Table 3.1 in 3.2.3).

what *styles* and *genres* of film (or music, or dance) you would draw on. (You might, of course, opt for film *with* music and/or dance, etc.; see 5.3.L).

Notice, too, that all of these essentially formal, tactical decisions would ultimately depend upon larger strategic decisions to do with overall interpretation and evaluation, as well as intended viewers and audience. What overall vision or version of events would you be aiming at, and for whom? Given the 'split' nature of the base text, this is likely to hinge on structural contrasts or complementarities. Perhaps water and land? Or sensuality and shame? Or adolescent voyeurism and womanly pragmatism? Or polished lyricism and rough drama – or even the different language varieties and cultures as such? In any event, the question still remains, as in the base text: just how convergent or divergent do you see these two versions and visions of the world to be? And who, where and when is doing the seeing? One event, language, discourse, culture? Or more than one? You, as the most immediate and crucial reader, re-writer and re-viewer, must decide.

(Note: The above passage is an extract from a longer text. Before going on to any larger-scale re-textualisation you are naturally advised to read the poem as a whole and to set about understanding its larger cultural contexts. Perhaps start with the text and surrounding notes in Allnutt *et al.* (1988: 3–4, 47–8, 354); then follow up with the Caribbean-British readings suggested below in 4.6.)

Theoretical interlude

By way of both a break and a link between the last cross-cultural activity and the next, here is a theoretical interlude. It is on the *hybrid* nature of language, culture and history. Indeed, the writers drawn together here themselves represent something of a hybrid; for they include a Caribbean poet, a Russian linguist and a German playwright. A summary proposition is supplied at the end for you to debate and modify as you see fit.

The Barbadian poet, performer and professor Edward Kamau Brathwaite describes the complex linguistic and cultural situation of modern Caribbean peoples as follows (Brathwaite 1984: 5–6):

> All Caribbean people partake in multiple cultures. They partake in the American culture. Some of us partake in the Latin American culture. Then there's the European culture and the Caribbean culture. [. . .] We are at the stage Chaucer was in his time. That's my assessment of it. Chaucer had just started to gel English, French and Latin. We are doing the same thing with our creole concepts, our Standard English, our American, and our modernism.

Now consider this observation in the light of the following theoretical account of linguistic 'hybridisation' offered by Bakhtin (1981: 358–9):

> What is hybridisation? It is a mixture of two social languages within the limits of a single utterance, an encounter, within the arena of an utterance, between two different linguistic consciousnesses, separated from one another by an epoch, by social differentiation or by some other factor.

Bakhtin then goes on to link 'hybridisation' to language change in general, observing that 'unintentional, unconscious hybridisation is one of the most important modes in the historical life and evolution of all languages':

> We may even say that language and languages change historically primarily by means of hybridisation, by means of mixing of various 'languages' co-existing within the boundaries of a single dialect, a single national language, a single branch, a single branch of such branches [. . .] – but the crucible for such mixing always remains the utterance.

And this in turn leads him to reflect upon what he terms 'artistic' or 'intentional' hybridisation. By this he means nothing less than the process whereby every consciously manipulated utterance is inevitably 'hybrid' in that it depends upon a critical and creative distance or difference between the language user and the language used. In this case 'hybridisation' is not so much a 'thing' as an 'activity': the superimposing of the writer's or speaker's design upon the available resources of the language:

The artistic image of a language must by its very nature be a linguistic hybrid (an intentional hybrid): it is obligatory for two linguistic consciousnesses to be present, the one being represented and the other doing the representing, with each belonging to a different system of language. Indeed, if there is not a second language-intention, then what results is not an image (*obraz*) of language but merely a *sample* (*obrazec*) of some other person's language, whether authentic or fabricated.

This 'artistic image of a language', it might be added, corresponds closely to Brecht's notion of drama as the 're-presentation' of an utterance and the theatrical 'gest' as the re-presentation of a gesture. That is, for Brecht, there had to be some more or less conscious distance, some visible and audible difference, between the dramatic representation of an event and the mere presentation of that event. It had, in Bakhtin's terms, to be an 'image of language' not merely 'a sample' (see above 4.1, pp. 125–6). These are all reasons why we have been so careful to expose and examine the precise nature and structure of our own 'dialogic' relation to the texts in hand. In the very act of uttering them we become conscious that in effect we are experiencing the tensions and contradictions of a 'hybrid': between the language as we find it and the language as we re-make it. What's more, in doing this we also expand our consciousness of the multi- and parti-coloured resources at our disposal. For only by recognising our very selves as 'hybrids' (i.e. infinitely differentiated and extensible subject/agents compounded of shifting configurations of 'self' and 'other') can we in fact change and grow. The constant hybridisation of language and culture is therefore an essential condition for our own growth.

Now debate the following proposition *for*, *against* and *alternative* (i.e. by fashioning an alternative proposition):

It is the task of the creative artist to explore the changing and hybrid nature of *cultures* – not to fix them into some single homogeneous entity called *Culture*.

Here is the final move in the present dialogue with/in 'Eng Lit.'. It is in the shape of an extract from a poem and performance-piece by Merle Collins (Cousyn, 1989: 51–3). This somehow succeeds in knitting together the main concerns of this section while still leaving them all teasingly undone. Languages and literatures; English/es – ancient and modern; hybrids and hi/stories; monologues and dialogues; narrative and drama; politics and pleasure; seriousness and fun; struggle and celebration; old and new wor(l)ds – they are all in here somewhere. All *we* have to do is find and make the connections – for ourselves and for one another.

Read over this piece quietly to yourself till you get the hang and the swing of it. Then read it out loud, good and strong.

No Dialects Please

In this competition
dey was lookin for poetry of worth
for a writin that could wrap up a feelin
an fling it back hard
with a captive power to choke de stars
so dey say
'Send them to us
but NO DIALECTS PLEASE'
We're British!

Ay!
Well ah laugh till me bouschet near drop
Is not only dat ah tink
of de dialect of de Normans and de Saxons
dat combine an reformulate
to create a language-elect
is not only dat ah tink
how dis British education mus really be narrow
if it leave dem wid no knowledge of what dey own history is about
is not only dat ah tink
bout de part of my story
dat come from Liverpool in a big dirty white ship mark
AFRICAN SLAVES PLEASE!
We're the British!

But as if dat nat enough pain
for a body to bear
ah tink bout de part on de plantations down dere
Wey dey so frighten o de power
in the deep spaces
behind our watching faces
dat dey shout
NO AFRICAN LANGUAGES PLEASE!
It's against the law!
Make me ha to go
an start up a language o me own
dat ah could share wid me people [. . .]

Ay! Ay!
Ah wonder when it change to
NO DIALECTS PLEASE!
WE'RE British!
Huh!
To tink how still dey so dunce
An so frighten o we power
dat dey have to hide behind a language

that we could wrap roun we little finger
in addition to we own!
Heavens o mercy!
Dat is dunceness oui!
Ah wonder where is de bright British?

Go on to use this piece for:

(a) a final work-out with activities (I)–(IX) on pp.143–5;

(b) further debate about the creative, critical and historical issues raised in the preceding 'theoretical interlude'.

Incidentally, on first reading the title of this particular section (4.4.4), some people expect it to feature Samuel – not Amryl – Johnson, and William or Wilkie – not Merle – Collins. It is instructive to ask 'Why?'

4.5 EXTENDED WORK-OUT: RE-PRODUCING *HAMLET*

This project explores different moments in the production and reproduction of 'the same text' (*Hamlet*) over some four hundred years. More particularly, it focuses on versions of the 'To be or not to be' speech. Notionally, this speech is a *monologue*. Indeed, it is that peculiarly theatrical kind of deliberately overheard dramatic monologue known as a *soliloquy*. And yet, time and again, what we shall be observing people doing with and to this monologue is always in practice a *dialogue*. There is always someone involved 'working on' and 'speaking through' the material; whether this someone is author, scribe, printer, actor, director, film-maker, painter, musician, dancer, critic, reader, audience, you, me, or anyone else. Moreover, this 'working on' and 'speaking through' is invariably done with someone else in mind: actual or imaginary addressees, readerships, audiences; people who in turn will articulate themselves through a slightly or very different dialogue with the materials. We shall therefore always, in practice, be engaging with this monologue as part of an overt or covert series of dialogues in history. And as far as possible we shall be dealing with 'text tokens': actual material instances of texts; particular editions, performances or critiques – *Hamlets* (plural). We shall therefore hardly be concerned with the notion of 'the text type': the general, immaterial, highly abstract idea of some quintessential – and strictly non-existent – *Hamlet* (singular). The same can be said of any text, of course. It's simply that such highly particular dialogic processes are more spectacularly obvious – and sometimes more subtly elusive – with a familiar theatrical text which has been worked over so many ways at so many moments in history.

Commentary will be kept to a minimum so that the passages can speak for themselves in their own terms – and so that you can speak to them directly in yours. Accordingly, the suggested activities are no more than that: suggestions. You may decide to read, analyse, re-write and interrelate these texts differently. Flick through the following pages to see the kinds of *Hamlet* we shall be dealing with. Go through all of them in this order, or pick on particular sections which answer to your present concerns. Either way, in each case, be prepared to recognise yourself as the most recent and, in some respects, the most crucial re-producer of yet another 'Hamlet'.

4.5.1 Alternative base texts

Below are two versions of Hamlet's soliloquy. Version A is from the first printed edition, the Quarto of 1603 (ed. Holderness and Loughry 1992: 60–1). Version B is a modern annotated and repunctuated edition based (as is conventional) on a 'diplomatic' collation of the Second Quarto (1604) with the First Folio (1623) (ed. Hubler 1963: 93–4, III.i.56–89). None of these texts, nor any text of any of the plays, is signed by Shakespeare. An autographed manuscript does not exist. Consequently, for the moment, you are invited to treat these two versions as equally authoritative and authentic. And if you *do* find one version more familiar, you are asked to reflect that it is not necessarily either the earliest or the best. (Defining what we mean by 'best' and for whom is the main point of the ensuing exercises.)

At this point in the play Prince Hamlet is being spied on by his uncle, King Claudius, and a court counsellor, called Corambis in the First Quarto and Polonius in later versions. They are watching to see if Hamlet's apparent madness is caused by love of Polonius'/ Corambis' daughter, Ophelia, or by something else. Ophelia is greeted at the close of these speeches.

Read through each speech a couple of times so as to get the feel of it. Then note the main differences and begin building up a provisional sense of preferences.

Version A: First Quarto (1603)

HAMLET: To be or not to be, I there's the point,
To Die, to sleepe, is that all? I all:
No, to sleepe, to dreame, I mary there it goes,
For in that dream of death, when wee awake,
And borne before an everlasting Judge,
From whence no passenger ever retur'nd,
The undiscovered country, at whose sight
The happy smile, and the accursed damn'd.
But for this, the joyfull hope of this,
Whol'd beare the scornes and flattery of the world,
Scorned by the right rich, the rich curssed of the poore?
The widow being oppressed, the orphan wrong'd,
The taste of hunger, or a tirants raigne,
And thousand more calamities besides,
To grunte and sweate under this weary life,
When that he may his full Quietus make,
With a bare bodkin, who would this indure,
But for a hope of something after death?
Which pusles the brain, and doth confound the sence,
Which makes us rather beare those evilles we have,
Than flie to others that we knowe not of.
I that, O this conscience makes cowardes of us all,
Lady in thy orizons, be all my sinnes remembered.

Version B: Second Quarto (1604)/First Folio (1623)

HAMLET: To be, or not to be: That is the question:
Whether 'tis nobler in the mind to suffer
The slings and arrows of outrageous fortune,
Or to take arms against a sea of troubles.
And by opposing end them. To die, to sleep –   60
No more – and by a sleep to say we end
The heartache, and the thousand natural shocks
That flesh is heir to! 'Tis a consummation
Devoutly to be wished. To die, to sleep –
To sleep – perchance to dream: ay, there's the rub*,   65
For in that sleep of death what dreams may come
When we have shuffled off this mortal coil*,
Must give us pause. There's the respect*
That makes calamity of so long life:*
For who would bear the whips and scorns of time,   70
Th'oppressor's wrong, the proud man's contumely,
The pangs of despised love, the laws' delay
Th'insolence of office, and the spurns
That patient merit of th'unworthy takes,
When he himself might his quietus* make   75
With a bare bodkin*? Who would fardels* bare
To grunt and sweat under a weary life,
But that the dread of something after death,
Th'undiscovered country from whose bourn*
No traveler returns, puzzles the will,
And makes us rather bear those ills we have   80
Than fly to others that we know not of?
Thus conscience* does make cowards of us all,
And thus the native hue of resolution
Is sicklied o'er with the pale cast* of thought,
And enterprises of great pitch* and moment,   85
With this regard* their current turns awry,
And lose the name of action – Soft you now,
The fair Ophelia! – Nymph, in thy orisons*
Be all my sins remembered.   90

65 *rub* impediment (obstruction to a bowler's ball)
67 *coil* (1) turmoil (2) a ring of rope (here the flesh encircling the soul)
68 *respect* consideration
69 *makes calamity of so long life* (1) makes calamity so long-lived (2) makes living so long a calamity
75 *quietus* full discharge (a legal term)
76 *bodkin* a dagger
76 *fardels* burdens
79 *bourn* region
83 *conscience* self-consciousness, introspection
85 *cast* color
86 *pitch* height (a term from falconry)
87 *regard* consideration
89 *orisons* prayers

Clearly, these are not just different versions of supposedly 'the same text'. They are in various ways quite different texts. Even leaving aside differences of 'content', the texts are presented and processed very differently. Version A is virtually as it appears in the First Quarto: spelling and punctuation (with the exception of the 's') follow early seventeenth-century writers' and printers' usages; there are no line numbers and no notes. Version B, on the other hand, is not only a collation of two distinct texts (hence, in part, the increased length); it also uses modern spellings and is thoroughly repunctuated (! – ; and , are liberally inserted). Moreover, Version B is extensively glossed and annotated so as to provide the modern reader with help in understanding and interpreting unfamiliar words, constructions and discourses – sporting, legal, etc. (Many editions do this even more, e.g. the New Oxford and Arden.)

Our first activities, therefore, are designed to expose this situation. We shall recognise the processes of editorial representation and reproduction that are at work by inverting them. Version A will be processed like Version B, and vice versa.

(1)

(a) Modernise and standardise the spelling and punctuation of Version A so as to make it look more familiar and make more immediately plausible sense. (Hint: remember that Hamlet appears to be mad. Consequently, as in Version B, the trick is to use punctuation such as commas, dashes and exclamation marks to construct a sense of a mind and a speech hovering near – but not over – the brink of madness.) Label the resulting text Version A1.

(b) Go on to add line numbers and brief annotations to your Version A1. Some of the latter can simply be transferred from those for Version B. Otherwise just add an asterisk where you feel a note might explain – and maybe explain away – a difficult word, construction or concept. Check with the *Oxford English Dictionary* where possible.

(2)

Strip away *all* the existing punctuation from Version B and re-punctuate it using only commas, full stops and question marks. Aim to make the structure of thought and speech less logical and clear, and perhaps less 'acceptable'. Go on to remove all the line numbers and annotations. The overall aim is to scramble the textual sense and the sense-making apparatus of Version B. Label the resulting text Version B1.

(3)

This activity can be done dialogically in the form of a debate or trial, or monologically through free-standing essay or speech.

(a) Mount a spirited defence of Version A (or A1) and an equally spirited attack on Version B (or B1) with regard to their relative effectiveness, significance and value. Invoke such criteria as simplicity and complexity; directness and indirectness; spare or dense imagery; ease or difficulty of delivery and performance; in/action; ease of understanding off the page; etc. Specify the kind of 'ideal' reader and/or audience each would be more effective for.

(b) Now do the reverse. Argue that Version B (or B1) is more effective than Version A (or A1). Draw on exactly the same differences but wield them so as to support an opposite preference. This will presumably also entail the construction of a different 'ideal' reader and/or audience from that envisaged in 3(a).

(4)

Finally, debate the following proposition in three ways: *for*, *against* and *alternative* **(i.e., in favour of a modified or different proposition):**

Students should only study from modernised, annotated editions which conflate the best texts.

4.5.2 Editors' and actors' responses

Here are two comments on Version A (the First Quarto). They use very different discourses to talk about 'the same text'. How would you characterise those differences?

(A2) In general there are three schools of thought: (1) the First Quarto is a badly reported version of an early draft of *Hamlet* as Shakespeare wrote it once and for all; (2) it is a badly reported version of an early draft of Shakespeare's play; and (3) it was expanded from some actor's parts of an early version. This last seems most likely [. . .] All three levels are to be found in the soliloquy beginning 'To be or not to be.'

(from 'Textual Note' in Hubler, 1963: 174–5)

(A3) *Christopher McCullough*: In my own experience of playing the text I couldn't perform 'I there's the point' by turning in on myself and pretending there wasn't an audience there. 'To be or not to be, I there's the *point*' actually only made sense if I said it *to the audience*. In fact I was using the soliloquy as a way of putting an argument to the audience as to what was going on in the narrative.

(from recorded interview with actor, cited in Holderness and Loughrey, 1992: 25–6)

Systematise and refine your analysis of these discourses by drawing attention to:

referential/experiential content – what each is about;

participants and functions – who is writing/speaking and why;

medium and mode – primarily printed or spoken; as part of monologue or dialogue;

linguistic features – predominantly first, second or third person ('inter/personalised' or 'depersonalised'); active or passive verbs; verbal and adverbial markers of tense, modality and aspect; kinds of linguistic cohesion and perceptual coherence.

Overall, then, how far do these two accounts reconstitute 'the same text' (the First Quarto) as in effect two different events? And are there any automatic grounds for preferring one version rather than another? More pointedly, do you prefer to treat a dramatic text as 'an object of historical scholarship' or as 'part of a performance process relating actors to audiences'? And is there necessarily an absolute difference between these positions?

4.5.3 Novelistic responses

Placing one text within another always generates a dialogue. Often this takes the form of 'known text' in 'new context', with the result that we see both text and context in a new light. This process is particularly marked in novels when they accommodate representations of 'literary classics'. For the novel as a genre tends to be concerned with the representation of contemporary realities, often with a strong sense of social context and a high degree of historical specificity. In such conditions a dialogue between the recalled 'there and then' of the re-presented classic and the pressing 'here and now' of the new context becomes acutely revealing. In fact we are forced to recognise that we can only ever respond to the effects and create the meanings of texts in specific contexts at specific moments in history. This is why Bakhtin was so fascinated by the 'dialogic' possibilities of the novel (see 4.4). The text for us *is* the one we read, see or hear *at that moment in those conditions for those purposes*.

In this section we explore the very different re-presentations and receptions of Hamlet's 'To be or not to be' speech in novels by Charles Dickens and Maya Angelou. For instance, here is how Dickens in *Great Expectations* (1860–1, ch. 31) describes the very active response to the soliloquy by a mid-nineteenth-century popular audience:

(B2) Whenever that undecided prince had to ask a question or state a doubt, the public helped him out with it. As for example: on the question whether 'twas nobler in the mind to suffer, some roared yes, and some no, and some inclining to both opinions, said 'toss up for it;' and quite a debating society arose.

This can be regarded as a prime example of a 'popular carnivalesque' response to a 'high culture classic' (cf. 4.5.6 below). It thwarts, inverts and sports with conventional proprieties and expectations. Some of the questions that arise, then, are these:

What are the conventional proprieties and expectations that are exposed by this treatment?

What is revealed about Hamlet's question by treating it as a real question?

How far does 'theatre' depend upon an agreed distance and difference between the play and non-play worlds, between actors and audiences? (The same applies to 'art' and 'life' in general.)

And are there any conditions in which it is permissible, desirable or simply fun to disagree about those distances and differences: to be *im*polite and *un*cooperative about the boundaries of 'theatre' ('art', etc.) (cf. 4.2)?

Here is another very different siting of Hamlet's 'To be or not to be' speech in novelistic discourse. It comes from Maya Angelou's autobiographical novel *I Know Why the Caged Bird Sings* (1969: 177–8). The scene is speech day in an all-black Southern States school in 1940. Henry Reed, a final-year pupil, is delivering his painstakingly polished valedictory address. This follows hard upon a deeply patronising speech in which the guest of honour, a white man running for state senator, has sought to inspire the school with examples of black sportsmen and popular musicians. The narrating 'I' is amongst the audience.

As you read, notice how the Shakespeare text is being reconstituted by the play of voices and discourses within, through and around it.

(B3) There was shuffling and rustling around me, then Henry Reed was giving his valedictory address, 'To Be or Not to Be'. Hadn't he heard the whitefolks? We couldn't
be so the question was a waste of time. Henry's voice came out clear and strong. I
feared to look at him. Hadn't he got the message? There was no 'nobler in the mind'
for Negroes because the world didn't think we had minds, and they let us know it.
'Outrageous fortune'? Now, that was a joke. When the ceremony was over I had to
tell Henry Reed some things. That is, if I still cared. Not 'rub,' Henry, 'erase.' 'Ah,
there's the erase.' Us.

Henry had been a good student in elocution. His voice rose on tides of promise
and fell on waves of warnings. The English teacher had helped him to create a
sermon winging through Hamlet's soliloquy. To be a man, a doer, a builder, a
leader, or to be a tool, an unfunny joke, a crusher of funky toadstools. I marveled
that Henry could go through the speech as if we had a choice.

(1)

**Explore the vocal and interpersonal dynamics of this passage using the 'audi-
ble' and 'visible structure' methods used with previous novels** (see 4.4.1). This
will help you to realise, dramatically and graphically, just how many complex and multi-
layered dialogues are in play here: with Hamlet's speech; with the speaker of the valedictory address, Henry Reed; with the preceding speech by the guest speaker; and with the
words of the English teacher of elocution. There is also an implicit dialogue between two
parts of the writer as narrator: the adult author communing with and recreating her childhood self. In Vygotsky's terms, there is a remarkably subtle interplay of 'inner (private)
voices' and 'outer (public) voices' (see 5.1).

(2)

**On the basis of your readings of the Angelou and Dickens passages, go on to
debate a couple of the following propositions. Again, do this in plural ways:
for, *against* and *alternative*.**

(a) Apparent monologues always turn out to be dialogues.

(b) Particular texts cannot be fully understood outside particular co-texts and contexts: there is no
such thing as 'the text'.

(c) Discourses of 'the self' are always constituted through discourses with 'others'.

(d) 'Inner voices' (half-expressed feelings, thoughts, etc.) are as much a part of any cultural history
as 'outer voices' (public speeches and records) – because the one is a refraction of the other.

(3)

**Use the instances of public heckling in Dickens or of silent resistance in
Angelou as initial models for developing your own critical-creative responses
to a particular text.** For instance, you might imagine (or recall) yourself and some friends
at some performance, reading, speech or lecture (of anything from a Shakespeare play to
last week's lecture or last night's gathering round the TV). How might you – or did you –
respond: collectively or individually; audibly or silently; approvingly, sceptically or resis-
tantly. And what might the visible effect be – if any – on the development of that event?

The main thing is to explore some text or part of a text in an overtly dialogic mode: recognising it as a site of potential celebration or conflict; a 'space' ceaselessly subject to the play of differences and the expression of preferences. This is, if you like, simply a narrative or dramatic way of contextualising and motivating the kinds of comment that people make all the time informally in the margins of pages, under their breaths, or in the corners of their minds. The difference is that the act of critical-creative composition brings them into the foreground and puts them centre-stage or page.

4.5.4 Earlier and later twentieth-century critics

We now turn to versions of 'Hamlet' offered by three bastions of the early twentieth-century Anglo-American theatrical and literary establishments: A.C. Bradley, Harley Granville-Barker and T.S. Eliot. These were all, in their respective capacities as professor of poetry, theatre director/critic, and poet/editor, highly influential in generating the kind of dominant cultural ethos breathed by the young Angelou (and everyone else) in 1940.

Read over these extracts a couple of times, trying to see each as simply a different 'version' of the *Hamlet* soliloquy. What 'worldview' does each assume or assert? Are there any 'key' terms? And are these instances of discourses you yourself would be happy to adopt or adapt? (If not, which terms and discourses would you prefer?)

(B4) *Hamlet* most brings home to us the sense of the soul's infinity, and the sense of the doom which not only circumscribes that infinity but appears to be its offspring [. . .] He [Hamlet] is meditating on suicide; and he finds what stands in the way of it, and counterbalances its infinite attraction, is not any thought of sacred unaccomplished duty, but the doubts, quite irrelevant to that issue, whether it is not ignoble in the mind to end its misery, and, still more, whether death would end it.

(Bradley, 1905: 128, 132)

(B5) 'To be or not to be, that is the question . . .' These unmodulated changes from storm to calm smack a little – and are meant to – of 'madness'. But how the man's moral quality shows in the fact that he can thus escape from his suffering to this stoically detached contemplation of greater issues.

(Granville-Barker, 1930: 70)

(B6) Hamlet's bafflement at the absence of objective equivalent to his feeling is a prolongation of the bafflement of his creator in the face of his artistic problem [which is] 'expressing emotion in the form of art' [finding an] objective correlative [. . .] a set of objects, a situation, a chain of events, which shall be the formula of this particular emotion.

T.S. Eliot, 'Hamlet' (1919) in Jump, 1968: 39–40.

(1)

Try 'translating' one or more of these passages into an idiom and a 'way of saying' with which you feel easier or are more familiar. What does this show up about the social and historical differences and distances between yourself and that writer?

(2)

Go on to develop a dialogue with one or more of these writers. This might be in the form of marginal glosses or commentaries on particular words and phrases, or in the novelistic or dramatic modes suggested by Dickens and Angelou in 4.5.3 above.

(3)

Convert the 'dialectical discourse questions' in 4.1 (p. 124) into specific questions addressed to each of these extracts. That is, *Whose wor(l)ds* are being represented – and mis-, under- or unrepresented? *Whose interests* . . .? *What preferences* . . .?', etc. Again, this might be textualised through a number of monologic or dialogic modes.

Earlier twentieth-century writers on Shakespeare don't have a monopoly on re-writing him in their own images. Discourses, ideological positions, rhetorical manoeuvres, assumptions and assertions, representation (mis-, under- and un-), the interplay of specific academic, aesthetic and political interests and preferences – manifestations of all these will be found in later twentieth-century critics too – or critics any time.

However, a distinctive feature of much contemporary criticism is that it is (or attempts or affects to be) theoretically 'up front'. Modern critics usually display at least some of their theoretical credentials at the outset. From one point of view this is very much to be encouraged. It prevents people claiming they're members of the only academic club (or 'interpretive community') there is. However, even being 'up front' has its problems, the main one being that older *assumptions* tend to be displaced by newer *assertions*. The premises are no longer veiled; they may indeed be vaunted. But that still leaves the critical reader the challenge of (a) identifying the premises of the model preferred; and (b) deciding how far s/he accepts them. The modern critical-theoretical game may be played more in the open and sometimes, ideologically at least, with 'gloves off' and 'no holds barred'. But the reader as critic still has to decide whose 'side' s/he's on. And, if s/he *doesn't* want to take sides in one particular game (model, debate), then s/he still has to say in what other game (model, debate) s/he *is* prepared to engage. The extracts which follow are chosen and framed with this in mind.

Again, as for the previous extracts, read over these passages, identifying assumptions and assertions, 'key' terms and preferred discourses. How far do you align yourself with such wor(l)ds? And, if not these, which?

(B7)   What it is to be a subject, in short, is a political problem for Hamlet, as it has once more become a political problem for us. Hamlet signifies the beginnings of the dissolution of the old feudalist subject, who is as yet, however, unable to name himself affirmatively in any other way. If we too are as yet unable to give a name to a different form of subjectivity, it is for the opposite reason – that we, unlike Hamlet, are the end-products of a history of bourgeois individualism beyond which we can only gropingly feel our way. Whatever the difference, this may be one reason why the (non-)character of Hamlet seems to speak to us more urgently than any other of Shakespeare's protagonists.

(Eagleton, 1986b: 75)

(B8) Or rather what does it mean to us that one of the most elevated and generally esteemed works of our Western literary tradition should enact such a negative representation of femininity, or even such a violent repudiation of the feminine in man? I say 'esteemed' because Eliot's critique [see (B6) above] has inflated rather than reduced *Hamlet*'s status. In 'Tradition and the individual talent', Eliot says the poet must 'know the mind of Europe [. . .]; Hamlet has more than once been taken as the model for that mind.' Western tradition, the mind of Europe, Hamlet himself, each one the symbol of a cultural order in which the woman is given too much and too little of a place. But it is not perhaps finally inappropriate that those who celebrate or seek to uphold that order, with no regard to the image of the woman it encodes, constantly find themselves up against a problem which they call femininity – a reminder of the precarious nature of the certainties on which that order rests.

(Jacqueline Rose, 'Hamlet – the "Mona Lisa" of literature' in MacCabe, 1988: 47)

(Note: As far as the 'To be or not to be' speech goes, this comment may fairly be attached to the last couple of lines. There Hamlet greets Ophelia as 'Nymph/Lady' and assigns her the role of praying for his sins.)

The next extract is a comparative analysis of two strikingly different film versions of *Hamlet*: Kozintsev's Russian version (1963) and Olivier's English version (1947). But whether you know the films or not, you can still consider this critical text as itself a highly mediated version of – not just a commentary on – the play.

(B9) Kozintsev's *Hamlet* (1963) was intended as an antithesis to the English actor's (Olivier's) psychological reading: a tragedy of a man caught in a climate of political corruption as opposed to one confronting his inner flaw. The landscapes of the two films bear this out. Olivier's Elsinore, despite its Expressionist construction, is a rigidly enclosed area. The camera's depth of focus, its occasional imitation of genre-art naturalism, and its frequent use of of high-angle shots to establish scenes, awards it the authority of an impartial observer clinically picking its way through the Prince's psychological problems. Kozintsev's landscape is vast, limitless and only partially comprehensible. There is a strong feeling of subjectivity (which was to be repeated in *Korol Ler*) behind the drifting viewpoint; the impression that the action, characters and text are part of a vast and intricate dream world.

(Collick, 1989: 135)

Go through the 'translation', 'dialogue' and 'discourse' procedures, as for the earlier twentieth-century critics ((1)–(3), pp. 170–1). Conclude by identifying your own 'key' terms and preferred discourses – and interrogating them too.

4.5.5 Theatrical de- and re-constructions

Hamlet, it is often said, is 'a play about play-acting'. We now look at the ways in which other playwrights have made 'other plays' out of Shakespeare's play. You are finally invited to make one too. This is therefore the time to read or see 'the whole' of Shakespeare's *Hamlet* – or re-read and re-view it. However, by now you will be well aware that different texts and editions exist, and that any performance on stage or film (or off the page and in the head) will also be in many respects unique and tied to a specific moment of reproduction. Nor will it be altogether 'Shakespeare's' play you see or read – whatever we take that to be. Consequently, we had better say that this is the time to (re-)read or (re-)view '*a whole Hamlet*'. Just how 'whole' and precisely 'whose' it is is itself part of the matter at issue.

'Hamlet: The Collage' (1966)

Here are some materials relating to a show put together by Charles Marowitz in association with Peter Brook and the Royal Shakespeare Experimental Group in the mid-1960s (Marowitz 1970: 93–4). They comprise: (a) the scene; (b) a passage from near the close of the play; and (c) part of Marowitz's own rationale. Read over these materials to get a general sense of what Marowitz and Company literally 'made' of *Hamlet*. Then try the activities which follow or devise your own.

(a)   *The scene* (Marowitz, 1970: 40–1)

The court at Elsinore. A plateau in the super-ego. The past as distorted by the present. The present as distorted by the past. A circus. An intellectual plane where various pieces of Shakespeare criticism commingle. Limbo. Heaven. Hell. A theatre.

(b)   *Closing passage* (Marowitz, 1970: 93–4. Look out for some famous lines – recast).

GHOST: . . . Thou comest in such a questionable shape
   That I will speak to thee. I'll call thee Hamlet.
   [*Puts toy sword under Hamlet's arm, like a crutch. The cast, now fully assembled, expresses its delight over the Ghost's send-up.*]
CLOWN [*acknowledging its wit*]: A hit, a very palpable hit.
GHOST [*still playing it up like mad*]: Speak, I am bound to hear.
   [*A long pause, during which everyone's sarcastic laughter gradually mounts*]
HAMLET [*weakly*]: To be or not to be, that is the question.
   [*All laugh*]
   [*weakly*] The play's the thing wherein I'll catch the conscience of the king.
   [*All laugh again*]
   [*vainly trying to find the right words*] There is something rotten in the state of Denmark.
   [*The laughter sharply cuts out. A powerful silence issues from everyone . . .*]

(c)   *Rationale* (Marowitz, 1970: 9–10)

No work of criticism that does not take into account the fact that the play has been around for about 400 years can begin to make sense of what the play means to modern audiences. [. . .]
   Is it possible to express one's view of Hamlet without the crutch of narrative? [. . .]
   Can a play which is very well known be reconstructed and redistributed so as to make a new work of art? [. . .]
   Must we forever be receiving Shakespeare; why can't Shakespeare *receive us*?

Here are some further questions and suggestions:

(1)

Where would *you* locate *Hamlet* conceptually and theatrically? And if not in the same times and spaces as Marowitz (see (a)) – when and where?

(2)

Follow up the lines gathered by Marowitz in (b) to their contexts in one of Shakespeare's texts (e.g. Hubler, 1963). What is the effect of redistributing and recontextualising them in this way? *Meanwhile, consider how legitimate and valuable 'collage' is as a critical-creative strategy.* What effects can it achieve that the conventional essay or commentary cannot achieve – and vice versa?

(3)

Debate each of the propositions in Marowitz's rationale (c): *for*, *against* and *alternative*.

Stoppard's Rosencrantz and Guildenstern are Dead *(1966)*

Whereas Marowitz cut up, redistributed and re-set *Hamlet*, Tom Stoppard in *Rosencrantz and Guildenstern are Dead* inverted and de- and re-centred it. The play was first performed as part of the alternative 'fringe' of the Edinburgh festival in 1966. The venue was apt; for the play takes a couple of very shadowy 'fringe' figures from Shakespeare's version (the courtiers Rosencrantz and Guildenstern) and puts them slap bang centre-stage. What's more, the stage is virtually empty. (Parallels with *Waiting for Godot* are numerous and acknowledged; cf. 4.3.2.) Accordingly, like the two tramps in Beckett's play, these two courtiers are companions who while away the time anxiously and comically trying to work out who and where they are, what they are supposed to be doing and why.

The play is quite well known and was turned into a film, with Stoppard himself adapting the script, in 1991. For this reason and for reasons of space, the extracts which follow (the initial scene and a closing passage) are brief. As with the previous 'collage', they are meant to be no more than illustrative of a particular strategy. Again, read over these materials to get a general sense of what Stoppard is doing with *Hamlet*. Some suggestions and questions follow.

The opening scene (Stoppard, 1967: 7)

> *Two ELIZABETHANS passing the time in a place without any visible character. They are well dressed – hats, cloaks, sticks and all. Each of them has a large leather money bag. GUILDENSTERN'S bag is nearly empty. ROSENCRANTZ'S is nearly full. The reason being: they are betting on the toss of a coin . . .*

Closing speeches The two anti-heroes are trying to sum up what they have (not) done and to grasp what they have (not) learnt about their relation to Hamlet, the plot and their own identities (pp. 80,91):

> Ros: The position as I see it, then. We, Rosencrantz and Guildenstern, from our young days brought up with him [Hamlet], awakened by a man standing on his saddle, are summoned, and arrive, and are instructed to glean what afflicts him and draw him on to pleasures, such as a play, which unfortunately, as it turns out, is abandoned in some confusion owing to certain nuances outside our appreciation [. . .]
>
> Guil: Our names shouted in a certain dawn . . . a message . . . a summons . . . There must have been a moment, at the beginning, where we could have said – no. But somehow we missed it.

[*He looks round and sees he is alone*]

Ros: —— ?

Guil: —— ?

Well, we'll know better next time. Now you see me, now you ——

[*And disappears*]

[*Immediately the whole stage is lit up, revealing, upstage, arranged in the approximate positions last held by the dead* TRAGEDIANS, the tableau of court and corpses which is the last scene of 'Hamlet']

Stoppard's play is a witty and highly instructive instance of the systematic de- and re-centring of a classic text. It is also very self-consciously 'playful' in its theatricality and its sporting with the boundaries between the 'play' and 'non-play' worlds. However, it must be insisted that Stoppard's is *not* the only possible de- and re-centring of Shakespeare's play. It does not realise the only alternative centres that may be inferred. And as with any text, however highly metatextual, there are some aspects of its own textuality it assumes or ignores. Consequently, it is also important to treat Stoppard's version of *Hamlet* not only as an alternative point of arrival but also as an alternative point of departure. What can we learn from it – for, against and alternative? The following activities should open up some more of the problems and possibilities.

On the basis of *your* **reading of** *Hamlet*, **what** *other* **alternative centres might be brought into the critical-creative foreground?** More particularly, what other focuses might there be in terms of, say:

gender (Gertrude, Ophelia, Ophelia's unmentioned mother . . .)?

class/rank (more from the soldiers (I.i); the grave-diggers (V.i); non-speaking servants . . .)?

race, nationality (more from the Norwegians; the Polacks – even the English . . .)?

At the same time, consider how you might textualise these possibilities. What strategies, genres and media might you draw on? 'Plays of plays' are only the most obvious possibility. Further novelistic or filmic re-centring and recontextualising are also conceivable (cf. Angelou in 4.5.3; and Collick in 4.5.4). And for a fuller array of possible textual modes, turn to 5.3.

Meanwhile, you might like to consider the following accounts of still other productions and reproductions of *Hamlet*. They point to methods, media and material so far hardly touched upon.

Feminist representations

Though she is neglected in criticism, Ophelia is probably the most frequently illustrated and cited of Shakespeare's heroines. Her visibility as a subject in literature, popular culture, and painting, from Redon who paints her drowning, to Bob Dylan, who places her on Desolation Row, to Cannon Mills, which has named a flowery sheet pattern after her, is in inverse relation to her invisibility in Shakespearean texts. . . .

But what can we mean by Ophelia's story? The story of her life? The story of her betrayal at the hands of her father, brother, lover, court, society? The story of her rejection and marginalisation by male critics of Shakespeare? . . .

In terms of effect on the theatre, the most radical application of these ideas was probably realized in Melissa's Murray's agitprop play *Ophelia* written in 1979 for the English women's theater group 'Hormone Imbalance'. In this blank verse retelling of the Hamlet story, Ophelia becomes a lesbian and runs off with a woman servant to join a guerrilla commune . . . [But] I can't proclaim that this defiant ideological gesture, however effective politically or theatrically, is all that feminist criticism desires, or all to which it should aspire.

(Elaine Showalter, 'Representing Ophelia: women, madness and the responsibilities of feminist criticism', in Parker and Hartmann, 1985: 77–8)

A socialist rehearsal strategy

Brecht encouraged the actors to explore the problems and possibilities of plays both through their own improvisation and through alternative scripts supplied by himself as director-writer (the *Dramaturg*). One of the results was a little 'parallel scene' developed from what Brecht saw as 'valuable fracture points' within the play. The purpose and substance of this rehearsal piece is explained at length in Brecht's *Work Journal* (1948), and neatly summarised by Margot Heinemann as follows:

> This is the point of the little 'parallel scene' Brecht wrote for actors in rehearsal. Hamlet, on his way to England in Act IV, reaches the coast and learns from the ferryman that relations between Denmark and Norway have now been settled by a treaty, whereby Denmark gives up the piece of coastline in dispute and Norway contract to buy Danish fish, so that a war has become unnecessary. Hamlet approves this change from old feudal to modern bourgeois behaviour. 'The new methods, friend. You find that now all over the place. Blood doesn't smell good any more. Tastes have changed'.

> The idea is not to act this to the audience, but to make the rehearsing actor aware that Hamlet is living in a time of changing values, and has a real choice.
>
> (Heinemann, 1985: 218; also see above 4.1, pp. 125–6)

Audience participation and intervention

Below is an actor's account of a remarkable moment in a production of *Hamlet* at Broadmoor high security psychiatric hospital in 1991. This production, part of a series which included improvisation and audience participation, was put on by a collective of volunteers from the Royal Shakespeare, National Theatre and Wilde Theatre Companies. It is offered here as a pointed and poignant instance of the ways in which the realisation of a classic text can be radically re-articulated in the consciousness of both actors and audiences.

Mark Rylance played Hamlet on this occasion. He is describing the effect both upon himself and the audience (all of whom were patients or their carers) of the way they played the 'graveyard scene' (Hubler 1963: V.i). I shall quote at length and without interruption. For this conversation is its own best brief chronicle of a deeply dramatic intervention and its profoundly personal and interpersonal consequences.

MARK RYLANCE: . . . That was a very good experience. The thing I remember most about it was doing the graveyard scene and allowing everyone else to take part, and just to imagine they were part of the society of Elsinore and had come to the funeral of Ophelia. It was an improvisation with the lines and we said, 'Come and stand around and imagine you are present and you haven't been there before and react – if you want to say anything or do anything, just go ahead'. One person fainted, I think, and sat down in a chair. There was an amazing moment when I said to Laertes:

> 'I lov'd Ophelia. Forty thousand brothers
> Could not with all their quantity of love
> Make up my sum' (V.1.273)

and one of the patients stood forward and said 'I believe you'. And it was extraordinary because my heart really choked up and tears flooded into my eyes and I thought – oh I really needed someone to say that. I thought about it afterwards and I always felt in that scene, when playing in front of an audience, while saying that line, that the women in the audience must think that I am such a prick. I had been so awful to the feminine in this play – to Ophelia, to Gertrude. I have transferred so much shit onto them and been so unreasonable with them and the feminine side of myself. I always expected someone to stand up and say 'Fuck off, you self-indulgent little bastard' [. . .] So when this man stepped forward I felt 'Yes, only perhaps someone like you would understand'. Perhaps that is part of why I wanted to go – or Hamlet in me wanted to go; a feeling that people would understand.

(from Cox, 1992: 41–2)

For many partial parallels, but within a fully scripted and choreographed framework, see Peter Weiss' *Marat/Sade* (1964), the subtitle of which is *The Persecution and Assassination of Marat as performed by the Inmates of the Asylum of Charenton under the direction of the Marquis de Sade.*

Two modern parodies

Here are extracts from two very different modern treatments of the 'To be or not to be' speech. Be appalled or delighted, offended or inspired.

(B10)
HAMLET [Alone]: To fuck or be fucked.
(*Enter* OPHELIA)
OPHELIA: My Lord!
HAMLET: Fuck off to a nunnery!

[*They exit in different directions*]
(from Richard Curtis, *The Skinhead Hamlet. Shakespeare's play translated into Modern English* (1982) in Brett, 1984: 318)

(B11)
PRODUCER: *Act 3* may be a bit long. In fact, generally, I think we've got a bit of a length problem [. . .] Some of that stand-up stuff in the middle of the action.
SHAKESPEARE: You mean the soliloquies?
PRODUCER: Yes. And I think we both know which is the dodgy one [. . .] To

be . . . nobler in the mind . . . mortal coil, that one. It's boring, Bill. The crowd hates it. Yawnsville.

SHAKESPEARE: Well, that one happens to be my favourite, actually.

PRODUCER: Bill, you said that about the avocado monologue in *King Lear*. And the tap dance at the end of *Othello*. Be flexible. [. . .] Give it some pizzazz. How does it begin that speech?

SHAKESPEARE: 'To be'.

PRODUCER: Come on, Bill.

SHAKESPEARE: 'To be a victim of all life's earthly woes or not to be a coward and take death by his proffered hand'.

PRODUCER: There, now, I'm sure we can get that down.

SHAKESPEARE: No, absolutely not. It's perfect.

PRODUCER: How about 'To be a victim or not to be a coward'?

SHAKESPEARE: It doesn't make sense, does it? To be a victim of what? To be a coward about what?

PRODUCER: OK, OK, take out 'victim', take out 'coward'. Just start 'To be or not to be'.

SHAKESPEARE: You can't say that. It's gibberish.

PRODUCER: But it's short, William. It's *short*. Listen to it – it flows. 'To be or not to be, that is the question.' Da da da da da da da da da da da.

SHAKESPEARE: You're damned right, it's the question. They won't have any bloody idea what he's talking about.

(from Rowan Atkinson and Hugh Lawrie, 'A small re-write'
in Fry, Mayer and Swann, 1991: 104–5)

Re-telling Horatio's tale

At the close of the play the dying Hamlet expressly enjoins his companion Horatio to 'report me and my cause aright / To the unsatisfied' (V.2, ll. 340–1). In fact, Hamlet spends not a little of his last breath spelling out precisely how this is to be done (ll.347–9):

> If thou didst ever hold me in thy heart,
> Absent thee from felicity awhile,
> And in this harsh world draw thy breath in pain
> To tell my story.

This is an an injunction with which his friend readily concurs. Surveying the final carnage, Horatio remarks (ll.378–81):

> . . . give order that these bodies
> High on a stage be placed to the view,
> And let me speak to th'yet unknowing world
> How these things came about.

Put your own name into the 'Horatio slot' – then tell it *your* way. Alternatively, put in the name of any other figure – inside or outside the play – whose potential version of events you consider valuable or interesting. The main thing is that you renegotiate and relocate the 'space' that is Horatio. For instance, some names that students have previously put in the 'Horatio slot' include: Austen, Dickens, Ibsen, Strindberg, Shaw, Brecht, Beckett, Osborne, Theatre Workshop,

Tarkovsky, Spielberg and Caryll Churchill. Each of these has thus been charged with the task of 'speaking to th'yet unknowing world'. And each has been made to do so in ways which involve not just the simple 'transfer' of Shakespeare's idiom, characters, situations and settings into those of another period and place, but a fundamental *transformation* of discourses and issues into those characteristically realised by another writer in another historical moment. As the commentaries invariably confirm, the critical-creative difference opened up by such 're-tellings' is highly revealing.

4.5.6   Hamlet the cigars!

This is the advert of the cigars of the myth of the play. It's about as far away from – and perhaps our most peculiar route back into – Shakespeare as we have time and space for here. The same crazily non/sensical path can be trod with any classic text. In fact, it perhaps *has* to be *re*-trod if we are really to make sense of such texts in their own terms and historical moments as well as our own. We cannot uncreate the present. And yet we are obliged in every sense to 'see through the present' in order to recreate the past. In the terms of contemporary cultural debates: we must 'see through' post-modernism with an eye trained on a radically historicist perspective.

For the past 30 years in Britain (since 1964) there has been a series of adverts for minia-ture cigars. The cigars are called Hamlet and the ads for them have become a familiar part of British popular culture (so much so that the tobacco company released a compila-tion video in 1992). The basic situation depicted is always the same, though precise figures and scenes vary considerably and, as usual with long-running ads, there is an increasing tendency towards knowing self-parody. What we are basically presented with is a man with a problem – or more precisely, *a man with a predicament.* Something goes wrong, and we are momentarily left asking 'What is he going to do about it?' A violinist is playing in an orchestra – and his violin disintegrates in his hands. King Canute is trying to stop the sea coming in – in vain. Napoleon stands on a battlefield – at the end of Waterloo. A man is entertaining a woman in a restaurant – and his toupee slips for-ward over his eyes. A man in a three-wheeler car accidentally knocks over a whole row of Hell's Angels' motorbikes – and they see him do it. And so on. In each and every case the man in question is left with a predicament. And so are we, the viewers, in so far as we identify with him. So how is this predicament resolved?

Cue Bach's 'Air on a G string' (slow, deep, moving bass; smooth strings). The man reaches into a pocket, pulls out a pack of cigars, lights one. And then, as the first puff of smoke and relief issues from his quietly smiling lips and his face lights up with satisfaction, a male voice-over (also 'mature' and 'mellow') says:

Happiness is a cigar called Hamlet.

The mild cigar. From Benson and Hedges.

Predicament solved. Satisfaction achieved. Cigar advertised.

Now, there are just a few, rather obvious observations I want to make about all this. How-ever, as they lead to conclusions about cultural processes and especially critical practices that may be less immediately obvious, they are perhaps still worth making. All of them involve 'Hamlets' of one kind or another.

(1) *'Hamlet' is a handy name for a miniature cigar* because it draws on a dual denotation: (a) it's the name of the tragic hero in the most famous play by the most famous English playwright, and therefore carries the connotation 'classic' (incidentally, there's a brand of miniature cigar called Classic too); (b) it's also the archaic word for a small village, usually with connotations of 'olde worlde' rustic charm (e.g. 'cosy hamlet').

(2) *'Hamlet' is a handy name for a series of situations where a man is in a fix.* What's more, like the hero of the play, he is always alone and his predicament is all but impossible. According to the current popular view at least, Hamlet is frozen in the moment where he weighs 'To be or not to be' – and his subsequent decisive plans and actions are ignored (as they are in much traditional criticism in fact). For *this* Hamlet at least, there is seemingly no way out. And yet . . .

(3) *'Hamlet' is a handy name for the temporary solution of that problem because it shows that, after all, there is a way out.* Apparently the answer to burning questions is to smoke a cigar! Notice, therefore, that, in common with most popular cultural forms (whether traditional or highly mediated) this is a distinctly comic and anti-heroic resolution – not a tragic and heroic one, as in the conventional 'high-art' version.

There are of course dialectical converses to all these statements: negatives that they imply and, more actively, negations that they invite. For each one of the above statements begs a question, and if we really want to know what all these various *Hamlets* mis/represent we shall have to ask them vigorously: that is, both attentively and assertively. Some systematic counter-hypotheses ('what if's) should do the trick.

(1) *What if* these miniature cigars were *not* called Hamlet but were called, say, The Taming of the Shrew (slogan: 'the wild's woman's smoke – with filters'?!); or Five Concentrated Cancer Sticks; or Pollutant Pack; or Cash Crop; or More leaves you can't eat; or Urban Overspill (the new Tower Hamlets project)?

(2) *What if* the man – or woman – in the fix looked for an alternative way out of his or her predicament? Not through the quick and costly fix of commodity aesthetics, but through attempting to do something positive about the situation – to challenge and maybe change it. The violinist could mend his violin. Canute could find out when a particularly low tide was due. The man in the toupee could get one that fitted properly – and stop posing for women in restaurants. Even Napoleon could comfort himself by enrolling for a course in 'counterfactual history'! And so on. The serious point, of course, is that people can make and do things and do not have to depend upon what is made and done for them – at a commercial, social and ecological price. To adapt Marx's most famous thesis on Feuerbach: 'the point is to change the world (preferably for the better) – not to consume it (for the worse)'.

(3) *What if* popular 'comic', 'carnival' and 'parodic' impulses were *not* appropriated by advertising agencies so as to serve a totally commodified view of people's relations to themselves, one another and the rest of the natural world. What if they were – as sometimes they are – the expressions of a genuine counter- or alternative culture: *not* fed on (or up with) endless re-hashings of some bogus versions of national heritage but celebrating a culture made by and for ourselves.

Finally, then, *what if* people were encouraged to meet many of the possible real – and really contentious – Hamlets (see previous sections). What if people recognised their power to make 'Hamlet' their own – and 'Hamlets' of their own – and works that did not aspire to be 'Hamlets' at all – simply different and richly their own. That would make a real change from the ad of the cigar of the myth of the play of the man that never was.

4.5.7 A post-post-modernist historical puzzle

This last section will leave us firmly in the 'historical' rather than the 'post-modernist' domain. It takes the form of a hybrid puzzle: a game, a research project, and a cross-cultural, intertextual dialogue. It is also a kind of summary of many of the concerns of this and other chapters (esp. 4.4).

What historical connections can you retrace between Hamlet and: (a) the two texts below; (b) cigars; (c) the slave trade; and (d) the development of a variety of institutions and social processes called 'English' and 'Language' and 'Literature'?

> Which way this time? Me killem die finish body b'long me Or me no do 'im? Me no savvy.

> Foh bi foh dis graun oh noh bi sehf – dat na di ting wei i di bring plenti hambag.

(*A clue*: both lines are modern Pidgin English versions of the 'To be or not to be' speech. The first is from The British Solomon Islands; the second from the Cameroon. Both can be found in Todd, 1984: 272–3.)

FURTHER RE-WRITING AND READING

A. Plotting alternative outcomes in conversation and drama (cf. 4.3)

(1)

Transcribe an instance of an interaction in which you yourself are involved (preferably on the basis of a recording). Then cut it at a strategic point part way through so as to plot some of the potential alternative developments. Do this systematically with an eye to the 'preferred outcomes' for each of the participants. What, then, was the precise interplay of power relations in the initial interaction which led to the actual outcome? And how, tactically and strategically, was this achieved?

(2)

Experiment with alternative endings in a play that you know well. Do this with a view to exploring (i) the specific kinds of problem the play 'solves' (and those which by implication it does not); and (ii) the kinds of interaction that are – and are not – expected or acceptable.

B. Further cross-cultural dialogues in and with the novel (cf. 4.4)

Return to the materials in 3.3 and use these for further explorations of the kinds of dialogue with/in 'Eng. Lit.' featured in 4.4. That is, apply the same 'dialogic' methods to the extracts from novels by Defoe, Tournier and Coetzee, etc. as were applied to extracts from novels by Trollope, Austen, Brontë and Rhys. Also consider Behn's *Oroonoko* (3.3.5) as a 'pre-text' in a very peculiar and particular kind of dialogue with the representations of colonialism and gender in Defoe.

C.   Classic re-production (cf. 4.5)

Use the pattern of activities devoted to exploring moments in the production and reproduction of *Hamlet* as a general model for the exploration of other 'classic' texts. Perhaps the best way of doing this is to design activities to help *other people* (and incidentally yourself) grasp what is – and isn't – going on. Consider the possibilities of:

alternative base texts and textual transmission;

critical reception (and perhaps theatrical production);

allusions and contextualisation in other works;

parodies and adaptations;

forms of post-modernist deconstruction and historicist reconstruction.

Go on to revise and refine these activities on the basis of the experience of actually doing them.

Useful brief introductions to *dialogue* in and out of literature are Burton in Carter and Burton (1982: 86–115) and Traugott and Pratt (1980: 226–71). Fuller studies are Pratt (1976) and (Burton, 1980); also see Sell (1990). *Bakhtin's* conception of the *dialogic* nature of all language use, and the related notions of 'heteroglossia', 'travestying' and 'carnival', pervade the present method. Therefore see Bakhtin (1981, 1984, 1990) and Voloshinov (1973) also Vygotsky (1934). Commentaries on and dialogic transformations of Bakhtin's words include: Todorov (1984), Holquist (1990), Lodge (1990) and Hirschkopf and Shepherd (1988). Debate on Bakhtin is currently intense. The main parameters of that debate are established in Bennett (1979: 75–97), Morson and Emerson (1989), Pechey in Barker *et al.* (1986: 104–25) and Hirschkopf and Shepherd (1988: 1–38, 195–202).

Brecht's theories and practices of 'drama as telling', 'making strange', and the active 'grasping' of meaning also pervade the present method. Therefore, see Brecht (1964, 1965) and the commentary on Brecht by Benjamin (1977). Other relevant commentaries and applications are: Wright (1989), Brooker in Brooker and Humm (1989: 73–89) and Heath in Mulhern (1992: 230–257). Other work on *drama* that has been drawn upon includes: Hunt (1974), Barker (1977), Elam (1980), McGrath (1981), Pavis (1991), Boal (1992) and Kershaw (1992).

Non/cooperative principles and *conflictual/consensual models* of language and society are reviewed briefly in Fairclough (1989: 6–14) and Birch (1989: 1–5, 47ff.) and more fully in Williams (1992). Tannen (1992) approaches conversation from a generally *assertive* and specifically *feminist* perspective; as do Cameron (1985, 1990) with respect to language in general. Sceptical traditions of linguistic philosophy are represented by Habermas (1990) and Rorty (1989), more radically by Wittgenstein (1953) and Taylor (1992); also see Kasulis (1981). Such studies usefully complement mainstream work in *pragmatics* by Leech (1983), Levinson (1983), Brown and Yule (1983), Sperber and Wilson (1986) and Blakemore (1992); also work by the founding 'fathers' of *speech act* theory such as Austin (1976), Searle (1969) and Grice (1975). *Discourse* is usefully defined in O'Sullivan *et al.* (1993: 72–6), Kress (1989: 6–7) and Carter and Simpson (1989: 8–13); and more fully explored in Macdonnell (1986) and Jan Mohammed and Lloyd (1990). For *dialectic* see Williams (1983: 106–8), Sharratt (1982).

Cross-cultural dialogues with/in 'English/es' can be picked up in such anthologies as Moore and Beier (1984), Burnett (1986), Allnutt *et al.* (1988) and Markham (1989); and supported by commentary from Brathwaite (1984), Ashcroft, Griffiths and Tiffin (1989), Dabydeen in Michaels and Ricks (1990: 3–14), Bhabha (1990, 1994), Spivak (1987, 1990, 1994) and Said (1993). When *re-producing Shakespeare*, see Kott (1967), Cohn (1976), Longhurst in Widdowson (1982: 150–63), Collick (1989), Holderness (1988), Dollimore and Sinfield (1985), Marowitz (1991), Cox (1992) and Hawkes (1986, 1993); also Heylen (1993).

5 Review of theories and practices

5.1 RELEVANT AND USABLE THEORY – A BIBLIOGRAPHICAL ESSAY

> The mistake we make when we choose a model is that we choose the point of arrival.
>
> (Anaïs Nin, cited in Ward-Jouve (1991: 9))

> After the final no there comes a yes
> And on that yes the future world depends
>
> (Wallace Stevens, *Collected Poems* (1957))

This section offers a brief overview of the main theoretical writings relevant to the present approach. Its function is simply indicative: to highlight some key terms and concepts, and to supply references for the reader to follow up for her- or himself. Fuller references to theory associated with certain topics can be found in the bibliographies of earlier sections: 'subjects' and 'agents', 'selves and others' in 2.8; 'narrative' and 'narratology' (including film) in 3.4; 'dialogue', 'dialectic' and 'discourse' in 4.6. My aim here is therefore no more than to supply some cues and clues as to the main theoretical positions and movements that seem to me to be most useful. Many of them can be associated with the kinds of functional and creative models of language referenced in 1.3.4. And all of them are grounded in what might be called *theories of practice and performance* or, more formally, **praxis**. For all the theories and theorists featured here are in one way or another concerned with realising the *processes* that lead to and from *products* (textual or otherwise). And all depend upon notions of *experience constituted through experiment, re-creation constituted through reflection and research*, and *dialogue as a form of dialectic*. Another phrase for all this is **heuristic interactive learning**. And by definition this resists any attempt to institute 'Theory' as in some way singular, monologic and in any worthwhile sense 'pure'. Theory you cannot actually use to test, probe, model and modify your own practice – both individual and collective – is quite literally 'useless' and 'irrelevant'. And our concern is, above all, relevant and usable theory.

First, then, and only apparently paradoxically, let's ground our approach to theory in approaches to practice. Until recently, systematic attention to the practice of learning in English studies has not been a strong element in higher education. Certainly this is generally the case in Britain (though for valuable counterexamples and arguments, see Batsleer *et al.*, 1985; Fowler, 1986: 178–80; Short, 1989; Brooker, in Brooker and Humm, 1989: 73–89; Durant and Fabb, 1990). It has also traditionally been the case in Australasia and America, outside the first-year composition classes and the courses specifically devoted to 'creative writing' (though see Moffett, 1968, and Scholes, 1985, 1988).

Nor has there been much willingness to feature student work as an object worthy of methodical study and publication in its own right, notwithstanding the universal tendency to assess and grade it. To be sure, a substantial and valuable tradition devoted to exploring the processes of student/pupil work exists for primary and secondary education, most relevantly in the various movements associated with *redrafting* (see Reid, 1984; Benton and Fox, 1985; Greenwell, 1988; Brown and Gifford, 1989; Corcoran and Evans, 1989; Moon, 1990; Brookes and Grundy, 1990). Moreover, communication and cultural studies at all levels, virtually from their inception, have often encouraged and drawn upon various kinds of interactive and group project work (see below). None the less, in 'Eng. Lit.' in higher education it still seems that 'academic work' almost automatically means *finished written products submitted by individuals, invariably in very specific sub-genres of essay, commentary and, sometimes, dissertation* (though see Fabb and Durant, 1993 for valuable practical guidance in these areas). Clearly, then, there is not a general atmosphere conducive to sustained attention to textual study as 'praxis'; i.e. *writing in process generated through negotiation in groups, often in a heterogeneous range of genres, materials and media.*

In a sense this situation is surprising. The chief instigator of *Practical Criticism*, I.A. Richards, based his highly influential book of that name on a review of the responses ('protocols') of undergraduate literature students to a number of 'unseen' texts (Richards, 1929). However, as Richards' chief aim seems to have been to demonstrate that students needed guiding towards a specific model of literary taste and judgement (his own and that of his cultural group), it is perhaps not surprising that the experiment has rarely seemed worth emulating so overtly. And yet, arguably, a rather similar project characterises the subsequent traditions of 'practical criticism' and 'close reading', only more covertly instituted. Encouraging a 'personal response to the words on the page' may have been the official line of much twentieth-century criticism. But woe betide the students who came up with a response which was *too* personal, or *differently* personal, or downright *political*, especially if it was at variance with the observations, values and judgements of their teachers/lecturers. The practice of 'close reading', especially when informed by systematic 'stylistic' analysis, has a lot to recommend it. But the common spectacle of aspiring novices learning first to guess and then to mimic the methods and tastes of their mentors is not one of them.

A notable exception is David Bleich's *Subjective Criticism* (1978), where the creative plurality of student responses is both valued and analysed in detail. Bleich's model, however, is essentially 'subjective' in the narrow sense of being premised upon psychologised individuals limited to the arena of group interaction in situations. The larger social and especially ideological contexts wherein individuals and groups are articulated are ignored or remain ultimately consensual and non-historical. The underlying model is thus phenomenological and 'given' rather than materialist and '(re-)made'.

Meanwhile, other theorists whom it might be assumed would have strong interests in the responses of actual readers (other than themselves) often fail to give any concrete instances. *Reader-response* theorists such as Iser, Jauss and Fish can be very useful in setting up a number of general models. So it is with Jauss's notion of *horizons of expectation* (the shifting interface at which the 'there and then' of the text and the reader's 'here and now' meet; Jauss, 1982); also Iser's notion of reading as a constant re-negotiation between positions occupied by textually 'implied' and historically 'actual' readers (Iser, 1978; cf. 3.1.5); and even Fish's notion of *interpretative communities* (the institutionalised bodies of readers who privilege and legitimise particular readings and reading strategies (Fish, 1980)). Notwithstanding, in all these cases, as with Richards, the bottom line is invariably the one drawn by the particular reader-response theorist. Time and again 'the reader' – invariably singular and individual – stands in for 'the ideal reader', and s/he in turn is a thinly disguised version of 'the particular theorist who reads' (i.e. Jauss, Iser or Fish). And for all the insistence on shifting 'horizons of expectation' and 'actual readers', there is little or no acknowledgement of real, historical differences of opinion based upon genuinely differing social, cultural and political interests. There is therefore no mechanism or organism for *change* – radical or otherwise – within the model, and therefore no real explanatory power. Fish's 'interpretative communities' are irretrievably inert and self-sufficient in this respect. Their values just *are* – whether you as an individual and a member of a potentially counter- or alternative group hold them or not. Moreover, this is a reader who, many critics would add, is implicitly as well as actually male, white and middle class. (For a critique, see Eagleton, 1983: 45–91; and Holub, 1984; also Fetterley, 1991.) McGann (1983), however, offers a more searchingly and sensitively historical application of reader-response methods to the elucidation of textual transmission and transformation.

For all the above reasons, signs of a relatively recent, albeit partial, shift towards methods and models based on openly negotiated group work make a refreshing – often inspiring - change. Classic examples in cultural studies are associated with the early work of the Birmingham Centre for Contemporary Cultural Studies; the Glasgow Media Group and various projects initiated by *Screen* and *Screen Education*. More recently, the practices of many kinds of women's, black and community writers' groups both inside and outside formal education have shown the way towards a renewed recognition of the supportive and explanatory power of such corporate – though not necessarily 'cooperative' – meaning-making (see Thompson and Wilcox, 1989; Milloy and O'Rourke, 1991; Wall, 1989). Similarly, 'creative writing' and 'performance' courses and workshops generally use group interactions, or at least individual variations on a common theme, as their chief modes of exploration and expression (see Barker, 1977; Boal, 1992; Fairbairns, in Brooker and Humm, 1989: 205–20; Monteith and Miles, 1992; Birkett, 1993).

Also relevant here are certain *games theories* and *role-playing* strategies. Though it must be insisted that I only intend those which have a positive emphasis on theories of productively 'deviant' behaviour, counterfactual and hypothetical 'what if' strategies, and constructive 'sabotage' – as distinct from mere 'imitation' and 'training simulations' of purportedly 'real-world' situations (see Jones, 1988; Crookall and Saunders, 1988). In this respect such games relate directly to theories and practices of *creativity* devoted to the blending and extending of given frames of reference, rather than merely 'playing the game' according to established rules (see Koestler, 1976 and Carse, 1987 for the former view of creativity).

Standard works on the *psychology of play* have also been drawn on, especially those concerned with explorations of 'self–other', 'subject–object' relations, and Gestalt methods of refashioning situations through the recognition of options and the exercise of choice (see Millar, 1968; Winnicott, 1974).

Textual intervention is the catch-all phrase used to designate the various creative-critical practices used in this book. All of them have to do with challenging and changing texts so as to recognise their distinctive strategies and preoccupations; and actively generating differences so as to establish firmer grounds for critical preferences. While such a method is not common in literary studies in higher education, partial parallels exist in cultural and communication studies. There the phrases *commutation – or substitution – techniques* are used to describe the act of changing a single element in an image, other artefact or situation (see O'Sullivan *et al.*, 1993; Fiske, 1982: 111–12). The aim is to disturb and thus highlight constitutive differences; e.g. by inverting gender or race roles, changing postures or back-grounds, affixing alternative captions, etc. Usually, however, as the word 'technique' suggests, this is a localised, ancillary practice, not an overall strategy of thoroughgoing transformation. It is more like opportunistic graffiti than radical critique. Theoretical arguments for this practice of 'semiotic guerrilla warfare' can be found in Eco (1986: 138–45); and for the broadly equivalent practice of 'stressed readings' applied to modernist 'high art' texts, see Caws (1989).

In cultural studies there is also a developed sense of the value of *counter- and alternative* (or 'aberrant') *decoding*: reading against or across the grain of the text so as to produce a response which is revealingly at variance with the dominant reading apparently expected of an 'ideal (i.e. submissive) reader' (see the classic essay by Hall in During, 1993: 90–103; also O'Sullivan *et al.*, 1993). A relevant three-part model of subject/agent positions in so far as they can involve different kinds and degrees of *identification, counter-identification* and *disidentification* (i.e. alternative identification) is offered by Pêcheux (1982; also see Selden, 1989b: 108). Perhaps even more relevant, because more fully plural and historicised, is the whole area of cultural studies concerned with *uses and gratifications* (see Brunsdon and Morley in Bennett *et al.*, 1981: 118–41; Fiske, 1987:62–83, 316–26). For there the focus is shifted to the very different ways in which different people actually *use* the same cultural products and practices, what various kinds of *gratification* they get from them, and how they routinely fit into their lives. For it must be recognised that there are very many ways in which actual readers/viewers engage with and derive pleasure or displeasure from, say, a series of TV ads or a Shakespeare play. Consequently, the whole idea of a particular product or practice having a single dominant meaning that can be 'decoded' has to give way to a more pluralised and relativised notion of it as a multifunctional site of activity (for instance, contrast the approaches to advertising in Williamson, 1978 and Cook, 1992). Functionally speaking, then, a cultural product or practice *is* the many things it *does*. It is therefore not properly an 'it' at all, but a 'them' – and not a product but a set of processes.

However, whether we are thinking in terms of 'de-coding' or 'gratifications and uses', there tends to be a common limitation. The emphasis is still upon *interpretive* acts of decoding (however opposed or alternative) and upon 'use' as *consumption* (however varied in mode). There is less encouragement actually to re-write and transform the text – in Barthes' phrase 'to change the object itself' (see Barthes, 1977: 165–9). By contrast, textual inter-vention as understood and practised in the present method always involves *critique through transformation* as well as interpretation and analysis; *re-coding* as well as de-coding; gratifi-cation through *re-production* as well as consumption; and *re-creation* in a genuinely active sense rather than 'recreation' in the sense of more or less passive leisure.

Other theories that can be invoked to justify all the above 'praxes' are necessarily diverse and themselves often contentious. I shall simply highlight those I find most relevant and stimulating. Educationally, the most deeply influential is that of Vygotsky (1934). His insistence that the *inner voices* of consciousness are constantly articulated through negotiation with the *outer voices* of others in the public domain has left a deep impression on the present method (e.g. 'an *inter*personal process is always transformed into an *intra*personal process' (1934: 57)). So have the early sociological studies of the shifting and reciprocal relations between 'self' and 'other' in the work of Herbert Mead (1934), and more recently Giddens (1991). More arcanely psychologised – even mythicised – counterparts are offered by Lacan (especially his notion of 'the entry of the human subject into language'; see Lodge, 1988: 79–106) and, in a more politically determined frame, by Althusser (especially his notion of the 'interpellation'/'hailing' of the human subject by ideology; see Althusser, 1917: 160–6). Coward and Ellis (1977) and Belsey (1980) offer valuable syntheses and critiques of all these notions of 'the subject'. However, it is the sheer power, flexibility and lucidity of Vygotsky's model of human subjects ceaselessly involved in 'self-making', both *against* and *with* others, that continues to recommend it as a dynamic alternative to, for instance, Piaget's more uniformly developmental, hierarchically staged account of the learning process. Vygotsky's pluralistic and relativistic notion of the 'zone of proximal development' (being the adjacent yet excluded frame of reference which the learner must grasp if s/he is to learn) is far more subtly organic than the relatively mechanistic and uniform developments looked for by Piaget and his more programmatic followers. Bruner (1986) provides a readable synthesis of Vygotsky's work in relation to contemporary education in general and literary studies in particular.

A more radical application of a dialectical model of internal–external, self-other negotiation to education can be found in the work of Paolo Freire (1972). His practical commitment both to where people start from (personally, culturally and historically) as well as to where they realise they need and want to go to (politically) makes for a peculiarly urgent and energised educational dialogue. So does his insistence on a 'bottom-up' rather than 'top-down' model of hierarchic change – and, indeed, on the dissolution of hierarchies as such.

'Dialogue', and especially what has come to be called *dialogics* or *dialogism*, brings us to Bakhtin (1981; 1984; 1990; and see 4.6; also Griffith, 1987; 1991). Bakhtin, it seems, was not particularly interested in either pedagogy or radical democracy. But he was fascinated by the re-presentation of different 'discourses' within the novel: the ways in which novelists constantly renegotiate the meanings and values of words by placing them in different people's mouths, refracting them through different people's minds, and siting them in different literary and social historical contexts (see above 4.4). A key concept is *another's words in one's own language* (Bakhtin, 1981: 303ff.). Bakhtin concentrated on the novel; but, arguably, the principles can be extended to all forms of 'intertextuality' in poems and plays as well, in fact in any language use where existing usages are brought to bear on and in immediate situations. Ultimately this means that virtually all language use enacts a creative tension between 'another's words' and 'one's own language'. The words we speak, write or otherwise record are never wholly our own. And yet, crucially, in the moment of use they are turned towards our own ends, whether these ends are overt or covert, conscious or unconscious. In a similar sense, Voloshinov (which may be Bakhtin's pseudonym) writes that 'word is a two-sided act', always suspended in meaning and function between speaker and listener (Voloshinov, 1973: 86–7).

Bakhtin supplies us with many other key terms and concepts, notably *heteroglossia, carnival,* and *travestying* (for useful glossaries, including some alternative translations, see Bakhtin, 1981: 422–34, and Hirschkop and Shepherd, 1988: 190–4). *Heteroglossia* or 'varied-tonguedness' (*raznorechie*), refers to the fact that the language use of any one person and of any one national language is both highly various and constantly on the move. That is, there is strictly no such thing as *the* idiolect of an individual or, say, '*the* English Language'. Rather, each is constituted by a variegated and variable bundle of attributes, depending on the specific history, and the immediate function and context. In this respect Bakhtin's (and Voloshinov's) linguistics make the particular usage primary as a site of converging or diverging interests. They are less concerned with and convinced by the notion of Language (capital 'L' and singular) as a notional and potentially fixed whole. This position is the broad converse of Saussurean (and traditional generative) linguistics, where it is the *langue* as whole system (or 'deep structures' and 'competences' as underlying principles) rather than the *parole* as particular utterance (or 'surface structure' and 'performances' as actual realisations) which is primary. Strictly speaking, this dichotomy is unnecessary. In many modern fully functional and pragmatic-generative models of language it can be substantially avoided (see the references on p. 182). Moreover, any comprehensive model of language must in some way seek to relate the *diachronic* axis of historical change (and therefore 'openness', 'unfinishedness') to the *synchronic* axis of contemporary use of the system as system (and therefore, in a provisional sense, 'closed' and 'finished'). Every model has an emphasis, however. So it is worth pointing out that the one preferred here is primarily material, particularistic and founded in ceaselessly renegotiated functions and values – not idealist, generalised and fixedly reified. For this reason, the reader with a philosophical bent is also urged to read the rigorously random and profoundly suggestive meditations on language in Wittgenstein's *Philosophical Investigations* (1945–9), rather than his earlier, monumentally totalising and largely superseded *Tractatus Logico-Philosophicus* (1921) (see Wittgenstein, 1953; Harris, 1988; and references in 1.3.4).

Carnival, especially as used by Bakhtin in his book *Rabelais and his World* (1968), refers to the general practice of inverting or subverting all workaday, official norms of proportion, propriety and 'sense' so as to celebrate a repressed or suppressed culture of playful, holiday a-normality, grotesquery and positively charged 'non/sense' (cf. 3.2 and 1.3). Bakhtin himself defines it thus: 'carnival celebrates the temporary liberation from prevailing truth and from the established order: it marks the suspension of all hierarchical rank, privileges, norms and prohibitions' (ibid.: 10). The practice is therefore 'an-archic' in a primitive etymological sense: 'without' or 'alternative to' – and not simply 'opposed to' – prevailing order. Partial psychological parallels may be found in Freud's notion of the power of the unconscious to always 'return the repressed' in one form or another. In fact, Kristeva's notion of 'semiosis' as a flux always ready to flow into and inform the 'symbolic' represents a suggestive attempt to meld Bakhtinian notions of 'carnival' with Freudian (and especially Lacanian) notions of the precariousness of the sign subject to subconscious pressures of fragmentation, dispersal and deflection (see Kristeva, 1980; 1984). *Travestying* is 'parody' in an enlarged sense. It refers to the activity of openly wrenching another's meanings to one's own ends and in relation to one's own situation. At best it registers the simultaneous interplay of different moments and modes of production and reproduction; and characteristically sets up intertextual tensions which are variously comic, satiric or ironic (see Bakhtin, 1981: 51–83; also Hutcheon, 1985; Nash, 1992: 83–98, 132–55; and Purdie, 1993).

Both the general practice of 'carnival' and the specific practices of 'travestying' and 'parody' are radically dialogic in that they involve sporting with what is given and re-making it, resisting mere transference and celebrating the power of transformation – often to shocking and exhilarating effect.

In this respect (or perhaps we should say 'disrespect') two other writers should be mentioned. One is Walter Benjamin and his stirring insistence that we read history 'against the grain' so as to recognise what has been officially marginalised, suppressed or ignored (see Benjamin, 1970; also Eagleton, 1986b). The other is Bertolt Brecht, whose most relevant theories and practices are treated at length in 4.1, seen in practice in 4.5.5 and referenced on p. 182. All that need be reiterated here is that Brecht's commitment to 'the *making strange*' (*Verfremdung*) of that which is assumed or accepted is fundamental to the present approach. So is his invitation to engage in an active *grasping* (*Eingreffung*) of meaning. Crucial to both is the critical re-presentation and opening up of that which was assumed to be finished or fixed. For only if we can creatively conceive of a story or history as an interaction that might have been otherwise can we exercise our critical judgements as to the implication and consequences of the actual hi/story as told or enacted. Such acts of 'making strange' and 'grasping' meanings are thus morally and politically charged. And in this respect they differ from the notion of *defamiliarisation* propounded by some formalists (e.g. Shklovsky in Lodge, 1988: 15–31). There what is at issue is often a more narrowly linguistic and perceptual distinction between what constitutes 'ordinary language use' ('familiar') and 'literature' ('language defamiliarised'). Both the connections and distinctions among Bakhtin, Brecht and the so-called Formalists are well examined by Bennett (1979: 93–110).

Consistent with Benjamin's and Brecht's projects is Macherey's method of reading the *gaps and silences* within and around a text: what it would not or could not say then and there, first in its initial moment of production and then in its subsequent moments of reproduction (Macherey, 1978: 85–96). The above readings and re-writings of Robert Browning's 'My Last Duchess' (1.2), Defoe's *Robinson Crusoe* (3.3) and *Hamlet* (4.5.5) are thus 'Machereyan' in this respect. In other respects, Macherey's position is the necessary obverse – though not necessarily flat contradiction – of, say, Lukacs'. For the latter it is precisely the 'world-historical totality' of the world carved out by literary works (especially novels) which is the object of study: what in its plenitude the text *did* manage to say and what contradictions it *did* attempt to articulate and resolve (see Lukacs, 1962). Broadly speaking, then, whereas Macherey works through *negation*, Lukacs works through *positive* identification. Both methods have their place in a fully dialectical model of the way we make sense of texts in history. From one point of view we must try to see through the textual and historical 'holes' by probing them with awkward and even anachronistic questions. At the same time we must try to grasp texts and histories as 'wholes' on their own terms and in their own times (see 3.1.4 and 3.2.5–6).

Other theorists whose methods and models pervade the present method are Roland Barthes, Jacques Derrida and Michel Foucault. Barthes' work on the post-structuralist analysis of narratives is referred to in 3.4. Of more general importance is his recognition that *all* texts (not just certain privileged ones) are potentially *writerly* ('scriptible') in that the reader is never merely a passive consumer of meanings but always reworks them to her or his own ends. Barthes' previous distinction between what he called 'writerly' and 'readerly' texts (respectively, those texts which do and those which don't invite the reader to recognise the textual play in which s/he is engaged) was thus shifted in emphasis. 'Play' became more a power and responsibility to be exercised by the reader, part of the process of reading, rather than a property of the text as a supposedly finished product. In fact both the early and later formulations prove valuable. Certainly some texts do invite a more 'playful' engagement than others (Shakespeare's *Hamlet* compared with a 'government health warning', for instance). At the same time we do well to remember that both can be and, indeed, are sites constituted by the play of innumerable differences and expressive of very variable preferences. *Hamlet* is constantly subject to 're-writing' in editing, performance and criticism (see 4.4); 'government health warnings' change with governments and with changes in the construction of 'health' (see 1.3.2).

Derrida is valued here for a clutch of related and now fairly familiar concepts (for which see Derrida, 1976; 1978 and the influential essay 'Structure, sign and play in the discourse of the human sciences' in Lodge, 1988: 107–23). Chief amongst these are:

> *différance*, meaning both 'difference' and 'deferral', and pushing Saussure's observation that meaning is constituted through 'a play of differences without a positive term' to its logical – some would say illogical – conclusion. Consequently, we must look between and beyond terms for their meanings, not at or into them; meaning is relational and ultimately ineffable, not essentialist and immediately apprehensible.

> *trace*, the connected observation that all meaning exists as a 'trace' or 'resonance' of anterior meanings, none of which has an absolute and identifiable source or origin.

> *writing 'under erasure'* (*sous rature*), the partial deletion and replacement of words so that both the words replaced and the words doing the replacing are still legible. In this way, as with a writer's draft in process, the actual order of decision-making, resolving differences into preferences, can be retraced by the reader.

> *de-centred subject*, drawing attention to the observation shared by Marxist and Freudian models alike that 'human beings', whether considered collectively or as individuals, only really exist as 'human becomings', without a single centre or fixed identity. Consequently, it is the ceaseless movement *amongst* 'centres' (whether these be conceived in psychological, philosophical, religious or political terms) and the 'trace' which that movement makes, which constitutes the *subject in process* – not the subject as a fixed point of departure or arrival.

There is, however, a crucial difference in emphasis between Derrida's approach and that practised here. Whereas Derrida is usually identified with processes of **de**-*centring* and **de**-*construction*, the stress here is on **re**-*centring* and **re**-*construction*. Hence the insistence throughout the book that

Any play of differences must finally be resolved into sets of negotiated preferences – however provisional. (cf. 1.1.3)

also that

the potentially endless 'deferral' of meaning must be tied down at some time with 'referral/reference' to extra-textual realities – again, however provisionally.

Derrida sometimes says as much (see above p. 14). But apparently not loud or long enough for some of his critics.

Foucault's influence is also pervasive, though again modulated (see Foucault 1972; 1980; 1986; his 'The order of discourse' in Young, 1981: 49–78; and 'What is an author?' in Lodge, 1988: 196–210; also the comprehensive study by During, 1992). Foucault's commitment to exploring knowledges as forms of *discourse* and *power* is particularly central (see 4.1). Certain ways of saying, seeing and being are privileged and become dominant at particular times only by displacing or replacing others. What Foucault initially calls 'archaeological', and subsequently 'genealogical', shifts are a part of cultural-political, not merely intellectual, history. What's more, it is always a history we speak from within. There is no absolutely privileged and impartial vantage point from which essentially 'true', 'factual' and 'objective' histories may be written. The 'will to truth' is a 'will to power'. 'True' and 'false', like 'fact' and 'fiction' (compounded as *faction*), become movable counters in a an ongoing power-play. The challenge, therefore, is to try to understand and manipulate the changing rules of the game.

This brings us to some of the debates and practices currently associated with *post-modernism*, references to which are made at various points in the book. Chief amongst these are engagements with:

faction, counterfactual history and *fictional meta-history*, being the splicing or framing of conventionally 'factual' with conventionally 'fictional' materials, to the point where the arbitrariness of the distinction is exposed, and sometimes exploded (Marshall, 1992: 147–78).

reading and re-writing 'high-art' forms through 'popular' forms, and vice versa, again with an emphasis on the exposure and explosion of differences so as to produce fresh grounds for the expression of preferences (see Hutcheon, 1989; and Bourdieu, 1984).

the recognition that a *copy, reproduction* or *imitation* can have a claim to attention equal to (though different from) some supposed *original* or *source* (see Lyotard, 1984).

Finally, if all the above theory is to be really usable it must in some sense be recognised as personally relevant. And that means it must be seen through lenses which focus not on grand generalities but on the particularities of certain people in certain times, places and institutions. And that means finishing – or perhaps starting – with immediate situations and orientations. Mine and yours, for instance. Speaking for myself as a white, early middle aged, European male in an institutionally privileged position, I must come to terms with some of the mass of challenging work produced over the last decades by writers who are self-consciously women, coloured, non-European and institutionally un- or under-privileged (e.g. students, as well as people denied access to higher – or any – education). The following works I have found both stimulating and formative. Whatever your particular situation or orientation, you may find them so too, albeit differently.

Cameron and others (1985; 1990) offer some forceful reminders that not only language but also systems for describing and analysing language are constituted through the play of highly contentious differences. In this case the primary axis is that of *gender* in general and *feminism* in particular. Jardine and Smith (1986) offer some food for thought, and practical action, to academic men in search of preferable roles.

Meanwhile, Said (1978; 1993) reminds every white European to look elsewhere – or at the same things differently – to see how we/they have defined our/themselves against non-European 'others'. The growing pre-eminence of the Middle East and Islam as a studiously cultivated 'others' and potential adversaries (replacing the former Soviet Union in this respect) makes Said's emphases and theses especially urgent. Meanwhile, Ashcroft *et al.* (1989) and Bhabha (1990; 1994) amongst many others, remind us of yet other arenas in which our foremothers and forefathers performed and we, in our ways, still perform. In this respect the critic who has most recently and powerfully affected my own sense of position and method is Gayatri Spivak (1987; 1990; 1994). For the sake of some labels, she can be called a Marxist-feminist-deconstructionist with a strong commitment to post/colonial writing and interactive teaching. However, as the starting – and sometimes the end – point for many of her arguments and analyses is precisely the dynamic of her own and her students' orientations in a complex and contentious arena of shifting subject/agent positions, such labels are both inadequate and contestable. Consequently, she offers not so much a single homogeneous theory as a flexible way of theorising (most revealingly through dialogue and interview); and not so much a specific critical position as a series of critiques.

I too prefer to tread such a path – though necessarily mine not hers. If you do too, you will also find the theory referred to in this chapter usable.

Relevant *introductions to theory* which prove both readable and stimulating are Belsey (1980); Eagleton (1983); Tallack (1987); Allen (1987); Griffith (1987); Selden (1989a; 1989b); Easthope (1991). Relevant *anthologies* are Bennett *et al.* (1981); Rylance (1987); Lodge (1988); Walder (1990); Corner and Hawthorn (1993); and During (1993). Necessarily, these theories and their associated practices span what are variously constructed as 'literary', 'cultural' and 'communication' studies. Such distinctions are signalled elsewhere in the book. At this point, looking to the existence of something(s) that might be called 'textual studies' or, still better, 'textual practices', I prefer to ignore them. Therefore, also see the journal *Textual Practice*.

5.2 STYLISTIC CHECKLIST

Here is a basic checklist of stylistic features, mainly at the 'micro-linguistic' level of word choice and combination, sound-patterning and visual presentation (cf. Leech and Short, 1981: 75–82; Toolan, 1988: 111–15; Fowler, 1991: 66–90). Use it in conjunction with the introduction to textual analysis in 1.3 when you are engaged in detailed work on verbal texture and structure. This checklist is prefaced by some more general questions on 'macro-textual' aspects such as medium, genre, discourse, etc. These are a reminder to relate linguistic form to communicative function, and verbal detail to larger social-historical processes. The presence of counter- and alternative questions throughout this checklist is a further reminder to read and re-write dialectically: to sharpen the experience of what is 'there' in a given utterance or text by experimenting with what is not – but might have been or might still be.

First, the questions that overarch and underpin everything else. They are framed both positively and in a variety of negated and dialogic forms (cf. dialectical discourse questions, 4.1, p. 124):

Who is addressing whom about what, how, when, where and why?

Who else might have been addressing the same people about 'the same thing' – but differently and for different purposes?

How did the people addressed respond – or how might they have responded?

How do you respond – for, against or alternative?

Word choice

What sorts of vocabulary are being used? What others might have been used?

How far are the words:

short or long; monosyllabic or polysyllabic?

simple or complex?

concrete or abstract; particular or general?

common and everyday, or from a specific area of use (religion, technology, etc)?

literal or figurative; referential or metaphorical?

context-sensitive (i.e. pronouns and other deictics – e.g. 'here', 'now'), or relatively context-free?

heavily adjectival and adverbial, or relatively unmodified nouns and verbs?

Experiment by substituting, adding or deleting words.

Word combination

What are the main ways in which the words are grouped or organised? How else might they have been structured, and to what alternative effects?

How far are there:

familiar collocations (recognisable word-clusters) – or is much of it strikingly new?

speeches – quoted directly or indirectly, freely or precisely?

speech moves, turns and exchanges with specific structures?

long or short sentences – and how many words on average?

'fully' or 'incompletely' framed sentences?

coordinated and/or subordinated structures?

repetitions of words, or parallelisms of phrase and sentence structure?

lightly or heavily modified nouns – pre- or post-modified; in/definite articles?

predominantly common nouns, proper nouns or personal pronouns?

lightly or heavily modalised verbs – with auxiliary verbs and/or adverbs?

one or more verbal tenses and aspects – suggesting what frames of time, duration and frequency?

actives or passives? dynamic or stative verbs? in/transitives?

favoured sentence-types – stating, questioning, commanding or exclaiming?

explicit or implicit markers of textual cohesion and perceptual coherence (between as well as within sentences)?

Again, experiment with alternatives. What combinations have not been used – but might have been?

Sound-patterning and visual presentation

What kinds of 'music' or visual patterns do the words make, and with what effects? What other 'musics' and visual patterns might there have been – and with what alternative effects?

What do you hear, see, or infer with respect to:

stress, rhythm and intonation?

repetition or near-repetition of sounds or sights?

alliteration and assonance? rhyme and half-rhyme?

use of short or long vowels? plosives (e.g. /p, b, t/) or fricatives (/f, s/)?

rhythmic beats or metrical syllables to the line?

single or many voices – alternating or overlapping, in harmony or cacophony?

distinctive features of punctuation, typography and layout?

sound-editing or graphic techniques?

As always, experiment with alternatives in the same, different or mixed media.

Here, finally, are some general questions on **participants**, **processes** and **circumstances**. They are a further reminder to relate the above features of word choice and combination to the perceptual and ultimately ideological structures which a particular text proposes or presupposes – thereby marginalising or ignoring others.

How far does the base text project the world as if it were composed of:

(a) *Participants*: relatively stable entities and identities, fixed 'things' and 'persons', finished 'products' – most noticeably through realising experience in terms of nouns (nominalisation)?

(b) *Processes*: relatively fluid states and dynamic actions, the very processes of being, doing, happening, thinking, communicating, behaving, etc. – most noticeably through realising experience in terms of verbs (verbalisation)?

(c) *Circumstances*: relatively dependent attributes, qualities and orientations of the various participants and processes – most noticeably in the forms of adjectives supporting nouns and adverbs supporting verbs.

Consider ways in which you might make a heavily nominalised text (dominated by participants/nouns) more verbal (recast in terms of processes) – or vice versa. Then consider the effect of stripping away or adding adjectives and adverbs (thus altering the circumstance items).

Go on to interrogate the specific *kinds* of participant, process and circumstance in more detail. Again, this checklist may be used to assist active re-writing as well as analytic reading. Which precise configurations were not used but might have been – or may still be?

How far are the **participants**:

inanimate objects or animate beings?

passive subjects or active agents?

affected or affecting?

depersonalised or personalised?

abstractly generalised or concretely particular?

collective or individual?

(Conversely, who or what else may be involved – differently?)

How far are the **processes**:

material and dynamic (concerned with 'doing' and 'happening') or relational and 'state-like' (concerned with 'being' and 'having')?

externally communicated (concerned with 'saying', 'writing', 'reading', 'showing', etc.) or internally perceived (concerned with 'thinking', 'feeling', 'sensing', etc.)?

active or passive – respectively, 'doing' or 'done to', and with the agent responsible either in grammatical subject position or delayed and perhaps deleted (e.g. 'The timber company cut down the trees' as against 'The trees were cut down (by the timber company)')?

finite or non-finite – respectively, marked or unmarked for tense, number and person (e.g. 'She won' and 'You will win' compared with 'To win or not to win' and 'Winning')?

transitive or intransitive – respectively, involving 'carry-over' from one participant to another (e.g. 'She won a car'; i.e. participant > process > participant) or just one participant without 'carry-over' (e.g. 'She won'; i.e. participant > process)?

purposive or non-purposive – respectively, involving intention or not (e.g. 'look' or 'see'; 'listen' or 'hear')?

How far are the **circumstances** *to do with*:

quality or quantity – 'how good or bad' as distinct from 'how many or how much' (e.g. 'clever, happy people' as distinct from 'ten, twenty-year-old persons'?

intensification or qualification – 'very', 'extremely', 'always', 'a lot', 'most', etc. as opposed to 'slightly', 'rather', 'occasional(ly)', 'a little', 'not many', etc.

time or place ('now', 'then', 'previous(ly)', 'next year', 'often', 'continually', 'February 1848' as distinct from 'here', 'there', 'in Manchester', 'China')?

Overall, then, experiment with ways of realising participants as processes, and processes as participants; and explore the possibilities for different *kinds* of participant and process. Add, delete and modify the circumstances accordingly.

WHO? WHAT? WHEN? WHERE? HOW? WHY?...................... ELSE?

WHY .... NOT?

5.3 TYPES OF TEXTUAL INTERVENTION

There are many modes of critical-creative writing other than those of the traditional academic essay, analysis or dissertation. It is the purpose of this section to summarise and cross-reference the ones used in this book. This will be done here at the 'macro-textual' levels of genre, discourse, medium, narrative and dramatic intervention, etc. For a corresponding checklist of stylistic features at the 'micro-linguistic' levels of word choice and combination, and sound-patterning and visual presentation, see the previous section (5.2).

At the outset, however, it is worth briefly exploring what these so-called 'alternative' modes of writing are alternative to. And it should certainly be emphasised that 'alternative' does not mean opposed – but rather complementary and supplementary. First, then, let's acknowledge that there are many more varieties and sub-genres of the 'traditional' essay, analysis and dissertation than are commonly recognised or made explicit. *Essays* can be in varying degrees formal or informal, depersonalised or personalised (use of the 'I/we', 'you' or 'one', for instance, may be proscribed, allowed, or encouraged – as may the use of active or passive and other verb forms, and certain ranges of vocabulary and construction). They can use 'logics' which are linear, recursive, dialectical, dialogic, abstract or figurative. And they can involve various degrees and kinds of textual reference, illustration, analysis and allusion. Specific texts may be invoked constantly or hardly at all. Explicit theorising may figure prominently or hardly at all. *Analyses*, too, are of many varieties: written or spoken; individual or group; practical critical/close reading; personal response; textual-editorial; stylistic; discourse-ideological; historical-contextual; etc. Meanwhile, *dissertations* – which are substantially like *essays* only larger and usually more rigid in format – may be organised on many different lines and in many configurations: by text, author, topic, theme, period, genre, theoretical position, etc. (For guidance in all these areas, see Fabb and Durant, 1993.)

Having said all that, the fact remains that the great bulk of academic work in literary studies in higher education still tends to operate within a certain narrow – albeit rarely explicitly defined – range of writing and thought. Basically, it requires or assumes the operation of *linear or binary logic*, *positivist textual reference* and, perhaps above all, the ability of the *individual learner* to recognise and reproduce the *dominant critical orthodoxy* in a particular course. The emphasis on individual – not collective – written work is constitutive (seminar discussion is generally recognised as valuable but not essential); and there is a marked attention to essays, analyses or dissertations as *written products* rather than as *writing processes* (also see 5.1). This view of textuality extends to the 'set texts' which are the objects of study. They are just that: 'set' and 'objects' – given and apparently both unchanging and unchangeable.

For all these reasons, it is worth trying to summarise the types of textual intervention and critical-creative strategy explored in this book. For they *are* genuine *alternatives* to dominant practices. Though how far they are to be viewed as *counter*-practices is for learners and teachers themselves to decide. For ease of use, this summary is broken down into 'General Strategies' and 'Specific Techniques' and fully cross-referenced.

General strategies

Parallel, counter- or alternative texts?

How far are you writing 'with', 'against' or 'across' the grain of the base text as you perceive it? Inevitably, most forms of intervention and re-writing have a mixture of critical orientations. None the less, it is a good idea to ask yourself early on which of these three trajectories you are trying to follow. Asking yourself the same question at the end is very revealing too. For there is invariably a significant difference between aim and result. The actual process of composition often leads to a product subtly or markedly different from that initially conceived. Preferences shift in the very exploration of differences. (See 1.1.2; 1.3.2; 3.3; 4.4.1–3; 4.5.)

Monologue or dialogue?

How far and in what ways are you using one or more *voices* and *discourses*, consensually or conflictually? That is, basically, how far is the world of your text primarily 'monologic' or 'dialogic'? Both have their distinctive strengths and weaknesses. Instances of overtly or substantially *monologic* (one-way) modes are: lecture, sermon, set speech, diary, prayer, confession, advertising, news bulletin, mail shots, etc. Instances of overtly or substantially *dialogic* (two- or many-way) modes are: conversation, debate, interview, interrogation, exchanges of letters, reviews, critiques, marginalia, heckling, graffiti, etc. Live speech, or simulations of it in scripted form, tend to be more ostensibly dialogic because they are always potentially or apparently immediate and two- or many-way. Conversely, the written, printed or electronically recorded word tends to be more ostensibly 'monologic' in that it is primarily one-way – and only two-way (if at all) after a heavily mediated delay. These distinctions are initially convenient. Two qualifications must be added, however.

(1) There is no such thing as an absolutely unanswering or unanswerable 'monologue'.

For every utterance or text is always prompted by another, however indirectly, and every utterance or text is directed towards some kind of effect – even if an 'answer', as such, is not expected or wanted.

(2) Conversely, there is no such thing as an absolutely equal 'dialogue' and an utterly 'free exchange of information'.

For every dialogue is implicated in the imbalances and inequalities of power structures, however indirectly. Consequently, there is always something partly or potentially monologic and 'one-way' in the communication of any utterance or text.

For all these reasons, then, it is important to recognise that all texts – our own included – move dialectically *between* 'monologue' and 'dialogue'. In Bakhtin's terms, they are subject to the variable interplay of *centripetal* (monologic) and *centrifugal* (dialogic) pressures (see

Bakhtin, 1981: 272–3, 425). Apparently 'single-voiced' discourse always turns out to be many-tongued. And an apparent polyphony of voices always turns out to have a dominant harmony or melody. How far, then, and in what ways is your text dialogic and/or monologic? And through what kinds of monologue/dialogue are you engaging with the base text – which itself, in turn, is caught in its own play of one – or many – voices and discourses? Such questions are necessarily complex and contentious. But they must be if we are to grasp the full subtlety and power of openly intertextual strategies – and of any form of interactive critique. (See 2.5; 3.1.3; 4.1.)

De-centring and re-centring?

How far and in what directions and dimensions are you shifting or switching the *centres of interest* offered by the base text? And is this de- and re-centring being effected: (1) textually, in the margins of the base text; (2) contextually, in its larger social-historical context; or (3) cross-textually, in another – albeit relatable – text entirely? (See 1.2; 3.3; 4.5.)

Personal, interpersonal, depersonalised?

How far and in what ways are you intervening in the distinctive configuration of subject/ agent positions offered by the base text? Is your alternative text primarily articulated through an 'I/we' (*personal*, speaking subject); a 'you' (*interpersonal*, spoken-to subject); a 'she', 'he', 'they' or 'it' (progressively *depersonalised*, spoken-about subjects)? And are these the same 'I's, 'we's and 'you's, etc., as those you found? Put another way, how far are you reconstituting the various *selves* and *others* of the base text? And are you according greater or lesser *agency* to any of the available *subjects*? (See 1.2.1; 2.2; 3.1.3.)

Genre, medium, discourse?

How far is the alternative text you are producing different from the base text in terms of: (1) kind or type (*genre*); (2) material (*medium*); and (3) way of saying and seeing (*discourse*)? Moreover, as all these categories are plural and to some extent overlap, what particular *hybrids* do you recognise yourself to be involved with, both in the base text and in your own text? (See 1.2.4; 2.6; 3.2.4.)

Specific techniques

All the following techniques can be applied very variously and in ways which draw upon all the above strategies. That is, each and every one can involve various kinds and degrees of: *parallel, counter- or alternative text; monologue or dialogue; de- and re-centring*, and be textualised in various *genres, media and discourses* articulating various configurations of *personal, interpersonal and depersonalised subject/agent positions*. Precisely which will depend upon the materials you are working on and how you decide to work them up.

A.   Alternative summaries and the arts of paraphrase

Summarise the text in a variety of ways so as to draw attention to different aspects of its preoccupations or construction – and to your own methods of

paraphrase. For instance, a series of summaries varying between a phrase, a sentence, 50 words, and 100 words can be very revealing in establishing what you consider progressively more or less central in terms of themes, events, figures, strategies, etc. Each of these can then be compared with those of colleagues so as to identify areas of overlap and difference.

Devising posters, adverts, songs, trailers and reviews based on the text in hand is another, critical-creative way of exploring summaries.

Alternatively, you might 'paraphrase' the text drawing on one of a range of critical-theoretical discourses: Leavisite; 'Anglo-American new critical'; Marxist; feminist; psychoanalytical; post-/structuralist; post-/colonialist; post-/modernist; etc. In all these ways you would in effect 'translate' and thereby *transform* the base text. You would also learn to treat your own apparently 'merely descriptive' summaries as forms of discourse – and your own apparently 'natural' and 'neutral' discourses as specifically value-laden ways of categorising, labelling and explaining. Summary/paraphrase might then be recognised not so much as a 'heresy' but an 'orthodoxy'! (See Selden, 1989a: 28–9; also Carter and Long, 1987: 5–15; and Nash, 1992: 67–82; cf. 3.1.6; 3.2.4; 4.5.4.)

B. Changed titles, introductory apparatuses and openings

Intervene in these areas of the text so as to disturb and reorient them. Aim to cue the reader for a slightly (or very) different reading experience – one with slightly (or very) different expectations as to genre, centre of interest, discourse, outlet, market, communicative relations, etc. (See 3.2.4; 3.3.2; 4.5.5.)

C. Alternative endings

Alter the ending of the base text so as to draw attention to some option not explored or in some way foreclosed. Go on to explore the reasons why such an ending was not desirable, advisable or possible in the base text at its initial moment of production. Then consider why you, in your own moment of reproduction, opted for it. Notice that, like all the exercises, this is an opportunity to explore historical differences and not simply express personal preferences. Arguing vigorously both 'for' and 'against' all these endings, each in its own historical moment, is a good way of interrogating assumptions about 'progress' or 'regress', absolute 'preferences' and 'eternal values'. (See 3.2.6; 4.3; 4.5.5.)

D. Preludes, interludes and postludes

Extend the text 'before', 'during' or 'after' the events it represents so as to explore alternative points of departure, processes of development, or points of arrival. What overall premises, procedures and aims are highlighted by this strategy? And how far are you seeking to *complement* or *supplement* the base text? Really 'ludicrous' preludes, interludes and postludes often sport with a variety of historical moments as well as a variety of genres and discourses, and narrative and dramatic strategies. (See 3.2.6; 3.3.3–4; 4.3; 4.4.3; 4.5.5.)

E. Narrative intervention

Change some 'turning point' in the narrative so as to explore alternative premises or consequences. Also consider ways of framing or 're-focalising' the narrative so that the very process of narration is reoriented, and perhaps made more (or less) obvious. This method of exploring continuities and discontinuities, kinds of textual cohesion and perceptual coherence, can be applied to 'histories' as well as 'stories'. It can also be applied to single sentences and propositions, as well as to lengthy novels, films and treatises. It all depends how – and how far – you distinguish narrative from other modes of representation and exposition. (See 3.1.4; 3.2.5–6; 3.4.)

F. Dramatic intervention

Change the direction of a scripted drama or transcribed conversation by intervening in a single 'move' or 'exchange'. Also consider figures you might reorient or insert so as to alter the emphasis or choice of topic and the course of the action. This can be done in conjunction with E and G. (See 4.1–3; 4.5.5.)

G. Narrative into drama; drama into narrative

Explore 'showing' through 're-telling', and 'telling' through 're-showing'. And thereby examine the peculiar configuration of re/presentation in your base text (See 3.1.3; 3.2.3; 4.4).

H. 'Imitation'

Recast the base text in the manner – and matter – of another author (director, theatre or film company, etc.). This is no mere matter of 'slavish imitation', even if such a thing were practically or theoretically possible (which strictly it isn't). Rather, it entails transformations of fundamental issues and discourses, along with settings and contexts, etc. For it soon becomes obvious that re-writing, say, some Shakespeare 'in the manner' of Ibsen, Brecht or Churchill (or Austen, or Dickens, or Joyce, etc.) is no mere question of 'style'. It also entails transformations of 'matter' as well. Another's 'word' always implies a whole 'world'. Negotiating the different ways in which different authors or directors might work up ostensibly the same figures, situations and issues is an excellent way of seeing that they are not quite – or at all – 'the same'. A variation on this activity is to select some contemporary item (a news story, anecdote or joke) and work it up in the manner and matter of the base text under consideration. (See 3.2.4 and 4.4.3.)

I. Parody

Exaggerate some features of the base text, or introduce incongruous (perhaps anachronistic) frames of reference, so as to throw its characteristic style or preoccupations into relief. Crude parody is *burlesque*. Subtle parody can be so implicit and ironic that its parodic intent may be all but invisible. Both can be critically and creatively valid – and great fun. Either way, parody can be an act of affectionate

REVIEW OF THEORIES AND PRACTICES **201**

celebration of an author's work. It is not necessarily either negative or destructive. In fact, the most searching and revealing parodies are usually those grounded in a mixture of fascination and frustration with the base text. (See 1.3.1; 4.5.5; also Hutcheon, 1985; and Nash, 1992: 83–99.)

J. Collage

Gather a diverse and perhaps disparate range of materials directly or indirectly relevant to the base text: sources; parallels; contrasts; bits of critical commentary; relatable words, images, pieces of music, etc. – perhaps from other periods and discourses, etc. Then select from and arrange these materials so as to make a number of implicit statements about the base text. There is a fascination in both the finding and making of physical and perceptual patterns; and a skill – as well as serendipity – in inviting your reader or viewer to perceive meaningful differences and discern implicit preferences. 'Collage' is neither more nor less than the art of 'sticking together' – with your base text, your material and any prospective readers, viewers and audiences. It's as simple – and complex – as that. As always, the commentary should seek to make explicit what was implicit, and to lay bare the process of composition. (See 1.2.4; 2.3; 2.6; 4.5.5; also Hutcheon, 1989; and Montgomery *et al.*, 1992: 147, 173.)

K. Hybrids and 'faction'

Recast two or more related texts in a new textual mould so as to produce a compound – not merely a mixture. Compounding conventionally 'fictional' and 'factual' texts usually produces 'faction' – in every sense. (Alternative metaphors for this process include grafting a new plant from two 'parent' plants so as to generate a *hybrid*; or the biological process of *cross-fertilisation* between species.) In any event, experiment with ways of making texts coalesce as well as collide. In this respect the generation of 'hybrids' is distinct from the sticking together of 'collages'. There is more obviously the making of a 'new and organic whole' than a 'mechanical assemblage of old fragments'. (See 1.2.4; 2.3; 3.3.5; 4.5.7.)

L. Word to image, word to music, word to movement, word to . . . ?

This is a catch-all reminder that verbal texts can be very revealingly understood in the attempt to transform them into another medium, sign-system or mode of communication and expression. Film, video, photography, painting and sculpture; all kinds of music; dance, mime and numerous kinds of performance art; even clothes, architecture, smells, touches and tastes . . . These all offer alternative ways of 're-realising' and 're-cognising' the actual and potential meanings, effects and values of a particular string of words – long or short, epic or epigram, novel or one-liner, single sound or letter. A *transference* always entails a *transformation*. So these are all ways of interpreting and intervening in the text's play of differences and sorting out your own frames of reference in your own preferred modes and materials.

M.   *Your own permutations, extensions and additions . . .*

Suggested work-pattern

There are as many ways of re-writing and intervening in texts as there are texts to re-write and people to intervene. However, the following more general questions and suggestions seem to help.

1 *Do you want to do it on your own or with other people? And are you allowed or encouraged to do the latter?* Associations with others can be loose and informal, or close and formal (e.g. assessable). Working on your own may feel safe because it is familiar. But collective work can have real benefits in terms of sharing both the excitement and the burden of learning.

2 *'Brain-storm' the possibilities early on, throwing everything down on paper.* Running through the above list of strategies and techniques should help. Then focus on what seem to be some of the more promising ideas. Discuss these with colleagues and a tutor. The main thing is to blend intertextual activity with interpersonal activity, exploring the materials both dialectically and through dialogue.

3 *Plan and write a first draft.* This will allow you to pick out some principal differences and establish some provisional preferences. What, basically, are you trying to say or show about the base text? A rough first draft will move you along more quickly than endless prevarication. So, if in doubt – plunge in.

4 *Do some supplementary reading to help extend and refine the initial ideas.* Sometimes such reading may come first. But in general it helps if you sort out what, basically, *you* want to say and how *before* being drowned out by the voices and discourses of others. Reading with a provisional purpose is also much more valuable than reading aimlessly.

5 *Shape your text through subsequent drafts, adding, deleting and modifying as seems appropriate.* Again, the guiding principle is 'What am I/we trying to say or show about the base text?' There will be all sorts of refinements you can introduce so as to make allusions more subtle and discriminating – and perhaps teasing. Remember that your reader knows the base text you are working with, so you can afford to make implicit changes and challenges to it. More express sign-posting is the business of the commentary. So –

6 *Make sure you add a commentary.* This should include some explicit statement of overall aims and rationale: what you were trying to do, which textual strategy you chose and why. There should also be some insight into the possibilities thrown up and problems encountered over the course of conceiving, drafting and re-drafting your project. Critically, the false starts and dead ends are important too. So is an open acknowledgement of the problems as well as the advantages of group work. Add references and a bibliography, as for essays.

Further reading

The following books feature versions of many of the strategies and techniques reviewed above – and more besides: Carter and Long, 1987, 1991; Collie and Slater, 1987; Carter and Nash, 1990; Hackman and Marshall, 1990; Durant and Fabb, 1990. Also see the earlier references in 5.1.

Bibliography

Most of the following references are to books or parts of books. The following journals are also particularly relevant: *Textual Practice*; *Language and Literature*; *Style*.

Abrams, M.H. (general ed.) (1993) *Norton Anthology of English Literature*, vols 1 and 2 (6th edn), New York: W.W. Norton.

Allen, R.C. (ed.) (1987) *Channels of Discourse: Television and Contemporary Criticism*, London: Routledge.

Allnutt, G., D'Aguiar, F., Edwards, K. and Mottram, E. (eds) (1988) *The New British Poetry*, London: Paladin.

Andersen, R. (1988) *The Power and the Word: Language, Power and Change*, London: Paladin.

Angelou, M. (1969) *I Know Why the Caged Bird Sings*, London: Virago, 1984.

Althusser, L. (1971) *Lenin and Philosophy and other Essays*, trans. B. Brewster, London: New Left Books.

Armstrong, I. (1988) *Jane Austen: Mansfield Park*, Harmondsworth: Penguin.

Ashcroft, B., Griffiths, G. and Tiffin, H. (1989) *The Empire Writes Back: Theory and Practice in Post-Colonial Literatures*, London: Methuen.

Attridge, D. (1988) *Peculiar Language: Literature as Difference from the Renaissance to James Joyce*, London: Methuen.

Attridge, D., Bennington, G. and Young, R. (eds) (1987) *Poststructuralism and the Question of History*, Cambridge: Cambridge University Press.

Attridge, D., Durant, A., Fabb, N. and MacCabe, C. (eds) (1987) *The Linguistics of Writing: Arguments between Language and Literature*, Manchester: Manchester University Press.

Augarde, T. (1984) *The Oxford Guide to Word Games*, Oxford: Oxford University Press.

Austen, J. (1814) *Mansfield Park*, ed. T. Tanner, Harmondsworth: Penguin, 1966.

Austin, J.L. (1976) *How to do Things with Words*, rev. edn, Oxford: Oxford University Press.

Bakhtin, M. (1968) *Rabelais and his World*, trans. H. Iswolsky, Cambridge, MA: MIT Press.

—— (1981) *The Dialogic Imagination: Four Essays*, ed. M. Holquist, trans. C. Emerson and M. Holquist, Austin: University of Texas Press.

—— (1984) *Problems of Dostoyevsky's Poetics*, ed. and trans. C. Emerson, Manchester: Manchester University Press.

—— (1990) *Art and Answerability: Early Philosophical Works*, ed. M. Holquist, and V. Liapunov, trans. V. Liapunov, Austin: University of Texas Press.

Bal, M. (1985) *Narratology*, trans. C. Van Boheemen, Toronto: University of Toronto Press.

Barker, C. (1977) *Theatre Games: A New Approach to Drama Training*, London: Eyre Methuen.

Barker, F., Hulme, P., Iversen, M. and Loxley, D. (eds) (1986) *Literature, Politics and Theory: Papers from the Essex Conference, 1976–1984*, London: Methuen.

Barthes, R. (1970) *S/Z*, trans. R. Miller, London: Cape, 1975.

—— (1977) *Image–Music–Text*, ed. and trans. S. Heath, London: Fontana.

Batsleer, J., Davies, T., O'Rourke, R. and Weedon, C. (1985) *Rewriting English: Cultural Politics and Gender and Class*, London: Methuen.

Beckett, S. (1956) *Waiting for Godot*, London: Faber.

Belsey, C. (1980) *Critical Practice*, London: Methuen.

Belsey, C. and Moore, J. (eds) (1989) *The Feminist Reader: Essays in Gender and the Politics of Literary Criticism*, London: Macmillan.

Benjamin, W. (1970) *Illuminations*, ed. H. Arendt, trans. H. Zohn, London: Cape.

—— (1973) *Understanding Brecht*, trans. A. Bostock, London: New Left Books.

Bennett, T. (1979) *Formalism and Marxism*, London: Methuen.

Bennett, T., Boyd-Bowman, S., Mercer, T. and Woollacott, J. (eds) (1981) *Popular Television and Film*, London: Open University Press and British Film Institute.

Benton, M. and Fox, G. (1985) *Teaching Literature: Nine to Fourteen*, Oxford: Oxford University Press.

Benveniste, E. (1966) *Problems in General Linguistics*, Miami: University of Miami Press.

Bhabha, H. (ed.) (1990) *Nation and Narration*, London: Routledge.

—— (1994) *The Location of Culture*, London: Routledge.

Birch, D. (1989) *Language, Literature and Critical Practice*, London: Routledge.

Birch, D. and O'Toole, M. (eds) (1988) *Functions of Style*, London: Pinter.

Birkett, J. (1993) *Word Power: A Guide to Creative Writing*, London: A. and C. Black.

Blakemore, D. (1992) *Understanding Utterances: An Introduction to Pragmatics*, Oxford: Blackwell.

Bleich, D. (1978) *Subjective Criticism*, Baltimore: Johns Hopkins University Press.

Boal, A. (1992) *Games for Actors and Non-actors*, trans. A. Jackson, London: Routledge.

Bold, A. (ed.) (1970) *The Penguin Book of Socialist Verse*, Harmondsworth: Penguin.

Bolinger, D. (1980) *Language: The Loaded Weapon*, London: Longman.

Booth, W. (1961) *The Rhetoric of Fiction*, Chicago: Chicago University Press.

Bordwell, D. (1985) *Narration in the Fiction Film*, London: Methuen.

Bordwell, D. and Thompson, K (1990) *Film Art: An Introduction*, New York: McGraw-Hill.

Bourdieu, P. (1984) *Distinction: A Social Critique of the Judgement of Taste*, trans. R. Nice, London: Routledge.

Brantlinger, P. (1990) *Crusoe's Footprints: Cultural Studies in Britain and America*, London and New York: Routledge.

Bradley, A.C. (1905) *Shakespearean Tragedy*, London: Macmillan, 1950.

Brathwaite, E.K. (1984) *History of the Voice*, London: New Beacon Books.

Brecht, B. (1964) *Brecht on Theatre*, ed. and trans. J. Willett, London: Methuen.

—— (1965) *The Messingkauf Dialogues*, trans. J. Willett, London: Methuen.

Brett, S. (ed.) (1984) *The Faber Book of Parodies*, London: Faber.

Brooker, P. and Humm, P. (eds) (1989) *Dialogue and Difference: English into the Nineties*, London: Routledge.

Brookes, A. and Grundy, P. (1990) *Writing for Study Purposes: A Teacher's Guide to Developing Individual Writing Skills*, Cambridge: Cambridge University Press.

Brown, G. and Yule, G. (1983) *Discourse Analysis*, Cambridge: Cambridge University Press.

Brown, J. and Gifford, T. (1989) *Teaching 'A' Level English Literature: A Student-centred Approach*, London: Routledge.

Browning, E.B. (1856) *Aurora Leigh*, ed. C. Kaplan, London: Women's Press, 1980.

Browning, R. (1991) *Robert Browning: Selected Poetry and Prose*, ed. A. Day, London: Routledge.

Brumfit, C.J. and Carter, R.A. (eds) (1986) *Literature and Language Teaching*, Oxford: Oxford University Press.

Bruner, J. (1986) *Actual Minds, Possible Worlds*, Cambridge, MA: Harvard University Press.

Burgin, V. (1986) *Between*, Oxford: Blackwell.

Burke, K. (1945) *A Grammar of Motives*, New York: Prentice Hall.

Burnett, P. (ed.) (1986) *Penguin Book of Caribbean Verse in English*, Harmondsworth: Penguin.

Burton, D. (1980) *Dialogue and Discourse: The Sociology of Modern Drama Dialogue and Naturally Occurring Conversation*, London: Routledge & Kegan Paul.

Burton, D. and Carter, R.A. (eds) (1982) *Literary Text and Language Study*, London: Arnold.

Cameron, D. (1985) *Feminism and Linguistic Theory*, London: Macmillan.

—— (ed.) (1990) *The Feminist Critique of Language*, London: Routledge.

Carey, J. (ed.) (1987) *The Faber Book of Reportage*, London: Faber.

Carse, J.P. (1987) *Finite and Infinite Games: A Vision of Life as Play and Possibility*, Harmondsworth: Penguin.

Carter, R.A. (ed.) (1982) *Language and Literature: An Introductory Reader in Stylistics*, London: Allen & Unwin.

—— (1993) *Introducing Applied Linguistics: An A–Z Guide*, Harmondsworth: Penguin.

Carter, R.A. and Long, M. (1987) *The Web of Words: Language-based Approaches to Literature*, Cambridge: Cambridge University Press.

Carter, R.A. and Nash, W. (1990) *Seeing Through Language: A Guide to Styles of English Writing*, Oxford: Blackwell.

Carter, R.A. and Simpson, P. (eds) (1989) *Language, Discourse and Literature: An Introductory Reader in Discourse Stylistics*, London: Unwin Hyman.

Caws, M.A. (1989) *The Art of Interference: Stressed Readings in Verbal and Visual Texts*, Princeton: Princeton University Press.

Chapman, S. (1986) *Great Expectorations: Advertising and the Tobacco Industry*, London: Comedia and World Health Organisation.

Chatman, S. (1978) *Story and Discourse: Narrative Structure in Fiction and Film*, Ithaca, NY: Cornell University Press.

Coetzee, J.M. (1986) *Foe*, London: Secker & Warburg.

Cohan, S. and Shires, L.M. (1988) *Telling Stories: A Theoretical Analysis of Narrative*, London: Routledge.

Cohn, R. (1976) *Modern Shakespeare Offshoots*, Princeton, NJ: Princeton University Press.

Cole, T. (ed.) (1961) *Playwrights on Playwriting*, New York: Hill & Wang.

Collick, J. (1989) *Shakespeare, Cinema and Society*, Manchester: Manchester University Press.

Collie, J. and Slater, S. (eds) (1987) *Literature in the Language Classroom: A Resource Book of Ideas and Activities*, Cambridge: Cambridge University Press.

Cook, G. (1992) *The Discourse of Advertising*, London: Routledge.

Corcoran, B. and Evans E. (eds) (1989) *Readers, Texts, Teachers*, Milton Keynes: Open University Press.

Corner, J and Hawthorn, J. (eds) (1993) *Communication Studies: A Reader*, London: Arnold.

Cousyn, J. (ed.) (1989) *Singing Down the Bones*, London: Women's Press.

Coward, R. and Ellis, J. (1977) *Language and Materialism*, London: Routledge & Keegan Paul.

Cox, M. (ed.) (1992) *Shakespeare Comes to Broadmoor: The Performance of Tragedy in a Secure Psychiatric Hospital*, London and Philadelphia: Jessica Kingsley.

Crookall D. and Saunders, D. (eds) (1988) *Communication and Simulation*, Clevedon, PA: Multilingual Matters.

Crowley, T. (1989) *Politics of Discourse: The Standard Language Question in British Cultural Studies*, London: Macmillan.

Crystal, D. (1988) *Re-discover Grammar*, London: Longman.

Darnton, R. (1985) *The Great Cat Massacre, and Other Episodes in French Cultural History*, Harmondsworth: Penguin.

Davis, H., and Walton, P. (eds) (1983) *Language, Image, Media*, Oxford: Blackwell.

Davis, L. (1983) *Factual Fictions: The Origins of the English Novel*, New York: Columbia University Press.

Defoe, D. (1719) *Robinson Crusoe*, New York: Signet, 1960.

Derrida, J. (1976) *Of Grammatology*, trans. G.C. Spivak, Baltimore: Johns Hopkins University Press.

—— (1978) *Writing and Difference*, trans. A. Bass, Chicago: Chicago University Press.

Descartes, R. (1637) *Discourse on Method*, trans. F. Sutcliffe, Harmondsworth: Penguin, 1968.

Dollimore, J. and Sinfield, A. (eds) (1985) *Political Shakespeare: New Essays in Cultural Materialism*, Manchester: Manchester University Press.

Durant, A. and Fabb, N. (1990) *Literary Studies in Action*, London: Routledge.

During, S. (1992) *Foucault and Literature: The Genealogy of Writing*, London: Routledge.

—— (ed.) (1993) *The Cultural Studies Reader*, London: Routledge.

Eagleton, T. (1983) *Literary Theory: An Introduction*, Oxford: Blackwell.

—— (1986a) *Against the Grain*, London: Verso.

—— (1986b) *William Shakespeare*, Oxford: Blackwell.

Easthope, A. (1991) *Literary into Cultural Studies*, London: Routledge.

Eco, U. (1986) *Travels in Hyperreality*, London: Picador.

Elam, K. (1980) *The Semiotics of Theatre and Drama*, London: Methuen.

Fabb, N. and Durant, A. (1993) *How to Write Essays, Dissertations and Theses for Literary Studies*, London: Longman.

Fairclough, N. (1989) *Language and Power*, London: Longman.

—— (ed.) (1992) *Critical Language Awareness*, London: Longman.

Fanon, F. (1967) *The Wretched of the Earth*, trans. F. Constance, Harmondsworth: Penguin, 1976.

Farb, P. (1975) *Word Play: What Happens When People Talk*, New York: Bantam.

Fetterley, J. (1991) *The Resisting Reader: A Feminist Approach to American Fiction*, Bloomington, IN: Indiana University Press.

Fish, S. (1980) *Is there a Text in This Class? The Authority of Interpretive Communities*, Cambridge, MA.

Fisher, A. (1988) *The Logic of Real Arguments*, Cambridge: Cambridge University Press.

Fiske, J. (1982) *Introduction to Communication Studies*, London: Routledge.

—— (1987) *Television Culture*, London: Routledge.

Forster, E.M. (1927) *Aspects of the Novel*, London: Arnold, 1948.

Foucault, M. (1972) *The Archaeology of Knowledge*, trans. A. Sheridan-Smith, London: Tavistock.

—— (1980) *Language, Counter-Memory, Practice*, ed. and trans. D. Bouchard and S. Simon, Oxford: Blackwell.

—— (1986) *The Foucault Reader*, ed. P. Rabinow, Harmondsworth: Penguin.

Fowler, R. (1986) *Linguistic Criticism*, Oxford: Oxford University Press.

—— (1991) *Language in the News: Discourse and Ideology in the Press*, London: Routledge.

Fowler, R., Hodge, R., Kress, G. and Trew, T. (1979) *Language and Control*, London: Routledge & Kegan Paul.

Freire, P. (1972) *Pedagogy of the Oppressed*, trans. M. Ramos, Harmondsworth: Penguin.

Fromkin, V. and Rodman, R. (1993) *An Introduction to Language*, New York: Harcourt, Brace Jovanovich.

Fry, S., Mayer, L. and Swann, R. (eds) (1991) *Amassed Hysteria!*, Harmondsworth: Penguin.

Gates, Jr, H.L. (ed.) (1987) *The Classic Slave Narratives*, New York: Mentor.

Giddens, A. (1991) *Modernity and Self-identity*, Oxford: Polity Press.

Giddings, R., Selby, K. and Wensley, C. (1990) *Screening the Novel: The Theory and Practice of Literary Dramatisation*, London: Macmillan.

Giglioli, P. (1972) *Language and Social Context*, Harmondsworth: Penguin.

Goldman, R. (1992) *Reading Ads Socially*, London: Routledge.

Graddol, D. and Boyd-Barrett, O. (eds) (1994) *Media Texts: Authors and Readers*, Clevedon, PA: Multi-lingual Matters.

Granville-Barker, H. (1930) *Prefaces to Shakespeare*, London: Batsford, 1958.

Greenwell, B. (1988) *Alternatives at English 'A' Level*, Sheffield: National Association for the Teaching of English.

Grice, H.P. (1975) 'Logic and conversation', in P. Cole and J. Morgan (eds), *Syntax and Semantics 3: Speech Acts*, New York: Academic Press.

Griffith, P. (1987) *Literary Theory and English Teaching*, Milton Keynes: Open University Press.

—— (1991) *English at the Core: Dialogue and Power in English Teaching*, Milton Keynes: Open University Press.

Guerrier, D. and Richards, J. (1969) *State of Emergency: A Programmed Entertainment*, Harmondsworth: Penguin.

Habermas, J. (1990) *Moral Consciousness and Communicative Action*, trans. C. Lenhardt and S. Weber Nicholsen, Cambridge: Polity Press.

Hackman, S. and Marshall, B. (1990) *Re-reading Literature: New Critical Approaches to the Study of English*, London: Hodder & Stoughton.

Halliday, M.A.K. (1985) *An Introduction to Functional Grammar*, London: Arnold.

Halliday, M.A.K. and Hasan, R. (1989) *Language, Context and Text: Aspects of Language in a Social-Semiotic Perspective*, Oxford: Oxford University Press.

Harris, R. (1988) *Language, Saussure and Wittgenstein: How to Play Games with Words*, London: Routledge.

Hawkes, T. (1977) *Structuralism and Semiotics*, London: Methuen.

—— (1986) *That Shakespeherian Rag: Essays on a Critical Process*, London: Methuen.

—— (1993) *Meaning By Shakespeare*, London: Routledge.

Haynes, J. (1989), *Introducing Stylistics*, London: Routledge.

Heinemann, M. (1985) 'How Brecht read Shakespeare', in Dollimore and Sinfield (1985): 202–30.

Heylen, R. (1993) *Translation, Poetics and the Stage: Six French Hamlets*, London: Routledge.

Hillis Miller, J. (1992) *Illustration*, London: Reaktion Books.

Hintikka, J. and Kulas, J. (1983) *The Game of Language*, Dordrecht: Reidel.

Hirschkop, K. and Shepherd, D. (eds) (1988) *Bakhtin and Cultural Theory*, Manchester: Manchester University Press.

Hodge, R. (1990) *Literature as Social Discourse: Textual Strategies in English and History*, Oxford: Polity.

Hodge, R. and Kress, G. (1993) *Language as Ideology*, 2nd edn, London: Routledge.

Hoffmann, Y. (1977) *The Sound of the One Hand: 281 Koans with Answers*, St. Albans: Paladin.

Holderness, G. (ed.) (1988) *The Shakespeare Myth*, Manchester: Manchester University Press.

Holderness, G and Loughrey, B. (eds) (1992) *The Tragicall Historie of Hamlet Prince of Denmark* (First Quarto), Hemel Hempstead: Harvester Wheatsheaf.

Holdsworth, A. (1988) *Out of the Doll's House: The Story of Women in the 20th Century*, London: British Broadcasting Corporation.

Holquist, M. (1990) *Dialogism: Bakhtin and his World*, London: Routledge.

Holub, R. (1984) *Reception Theory: A Critical Introduction*, London: Methuen.

Hubler, E. (ed.) (1963) *Hamlet*, New York: Signet.

Hughes, P. and Brecht, G. (1978) *Vicious Circles and Infinity: An Anthology of Paradoxes*, Harmondsworth: Penguin.

Hunt, A. (1975) *Hopes for Good Happenings: Alternatives in Education and Theatre*, London: Eyre Methuen.

Hutcheon, L. (1985) *A Theory of Parody: The Teaching of Twentieth-Century Art Forms*, London: Methuen.

—— (1989) *The Politics of Postmodernism*, London: Routledge.

Ibsen, H. (1965) *The League of Youth, A Doll's House, The Lady from the Sea*, trans. P. Watts, Harmondsworth: Penguin.

—— (1984) *Plays: Two*, trans. M. Meyer, London: Methuen.

Iser, W. (1978) *The Act of Reading: A Theory of Aesthetic Response*, Baltimore: Johns Hopkins University Press.

Israel, J. (1979) *The Language of Dialectics and the Dialectics of Language*, Brighton: Harvester.

JanMohammed, A. and Lloyd, J. (1990) *The Nature and Context of Minority Discourses*, New York: Oxford University Press.

Jardine, A. and Smith, P. (eds) (1987) *Men in Feminism*, London and New York: Methuen.

Jauss, H.R. (1982) *Towards an Aesthetics of Reception*, trans. T. Bahti, Brighton: Harvester Press.

Jelinek, E. (1994) *What Happened After Nora Left Her Husband*, in *Plays for Women: Ten*, London: Methuen.

Jones, K. (1988) *Interactive Learning Events*, London: Kogan Page.

Jump, J. (ed.) (1968) *Shakespeare, Hamlet: A Casebook*, London: Macmillan.

Kanda, M. (ed.) (1989) *Widows of Hiroshima: The Life Stories of Nineteen Peasant Wives*, London: Macmillan.

Kasulis, T.P. (1981) *Zen Action / Zen Person*, Honolulu: University of Hawaii Press.

Kermode, F. (1968) *The Sense of an Ending: Studies in the Theory of Fiction*, London: Oxford University Press.

Kermode, F. and Hollander, J. (1973) (eds) *Oxford Anthology of English Literature*, vols 1 and 2, New York: Oxford University Press.

Kershaw, B. (1992) *The Politics of Performance: Radical Theatre as Cultural Intervention*, London: Routledge.

Koestler, A. (1976) *The Act of Creation*, London: Hutchinson.

Kott, J. (1967) *Shakespeare our Contemporary*, London: Methuen.

Kramarae, C., Schulz, M. and O'Barr, W.O. (1984) *Language and Power*, Beverley Hills: Sage.

Kress, G. (1989) *Linguistic Processes in Sociocultural Practice*, Oxford: Oxford University Press.

Kristeva, J. (1980) *Desire in Language*, trans. T. Gora, A. Jardine and L. Roudiez, New York: Columbia University Press.

—— (1984) *Revolution in Poetic Language*, trans. M. Waller, New York: Columbia University Press.

Labov, W. (1972) *Language in the Inner City*, Philadelphia, PA: University of Pennsylvania Press.

Laing, R.D. (1965) *The Divided Self*, Harmondsworth: Penguin.

Leech, G.N. (1983) *Principles of Pragmatics*, London: Longman.

Leech, G.N. and Short, M. (1981) *Style in Fiction: A Linguistic Introduction to English Fictional Prose*, London: Longman.

Leith, R. and Myerson, G. (1989) *The Power of Address: Explorations in Rhetoric*, London: Routledge.

Levinson, S.C. (1983) *Pragmatics*, Cambridge: Cambridge University Press.

Litzinger, B. and Smalley, D. (eds) (1970) *Robert Browning: The Critical Heritage*, London: Routledge & Kegan Paul.

Lodge, D. (ed.) (1988) *Modern Criticism and Theory: A Reader*, London: Longman.

—— (1990) *After Bakhtin: Essays on Fiction and Criticism*, London: Routledge.

Lukacs, G. (1962) *The Historical Novel*, trans. H and S. Mitchell, London: Merlin

Lyotard, J.F. (1986) *The Postmodern Condition: A Report on Knowledge*, trans. G. Bennington, Manchester: Manchester University Press.

MacCabe, C. (ed.) (1988) *Futures for English*, Manchester: Manchester University Press.

Macdonell, D. (1986) *Theories of Discourse*, Oxford: Blackwell.

McGann, J.J. (1983) *The Beauty of Inflections: Literary Investigations in Historical Method*, Oxford: Oxford University Press.

McGrath, J. (1981) *A Good Night Out: Popular Theatre, Audience, Class and Form*, London: Methuen.

Macherey, P. (1978) *A Theory of Literary Production*, trans. G. Wall, London: Routledge & Kegan Paul.

McQuail, D. and Windahl, S. (1993) *Communication Models for the Study of Mass Communication*, London: Longman.

Markham, E. (ed.) (1989) *Hinterland: Caribbean Poetry from the West Indies and Britain*, Newcastle: Blood-axe.

Marowitz, C. (1970) *The Marowitz Hamlet and Dr Faustus*, Harmondsworth: Penguin.

—— (1991) *Recycling Shakespeare*, London: Macmillan.

Marshall, B. (1992) *Teaching Postmodernism: Fiction and Theory*, London: Routledge.

Martin, J.R. (1989) *Factual Writing: Exploring and Challenging Social Reality*, Oxford: Oxford University Press.

Mead, H. (1934) *Mind, Self and Society*, Chicago: Chicago University Press.

Metz, C. (1974) *Film Language: A Semiotics of the Cinema*, trans. M. Taylor, New York: Oxford University Press.

Michaels, L. and Ricks, C. (eds) (1990) *The State of the Language*, London: Faber.

Millar, S. (1968) *The Psychology of Play*, Harmondsworth: Penguin.

Milloy, J. and O'Rourke, R. (1991) *The Woman Reader: Learning and Teaching Women's Writing*, London: Routledge.

Moffett, J. (1968) *Teaching the Universe of Discourse*, Boston, MA: Houghton Mifflin.

Montgomery, M. (1986) *An Introduction to Language and Society*, London: Methuen.

Montgomery, M., Durant, A., Fabb, N., Furniss, T. and Mills, S. (1992) *Ways of Reading: Advanced Reading Skills for Students of English Literature*, London: Routledge.

Monteith, M. and Miles, R. (eds) (1992) *Teaching Creative Writing*, Oxford: Open University Press.

Moon, B. (1990) *Studying Literature: Theory and Practice for Senior Students*, London: English Media Centre and Chalkface Press.

Moore, G. and Beier, U. (eds) (1984) *The Penguin Book of Modern African Poetry*, Harmondsworth: Penguin.

Morson, G. and Emerson, C. (eds) (1989) *Rethinking Bakhtin: Extensions and Challenges*, Evanston, IL: Northwestern University Press.

Mühlhausler, P. and Harré, R. (1990) *Pronouns and People: The Linguistic Construction of Personal and Social Identity*, Oxford: Blackwell.

Mulhern, F. (ed.) (1992) *Contemporary Marxist Literary Criticism*, London: Longman.

Nash, W. (1992) *An Uncommon Tongue: The Uses and Resources of English*, London: Routledge.

O'Sullivan, T., Hartley, J., Saunders, D., Montgomery, M. and Fiske, J. (1994) *Key Concepts in Communication*, 2nd edn, London: Routledge.

Ousby, I. (ed.) (1988) *The Cambridge Guide to Literature in English*, Cambridge: Cambridge University Press, 1993.

Parker, P. and Hartman, G. (eds) (1985) *Shakespeare and the Question of Theory*, London: Methuen.

Pascoe, L. (ed.) (1974) *Encyclopedia of Dates and Events*, London: Hodder & Stoughton.

Pavis, P. (1991), *Theatre at the Crossroads of Culture*, trans. L. Kruger, London: Routledge.

Pêcheux, M. (1982) *Language, Semantics and Ideology*, trans. H. Nagpal, London: Macmillan.

Posner, R. (1982) *Rational Discourse and Poetic Communication: Methods of Linguistic, Literary and Philosophical Analysis*, Berlin and New York: Mouton.

Pratt, M.L. (1976) *Towards a Speech Act Theory of Literary Discourse*, Bloomington IN: Indiana University Press.

Prince, G. (1987) *A Dictionary of Narratology*, Lincoln: University of Nebraska Press.

Purdie, S. (1993) *Comedy: The Mastery of Discourse*, Hemel Hempstead: Harvester Wheatsheaf.

Quirk, R. and Greenbaum, S. (1976) *A University Grammar of English*, London: Longman.

Reid, I. (1984) *The Making of Literature: Texts, Contexts and Classroom Practice*, Canberra: Australian Association for the Teaching of English.

—— (1992) *Narrative Exchanges*, London: Routledge.

Reps, P. (ed.) (1957) *Zen Flesh, Zen Bones*, Harmondsworth: Penguin, 1971.

Rhys, E. (ed.) (1927) *Edward Lear, Lewis Carroll and Others: A Book of Nonsense*, London: Dent, 1988.

Rhys, J. (1966) *Wide Sargasso Sea*, Harmondsworth: Penguin, 1968.

Richards, I.A. (1929) *Practical Criticism: A Study of Literary Judgement*, London: Routledge & Kegan Paul.

Ricoeur, P. (1984) *Time and Narrative*, trans. K. Laughlin and D. Pellamer, Chicago: Chicago University Press.

Rimmon-Kenan, S. (1983) *Narrative Fiction: Contemporary Poetics*, London: Methuen.

Rorty, R. (1989) *Contingency, Irony and Solidarity*, Cambridge: Cambridge University Press.

Rosen, H. (1985) *Stories and Meanings*, Sheffield: National Association for the Teaching of English.

Rylance, R. (ed.) (1987) *Debating Texts: A Reader in 20th-century Literary Theory and Method*, Milton Keynes: Open University Press.

Said, E. (1978) *Orientalism*, New York: Random House.

—— (1993) *Culture and Imperialism*, London: Chatto & Windus.

Scholes, R. (1985) *Textual Power: Literary Theory and the Teaching of English*, Binghampton: Yale University Press.

—— (1987) *Text Book: An Introduction to Literary Language*, London: St Martin's.

Scarle, J.R. (1969) *Speech Acts: An Essay in the Philosophy of Language*, Cambridge: Cambridge University Press.

Selden, R. (1989a) *Practising Theory and Reading Literature*, Hemel Hempstead: Harvester Wheatsheaf.

—— (1989b) *A Reader's Guide to Contemporary Literary Theory*, Hemel Hempstead: Harvester Wheatsheaf.

Sell, R. (ed.) (1990) *Literary Pragmatics*, London: Routledge.

Sharp, A. (1987) *The Story-Trails Book of Science Fiction*, Cambridge: Cambridge University Press.

Sharratt, B. (1982) *Reading Relations: Structures of Literary Production – A Dialectical Text/book*, Atlantic Highlands, NJ: Humanities Press.

Shaw, G.B. (1944) *The Black Girl in Search of God and Lesser Tales*, Harmondsworth: Penguin.

Short, M. (ed.) (1989) *Reading, Analyzing and Teaching Literature*, London: Longman.

Simpson, P. (1992) 'Teaching stylistics: analysing cohesion and narrative structure in a short story by Ernest Hemingway', *Language and Literature*, 1.1, 47–67.

—— (1993) *Language, Ideology and Point of View*, London: Routledge.

Sinfield, A (1992) *Faultlines: Cultural Materialism and the Politics of Dissident Reading*, Oxford: Oxford University Press, esp. ch.1.

Sperber, D. and Wilson, D.M. (1986) *Relevance: Communication and Cognition*, Oxford: Blackwell.

Spivak, G.C. (1987) *In Other Worlds: Essays in Cultural Politics*, London: Methuen.

—— (1990) *The Post-colonial Critic: Interviews, Strategies and Dialogues*, London: Routledge.

—— (1994) *Outside in the Teaching Machine*, London: Routledge.

Stallybras, P. and White, A. (1986) *The Politics and Poetics of Trangression*, London: Methuen.

Stibbs, A. (1991) *Reading Narrative as Literature: Signs of Life*, Milton Keynes: Open University Press.

Stoppard, T. (1967) *Rosencrantz and Guildenstern are Dead*, London: Faber.

Tallack, D. (ed.) (1987) *Literary Theory at Work: Three Texts*, London: Batsford.

Tannen, D. (1991) *You Just Don't Understand: Women and Men in Conversation*, London: Virago.

Taylor, T. (1992) *Mutual Misunderstanding: Scepticism and the Theorising of Language and Interpretation*, London: Routledge.

Thompson, A. and Wilcox, H. (eds) (1989) *Teaching Women: Feminism and English Studies*, Manchester: Manchester University Press.

Thompson, E. and Smith, D. (eds) (1970) *Protest and Survive*, Harmondsworth: Penguin.

Thouless, R. (1953) *Straight and Crooked Thinking*, London: Pan.

Todd, L. (1984) *Modern Englishes: Pidgins and Creoles*, London: Blackwell & Deutsch.

Todorov, T. (1984) *Mikhail Bakhtin: The Dialogic Principle*, trans. W. Godzich, Manchester: Manchester University Press.

Toolan, M.J. (1988) *Narrative: A Critical Linguistic Introduction*, London: Routledge.

—— (ed.) (1992) *Language Text and Context: Essays in Stylistics*, London: Routledge.

Tournier, M. (1967) *Friday, or the Other Island*, trans. N. Denny, Harmondsworth: Penguin, 1984.

Traugott, E.C. and Pratt, M.L. (1980) *Linguistics for Students of Literature*, New York: Harcourt Brace Jovanovich.

Trollope, A. (1857), *Barchester Towers*, ed. R. Gilmour, Harmondsworth: Penguin, 1983.

Voloshinov, V.N. (1973) *Marxism and the Philosophy of Language*, trans. L. Matejka and I. Titunik, New York: Seminar Press.

Vonnegut, K. (1963) *Cat's Cradle*, Harmondsworth: Penguin, 1973.

Vygotsky, L.S (1934) *Thought and Language*, trans. E. Hanfmann and G. Vakar, Cambridge, MA: MIT Press, 1962.

Walder, D. (ed.) (1990) *Literature in the Modern World: Critical Essays and Documents*, Oxford: Oxford University Press and Open University Press.

Wales, K. (1989) *A Dictionary of Stylistics*, London: Longman.

Wall, C. (ed.) (1989) *Changing Our Own Words: Essays on Cultural Theory and Writing by Black Women*, London: Routledge.

Ward-Jouve, N. (1991) *White Woman Speaks with Forked Tongue: Criticism as Autobiography*, London: Routledge.

Waugh, P. (1984) *Metafiction: The Theory and Practice of Self-Conscious Fiction*, London: Methuen.

Widdowson, P. (ed.) (1982) *Re-reading English*, London: Methuen.

Williams, G. (1992) *Sociolinguistics: A Sociological Critique*, London: Routledge.

Williams, R. (1983) *Keywords: A Vocabulary of Culture and Society*, London: Flamingo.

Williams, W.C. (1976) *Selected Poems*, ed. C. Tomlinson, Harmondsworth: Penguin.

Williamson, J. (1978) *Decoding Advertisements*, London: Marion Boyars.

Winnicott, D.W. (1974) *Playing and Reality*, Harmondsworth: Penguin.

Wittgenstein, L. (1953) *Philosophical Investigations*, ed. and trans. G.E.M. Anscombe, Oxford: Blackwell, 1978.

Wright, E. (1989) *Postmodern Brecht: A Re-Presentation*, London: Routledge.

Young, R. (ed.) (1981) *Untying the Text: A Poststructuralist Reader*, London: Routledge & Kegan Paul.

Index

Printed in the United Kingdom
by Lightning Source UK Ltd.
119527UK00005B/1